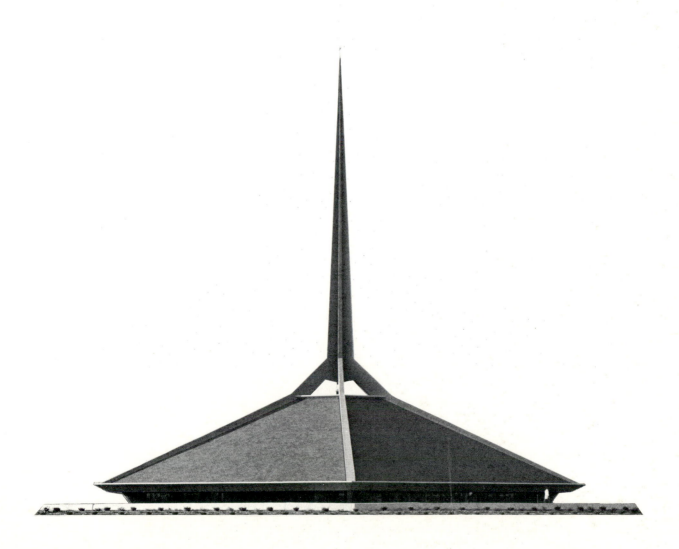

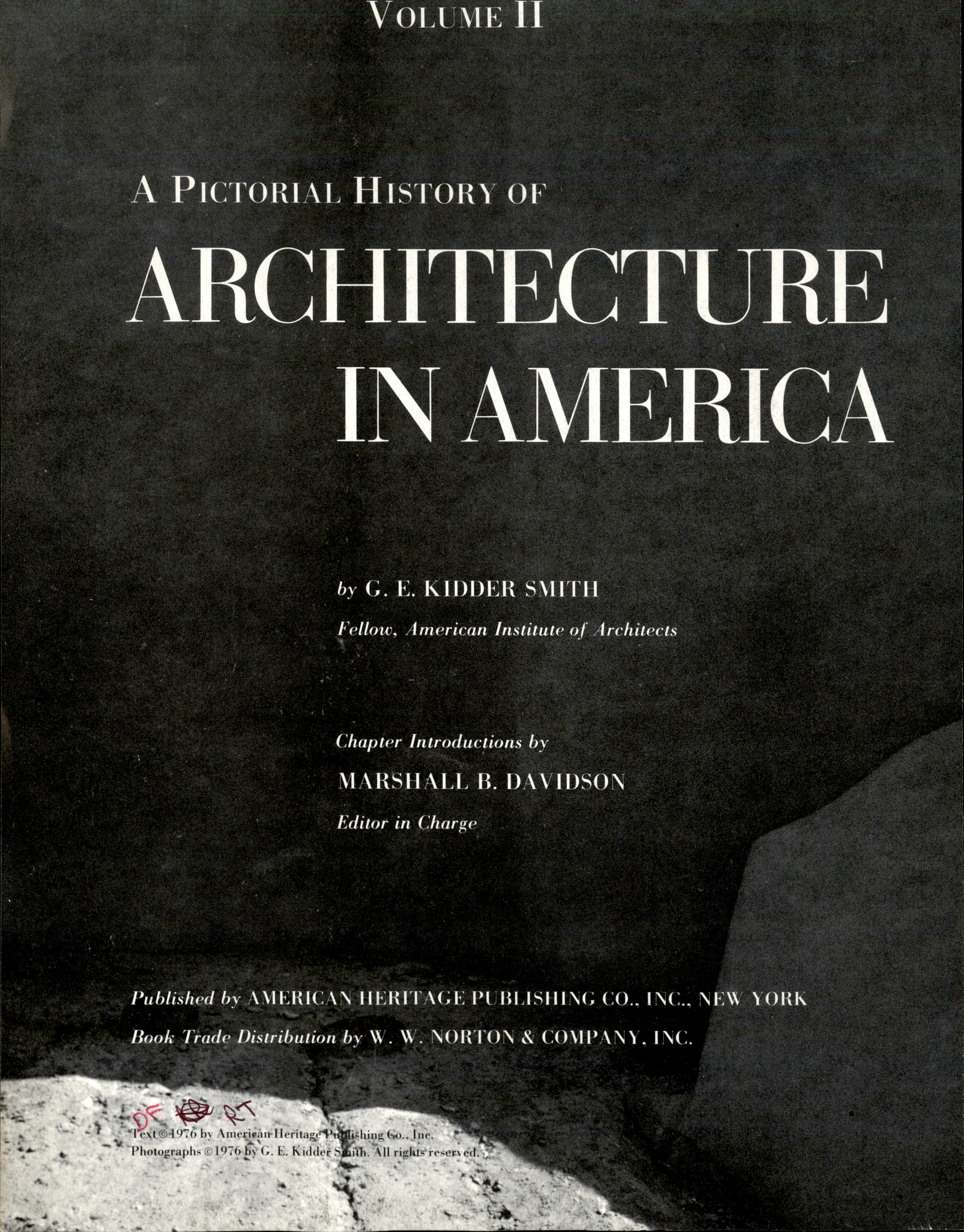

VOLUME II

A PICTORIAL HISTORY OF

ARCHITECTURE IN AMERICA

by G. E. KIDDER SMITH

Fellow, American Institute of Architects

Chapter Introductions by

MARSHALL B. DAVIDSON

Editor in Charge

Published by AMERICAN HERITAGE PUBLISHING CO., INC., NEW YORK

Book Trade Distribution by W. W. NORTON & COMPANY, INC.

CONTENTS

VOLUME I   **6**   EDITORIAL FOREWORD

   7   AUTHOR'S INTRODUCTION

   10   NEW ENGLAND
     Connecticut, Maine, Massachusetts, New Hampshire,
     Rhode Island, Vermont

   124   MID-ATLANTIC
     Delaware, District of Columbia, Maryland, New Jersey,
     New York, Pennsylvania

   274   SOUTH
     Alabama, Florida, Georgia, Kentucky, Mississippi,
     North Carolina, South Carolina, Tennessee,
     Virginia, West Virginia

VOLUME II   **422**   MIDWEST
     Illinois, Indiana, Iowa, Michigan, Minnesota,
     Ohio, Wisconsin

   530   SOUTHWEST
     Arizona, Arkansas, Louisiana, New Mexico,
     Oklahoma, Texas

   620   PLAINS & ROCKIES
     Colorado, Idaho, Kansas, Missouri, Montana, Nebraska,
     North Dakota, South Dakota, Utah, Wyoming

   702   FAR WEST & PACIFIC
     Alaska, California, Hawaii, Nevada, Oregon, Washington

   820   INDEX

MIDWEST

POWESHIEK COUNT

ILLINOIS

INDIANA

IOWA

MICHIGAN

MINNESOTA

OHIO

WISCONSIN

What is often referred to as the heartland of America has been given various boundaries. For the purposes of this publication it embraces the seven midwestern states here listed. Most of that large area was incorporated into the United States as the Northwest Territory shortly after the conclusion of the Revolutionary War, when it was largely a wilderness yet to be subdued. Its typical architectural form was then the fortified frontier post and in certain areas the simple homestead of the French *habitant*, who had been the first white man to settle in those remote parts. For years this had been contested ground, fought over by an assortment of Indian tribes and by their French and British allies, before the American colonists successfully challenged the others for possession and authority.

Today it is a land of apparent paradox. It contains some of the nation's most spacious and productive farmlands and also some of its greatest industrial complexes and urban centers. Midwestern cities are far from either ocean, landlocked in the center of the continent, yet Michigan, bordering its three great lakes, has one of the longest coastlines of any state in the United States and its cities and those of neighboring states have easy access to the major waterways of the outside world. Principally through the enterprise of Chicago and its environs, the Midwest has contributed enormously to the architectural heritage of America.

Daniel Webster once observed that no law in history produced more beneficent and lasting results than the Northwest Ordinance of 1787, which secured the administration of that territory. Its enlightened provisions banned slavery, going beyond the Declaration of Independence and the Constitution in that respect; it assured religious freedom over a wide area; and it actively encouraged education in all the land north of the Ohio River. It denied once and for all the ancient contention that colonial territories were subordinate to the mother country in their political and social interests. The future states of that area were to enter the Union "on an equal footing with the original states, in all respects whatever." In short, it announced a new, organic concept of empire, a concept that dictated the future history of the United States.

However, any fulfillment of that farsighted plan had to await the pacification of those borderlands. Although the Revolutionary War campaigns of George Rogers Clark had established America's claim to the territory, it remained hostile Indian ground for a decade and more to come. Many of the frontier forts continued to be under control of the British, who were allied with various Indian tribes. In the summer of 1794 this issue was largely settled when Anthony Wayne sallied forth from Fort Defiance, not far from the western tip of Lake Erie, to do battle. He was dubbed "Mad Anthony" because of his tactical boldness and his personal courage, but he was anything but mad, for he took elaborate precautions to ensure the success of his operation. In the sanguinary Battle of Fallen Timbers he broke the natives' resistance, and with this turn of events the British were forced to evacuate those border forts they had continued to occupy.

Now that the new frontier was relatively quiet, the westward movement of Americans took on a new momentum. Even before the Indian menace had been removed, migrants from the East were surging into Ohio by the thousands searching for new

Ornament detail, Poweshiek County National Bank, Grinnell, Iowa (1914). Louis H. Sullivan, architect

homesites at the risk of their scalps. Revolutionary War veterans established a settlement, named Marietta in honor of Marie Antoinette, on the north bank of the Ohio River as early as 1788. Here the little office of the Ohio Land Company, originally raised within a stockade, still stands, and is considered the oldest building in Ohio. In 1790 Gallipolis was first settled by hopeful Frenchmen lured into the West by speculative land jobbers. (George Washington, Benjamin Franklin, and others among the Founding Fathers owned tracts of land in the western country which they held and sold for whatever profit they might make.) These first settlers were but a trickle presaging the flood of humanity to follow. The pace of migration became spectacular, especially after the War of 1812, during which bloody turmoil again broke out along the borderlands. Then, with the extension of the National Road from Baltimore to the Ohio River and the opening of the Erie Canal, the floodgates were wide open. "All America seems to be breaking up and moving westward," one British traveler reported as he watched this great swarm of westering people. From New England and from Virginia came laments that the exodus might soon depopulate the older regions and leave them wastelands. Within less than a decade after Fallen Timbers, Ohio was populous enough to qualify as a state of the Union; by 1830 the western state had more inhabitants than the old New England states of Massachusetts and Connecticut combined.

In this new land Yankees and Yorkers mingled with Virginians and Pennsylvanians and with first generations of Americans from European countries to breed a typical New World civilization of mixtures within mixtures of people. The earliest settlers inevitably tended to perpetuate their separate and familiar cultures. Immigrants from Connecticut, for example, traveling westward through New York for the most part, soon laid out tidy village greens graced with steepled meetinghouses amidst the rolling hills of northern Ohio, and gave such good old Connecticut names as Greenwich and Norwalk to their newly established villages. The Virginians and Pennsylvanians took to the National Road as it pushed westward until they reached the Ohio River at Wheeling, West Virginia. (Traffic was so heavy, wrote one historian of that road, that it looked more like a leading avenue of a great city than a road through rural districts.) From Wheeling they moved on to easily accessible sites across the river to transplant their own architectural heritage. In those early years, the architecture of Ohio became to a large degree a recapitulation of the building styles and methods that had prevailed up and down the Atlantic seaboard for the preceding century.

Year after year what had been a West became an East with bewildering speed. To the west of Ohio, Indiana became a state in 1816, Illinois in 1818, Michigan in 1837, Iowa in 1846, Wisconsin in 1848, and Minnesota in 1858. Unlike great migrations of the past, this westering movement of Americans was not a wandering of tribes or, with important exceptions, the settlement of compact colonies. Individuals, families, and small groups, on their own initiative, found their way through the wilderness to new homes and new adventures. "How beautiful," Thomas Carlyle rhapsodized in a letter to Emerson, "to think of lean tough Yankee settlers, tough as gutta-percha, with most occult unsubduable fire in their belly, steering over the Western Mountains to annihilate the jungle, and bring bacon and corn out of it for the Posterity of Adam.—There is no *Myth* of Athene or Herakles equal to this *fact*."

Those who so quickly peopled the heartland wilderness were not, of course, all Yankees by any means—or even natives of other eastern coast regions. Immediately following the first wave of pioneers came Germans, then Irishmen, in turn followed by people from the shores of the Mediterranean, by Russians, Poles, and Balkan and Baltic immigrants. A great influx of Scandinavians settled the northlands of Michigan, Minnesota, and Wisconsin that so closely resembled their homelands. Meanwhile, Swiss came to Indiana and Wisconsin, Dutch to Michigan, and so on down a long list of nationalities, each adding another patch to this large and varied quilt of American life.

It was a world of promise and, in addition to the host of newcomers who came to realize their individual dreams, there were a number of organized groups of all descriptions and of both native and foreign conception who moved into the West, each intent on building a perfect community according to its lights. In 1817 a "holy experiment," the Separatists Society of Zoar, Ohio, was established by Germans who had emigrated from Württemberg and who laid out their vast central garden in a radial plan of the New Jerusalem envisioned in the Apocalypse. The community ceased to exist as such in 1898, but a number of its buildings, including a meetinghouse on a hill overlooking the town, still stand as witness to the lofty convictions of these enterprising immigrants. In Iowa there remain seven villages of the Amana Society, another German religious group who were led to America in 1843 by Christian Metz and moved into the West in 1855. (Amana is the biblical term for "remain faithful.") Descendants of the first colonists still live along the quiet streets of these towns. Amana itself is reminiscent of a German village.

The Shakers founded several communities, one on the site of what is now the prosperous Cleveland suburb of Shaker Heights. Mormons also looked for utopia in the heartland. At Nauvoo, Illinois, they laid the foundations for an extravagant temple in what had by then become the largest city in the state, but the structure was never completed because the Church's founder, Joseph Smith, was assassinated and his people moved on to Utah under the leadership of Brigham Young in quest of a site beyond reach of persecution.

One of the bravest of such efforts to reclaim man from social evils was the communitarian colony established in 1825 at New Harmony, Indiana, by the Scottish reformer Robert Owen. Owen had the good luck and good sense to find and prefer a site that had already been cleared and built upon by an earlier group of pioneering idealists, the German Rappists, who sold out to return east. Thousands of colonists from almost every state in the Union and from most of the countries of northern Europe came to the settlement. These hopefuls included numerous men of marked ability and high purpose. A vast and complex structure composing a square enclosure one thousand feet wide was envisioned as the nucleus of the settlement, but it was never built. The community dissolved. Those modest dwellings the members did live in for a while are preserved as a national historical landmark.

More practical and enduring were the cities that sprang up with such astonishing rapidity from one edge of the heartland to the other. With access to flourishing farmlands and with trade outlets to East, West, and South by ample waterways, Cincinnati became the crossroads of an active traffic, and would soon be aptly known as the "Queen City of the West." With a large number of Germans among its inhabitants, Cleveland, founded in 1796, was an outpost one day, a great lakeside port the next. The American flag was not raised over the frontier outpost at Detroit until 1796. When the settlement burned to the ground in 1805, it was only a cluster of wooden buildings covering a few acres of ground and surrounded by a stockade. But it, too, was on the main route to the West, and once the great migration started, the little village, almost as old as Philadelphia (it had been founded by the French in 1701), suddenly awoke from its long sleep. In 1836 one visitor remarked on the thousands of settlers who were pouring in every year, many of them Irish, German, or Dutch, pausing there to make money before working their way farther west.

Urban developments were far from predictable. A century ago Galena, in Illinois, was bright with the promise of future growth. Today its population is half what it was in 1856, and Galena remains an almost perfect prototype of the mid-nineteenth-century midwestern town. On the other hand, the growth of Chicago defied credulity. For nearly a half century after the founding of the nation, this tiny settlement remained almost invisible in the midst of a vast, undeveloped prairie. The small town was incorporated in 1833. After being burned down a few times, thought one English observer in 1846, the village might amount to something. No city on earth was to amount to something more suddenly, burn down more thoroughly, and rise again from the flames more lustily. Chicago's surging growth had its real beginning in 1852 when for the first time the railroad linked the future metropolis with the eastern seaboard. Four years later a Scotch visitor to Chicago encountered railroad lines then in the course of speedy construction that would open up 6,738 miles of trackage leading in all directions out of the city. At the center of what Abraham Lincoln termed the "Egypt of the West," Chicago was by then the greatest primary grain market in the world and was fast becoming the railway hub of the nation.

Then, in October, 1871, the booming city, already boasting a population of almost a third of a million people, burned level in one of the major catastrophes of the century. But that proved an incentive rather than a deterrent. Within less than a decade the city was not only rebuilt, but greatly enlarged. With a population of over one million people, it was America's second city. Chicago was classified with Niagara Falls as one of the great wonders of the United States. In a few years it would initiate contributions to American architecture that were in some ways greater than those of any other contemporary city, as its skyscraping structures would so proudly testify.

Generally speaking, the same sequence of styles that characterized developments along the eastern seaboard attended building in the Midwest, with some time lag in the beginning and with variations dictated by available building materials. (An exception to this was in those areas in the Mississippi Valley where the French had settled and for a time to come continued to build in their traditional manner, but this was largely a localized expression.) One important technological advance was apparently introduced by a Chicago builder in 1839. As earlier mentioned, for hundreds of years men had framed their wooden dwellings and other buildings of heavy timbers, often more than a foot square, that were mortised, tenoned, and pegged together, and then raised into position by group labor. As one traveler pointed out, in the headlong rush to occupy the land of the prairies, where heavy timber, labor, and carpentry skills were unavailable, homebuilders were obliged occasionally "to do with make-shift" to get a home at all. The Chicago-born innovation of the 1830's known as balloon framing was a construction of light two-by-four studs nailed, rather than joined, in a tight framework, the studs rising continuously from foundation to rafters. Uninjured by mortise or tenon, with every strain coming in the direction of the fiber of some portion of the wood, the numerous, light sticks of the structure formed a fragile-looking skeleton that was actually exceptionally strong.

This radically new method of construction, inevitable as it seems in retrospect, had awaited two technological advances: the mass production and distribution of dimensioned lumber and the production of cheap machine-made nails. With these available, a whole new order of speed and economy in wood framing was made possible. Balloon-frame houses were more than makeshift; the method has been generally used throughout the country ever since it was first conceived. Without its advantages, Chicago and other mushroom cities of the Midwest could never have risen, or been rebuilt, as fast as they did and were.

Practical and economic as it was for domestic building, the balloon-frame structure was hardly adequate to cope with the architectural problems created by the surging economic and industrial growth of the Midwest, pivoting on Chicago, in the late nineteenth century. For the accommodation of this booming commercial enterprise, planning and building had to be projected on a bolder scale and with more imagination than had yet been attempted. Chicago, after the Great Fire, provided an electric environment, an urgent demand for offices, an abundance of capital, and a progressive spirit of prodigious vigor. Out of this combination of circumstances emerged what has been called the "Chicago School" of architecture, ever since famed for accomplishments unmatched during the next several decades anywhere else in the nation.

Among the assemblage of brilliant talents who contributed to this phenomenal outburst of creativity, three men stand out with special distinction: Henry Hobson Richardson, Louis Henri Sullivan, and Frank Lloyd Wright. Richardson can fairly be called a prime mover. His work in the eastern states, some of it earlier discussed, spread its roots into the Midwest and came to fresh flowering in the advanced constructions of Sullivan and Wright. Richardson was keenly aware of the needs and circumstances of his time. He once exclaimed that he most wanted to design a grain elevator and the interior of a great river steamboat, two prime symbols of progress at the time. He never realized either of those aspirations, but among his many other accomplishments before his early death he did see to completion several memorable railroad stations, symbols of another mightily important aspect of the new industrial age.

In 1885 Richardson went to Chicago to design a wholesale store for Marshall Field. This massive, seven-story structure, solidly built of sandstone and covering an entire city block, was the greatest of Richardson's designs for the world of commerce. It was a magnificently simple building. The only ornament, if it could be called that, consisted of the placement of stones of various sizes and the graduated sequence of the building's round-arched window embrasures. But these façades precisely expressed the internal organization of the store. "Four-square and brown, it stands . . . ," Louis Sullivan observed admiringly, "a monument to trade, to the organized commercial spirit, to the power and progress of the age, to the strength and resource of individuality and force of character; it stands as the index of a mind large enough, courageous enough to cope with these things, master them, absorb them, and give them forth again, impressed with the stamp of larger and forceful personality."

When Richardson died in 1886 at the age of forty-eight he was at the height of his career. He had been a fundamental force in developing and dominating architectural trends, in private dwellings as well as in public edifices, occasionally in wood as well as in stone; what he might have accomplished had he lived longer can only be imagined. Brief as it was, however, his invasion of the Chicago scene with what Sullivan termed his "direct, large, and simple" construction was to have an important influence on the future of the city's architecture. Richardson died at the dawn of the age of steel-frame construction—the age of the skyscraper—and with his straightforward functional designs he had foretold its advent.

No one better appreciated the organized planning of Richardson's constructions than Louis Sullivan, who would for a brief time enjoy eminence as a prophet of modern architecture, the unchallenged master of the skyscraper. Richardson had opened Sullivan's eyes to a vision that was revolutionary for his generation. He was determined to create an architecture that would necessarily evolve from and express the American environment, and for him the center of that environment was Chicago, although he had been Boston-bred, the son of an Irish dancing master and a Swiss pianist. "The function of a building must . . . organize its form . . . ," he wrote, "as, for instance, the oak tree expressed the function oak, the pine tree the function pine." The Crystal Palace of the Exposition of 1851 in London, the Brooklyn Bridge in New York, and the Eiffel Tower in Paris had already indicated how large a part engineering and iron and particularly steel would play in this approaching day of giant buildings.

Sullivan had attended the Massachusetts Institute of Technology in 1872, worked in Philadelphia as a draftsman, and in 1874 enrolled in the École des Beaux-Arts in Paris to receive the highest training in architecture then available. As he remembered it in his autobiography, when he visited Chicago after the fire and during the panic year of 1873, he found the city "magnificent and wild: a crude extravaganza, an intoxicating rawness, a sense of big things to be done. For 'big' was the word . . . and 'biggest in the world' was the braggart phrase on every tongue . . . [the men of Chicago] were the crudest, rawest, most savagely ambitious dreamers and would-be doers in the world . . . but these men had vision. What they saw was real." Sullivan entered the great period of his career in the early 1890's. He had joined a fruitful partnership at Chicago with the German-born Dankmar Adler, whose knowledge of engineering and acoustics had earned him wide respect in the city. Assisted by Adler, and stimulated by the young Frank Lloyd Wright, who had joined the firm in 1887 and become his chief apprentice, Sullivan's genius came to flower.

Focusing his attention on the skyscraper, he pondered the problem of "How shall we impart to this sterile pile, this harsh brutal agglomeration, this stark, staring exclamation of eternal strife, the graciousness of those higher forms of sensibility and culture that rest on the lower and fiercer passions?" His solution was to combine the traditional elements of classic composition—proportion, scale, rhythm, and ornament, to name a few—with the new skeletal structure of the tall, steel-frame commercial buildings. Sullivan did not invent the steel frame or the many-storied building, but he produced outstanding examples which in their plans and their expressive façades were not substantially improved upon for another fifty years to come. His work, by no means confined to Chicago, consisted of more than one hundred buildings in various states, and through these highly diversified structures, ranging from tombs to department stores, and through his philosophical essays, he was for a time an important energizing force in the theory and practice of advanced American architecture. He provided a basic approach for the tall office building.

Sullivan also realized that the skyscraper represented a potential social menace when it was built in "surroundings uncongenial to its nature." "When such buildings are crowded together on narrow streets or lanes," he pointed out, "they become mutually destructive." That warning has since been largely ignored in the building and rebuilding of our large cities, with the unhappy consequences that he foresaw would result when the multitudes working and living in these great piles swarm in and out to choke the limited spaces available at street level.

Sullivan's later life was a sad anticlimax. When an economic depression caused the firm of Adler and Sullivan to dissolve, the sensitive architect no longer had his partner to shield him from the harsh world of business outside his drafting room. His commissions drastically diminished, and he was also beset by a series of humiliating personal tragedies that included the failure of two marriages, the loss of his country retreat, the auctioning of his art and furniture, and the removal of his offices where he had long done his work. He ended his days in a dingy hotel room on Chicago's South Side, all but forgotten, despondent and, not without reason, cynical about the immediate future of American architecture.

The financial panic of 1893 that led to the dissolution two years later of Sullivan's partnership with Adler coincided with the opening of the World's Columbian Exposition at Chicago. This great fair was staged to celebrate (one year late) the four hundredth anniversary of Columbus' discovery of America. It also celebrated (a few years early) the rounding out of a century of progress. By extension of that record, with its impressive displays of technological achievements, it forecast a more promising tomorrow for Americans and for the rest of the world. The fair, it was announced, would "awaken forces which, in all time to come, [would] influence the welfare, the dignity and the freedom of mankind."

If the industrial and scientific displays at Chicago foretold a future of progressive advances, the buildings that housed them gave no indication of such an outlook. Almost all of them turned back to models from the classical past for their inspiration—largely to the styles and canons of ancient Rome. A host of distinguished architects, sculptors, and painters had been brought together to create this "inconceivable scenic display," as Henry Adams termed it. The Chicago architect Daniel Hudson Burnham was charged with the allover planning, but most of the others were easterners of unassailable reputations. Richard Morris Hunt, famed for the magnificent châteaux he designed for the very wealthy in Newport and New York, was among them, as was Stanford White, of the prestigious firm of McKim, Mead, & White, whose buildings in period styles were renowned throughout the East. The result was a monumental midwestern extravaganza, with glittering façades of plaster of Paris rising with fluttering flags on the shores of Lake Michigan. This, remarked Burnham, was "what the Romans would have wished to create in permanent form." He also predicted that all America would soon be constructed in the "noble, dignified classic style," and in this he came close to the truth. In the years that followed, that style did become almost a standard brand for state capitols and official buildings in general, banks, libraries, railroad stations, and other types of public edifices.

Others viewed the Exposition scene differently. To a number of critics the thin veneer of classical order imposed on most of the buildings, and which bore little or no relation to the demonstrations within, seemed like a sickly-sweet frosting laid on by the chill, dead hand of the past. Predictably, Sullivan was appalled. (His nonclassical Transportation Building at the fair, in the designing of which he was assisted by his protégé Frank Lloyd Wright, was the one structure that caught the special attention of foreign observers.) He thought that the influences of the fair on American architecture would be all but disastrous. The epidemic of neoclassicism that had germinated in the East, he wrote, had spread westward, contaminating all that it touched. "Thus did the virus of a culture, snobbish and alien to the land of the free and the home of the brave, subvert the cause of progress. Thus ever works the pallid academic mind, denying the real, exalting the fictitious and the false, incapable of adjusting itself to the flow of living things." Architecture would be a living art, he was convinced, only when the form of a building was dictated by the function it was to serve.

No one can reasonably contest Sullivan's original contributions to the art and science of building. However, without stretching the point too far, his ideas could be viewed as an extension of much earlier American theories and practices. In 1851, the Yankee sculptor Horatio Greenough wrote to Ralph Waldo Emerson explaining his theory of structure, which he saw justified in the sailing ships of the time—the time of the magnificent clipper ships and the cup-winning yacht *America*—and which he thought offered a "glorious foretaste" of what could be accomplished elsewhere in the near future. "Here is my theory of structure," he wrote. "A scientific arrangement of spaces and forms to functions and to site—An emphasis of features proportioned to their *gradated* importance in function—Color and ornament to be decided and arranged and varied by strictly organic laws—having a distinct reason for each decision—The entire and immediate banishment of all makeshift and make-believe." Greenough was an outspoken functionalist before that word had been coined. "By beauty," he once wrote, "I mean the promise of function. By character I mean the record of function." In such a spirit he would remove design from the thralldom of the past.

When those words were written, the industrial revolution had not yet had any profound impact on American life, at least compared to the changed conditions that would result from the explosive growth of technology in the decades to follow. Greenough could not have visualized the new possibilities that would open up to architects and engineers of the next generation or two, technical developments that were far advanced when Sullivan voiced his protest on the occasion of the Chicago fair—his complaint against the "fraudulent and surreptitious use of historical documents" such as he saw there and that caused him to despair. In later years, from the depth of his despondency, as he awaited commissions that too rarely came, he confessed, "American architecture is composed, in the hundred, of 90 parts aberration, eight parts indifference, one part poverty, and one part Little Lord Fauntleroy. You can have the prescription filled at any architectural department store, or select architectural millinery establishment." He had lost all hope that his work or his ideas would be remembered.

The year that the fair opened, the young, Wisconsin-born Frank Lloyd Wright quit his apprenticeship under Sullivan to start a practice of his own. He was only twenty-four years old at the time, but he took with him a precious legacy from his six years of close association with his *lieber Meister*, as he reverently referred to Sullivan. Like Sullivan, Wright resolutely turned away from everything the classical buildings at the Chicago fair stood for. Those reactionary forces, however, put a harsh limit on the market for his brilliant but unorthodox proposals. Referring to those circumstances through which he would adamantly have to cut his highly individual way as his career progressed, Wright later remarked that "they killed Sullivan and they nearly killed me!" Like Sullivan, Wright was to know misadventures and tragedies, periods of failure, and frustration. But, whereas Sullivan's career was in effect over by 1910, Wright persisted, survived, and when he died in 1959 at the age of ninety he was widely recognized, even by some of his many critics and enemies, as the greatest American architect of the twentieth century.

Actually, Wright won quicker and greater critical acclaim abroad than in his own country. As early as 1910 and 1911 two reports of his architecture that were published in Germany spread his fame across Europe. An architect from Holland who came to the United States early in the century to see Wright's buildings at first hand and to talk with the man himself, went away "with the conviction of having seen a genuinely modern work, and with respect for the master able to create things which had no equal in Europe." That was a degree of recognition that few if any of his American colleagues at the time were ready to give Wright; and the American public at large was very far from understanding his aims.

As Wright repeatedly explained, his buildings looked the way they did on the outside chiefly because of what he did with them on the inside. He decried the box-within-box arrangement of rooms in earlier dwellings as a "cellular sequestration that implied ancestors familiar with penal institutions." Democracy, he claimed, "needed something basically better than a box to live and work in. So I started to destroy the box as a building." In his autobiography he wrote that he saw a house "primarily as livable interior space under ample shelter. . . . So I declared the whole lower floor as one room, cutting off the kitchen as a laboratory. . . . Scores of unnecessary doors disappeared and no end of partition. . . . The house became more free as space and more livable too. Interior spaciousness began to dawn." Like the medieval cathedral builders, Wright used light and space as the equivalent of natural building materials, in his public and commercial structures as well as in the private dwellings he designed.

Wright once remarked that the "real American spirit, capable of judging an issue for itself upon its merits, lies in the West and the Middle West . . . where breadth of view, independent thought and a tendency to take common sense into the realm of art, as in life, are more characteristic. It is done in an atmosphere of this nature that the Gothic spirit of building can be revived." However, for the better part of a generation, what Wright was propounding and his buildings themselves were all but ignored in America. About 1911 an issue of *The Western Architect* remarked that "none have gone so far into the realm of the picturesque, or failed so signally in the production of livable houses, as Frank Lloyd Wright." (Wright later confessed that he was "black and blue in some spot" almost all his life from too intimate contact with the furniture he had designed early in his career.) Nevertheless, he persevered and by constantly renewing his vision lived on to confound many of his critics, to win most of them over, and to irritate others with his everlasting innovations.

From the early years of the century to the dark days of the Great Depression, most traces of modernism as represented by Wright's work and that of some of his advanced contemporaries were eclipsed by conservative trends in America, trends that looked to "period" styles of accepted worth and attraction for solution to problems of design and style. Up until the beginning of that regression, Europe could offer no comparable achievements in progressive architecture to those that featured the height of the Chicago movement. However, during the years between the two World Wars, while America remained relatively isolated in its outlook, the avant-garde European architects developed the strictly modern, so-called "international style" that swept all before it overseas. It was in the early 1930's that Americans, architects and public alike, were first shocked by the realization of what had been transpiring on the Continent while, so to speak, their backs were turned. In no small part those developments stemmed from ideas that Wright had been expounding and that had found their way abroad, there to receive a more generous welcome than they had at home.

It was after World War II that the new architectural language was widely imported into the United States and rapidly found acceptance here. By the end of the war, as well, many of Europe's most forward-looking builders, including Ludwig Mies van der Rohe, Marcel Breuer, Walter Gropius, and others, were living in this country and giving fresh impetus to developments here. Once again the provocative but neglected or half-forgotten issues so much earlier raised by Louis Sullivan and Frank Lloyd Wright were brought out into open controversy. Wright himself was rediscovered by a new generation, and his subsequent years proved to be his most prolific ones. A new "Chicago School" was established, a movement sharply spurred by the influence of Mies van der Rohe, who took that city as the base for his operations, and by the continuing presence of Wright. "Chicago has reasserted its great building tradition," writes one critic of our day, "in a body of work that may be traced directly back to the days when the city launched the modern movement in architecture and structural techniques." What has regerminated there has spread over the entire Midwest and far beyond.

OVERLEAF: *Fort Michilimackinac, Mackinaw City, Mich. (as of 1715)*. In its duel with England for an empire in North America, France thrust its way through the heart of the continent from the rocky eminence of Quebec in the North down the length of the Mississippi to distant New Orleans in the South. At a vital point in their line of communication, near the site where the waters of Lakes Michigan and Superior unite with Lake Huron, early in the eighteenth century the French built the palisaded outpost known as Fort Michilimackinac. This roughly square enclosure, about 320 by 360 feet, was a primitive wood construction that has recently been as meticulously re-created as the technology of modern archaeology can contrive. Of basic architectural interest are the *poteaux*, or vertical posts, which were driven into the ground—a speedy method of building typical of the French frontier. However, unless the posts were of cedar, which resists the dampness underground, they tended to rot and disintegrate, as happened with the original structure at Michilimackinac. All the reconstructed buildings here, both within and without the enclosure, rest on their original foundations.

Church of the Holy Family, Cahokia, Ill. (1799)

Cahokia Courthouse, Cahokia, Ill. (1737)

The structures on these pages are survivors from the eighteenth century when the French controlled the Great Lakes-Mississippi Valley from Canada to New Orleans. In 1737 Captain Jean Baptiste Saucier built a dwelling in Cahokia, Illinois (opposite St. Louis), in the traditional early French *poteaux-en-terre* method—hand-hewn timbers set vertically in the earth and caulked with a mixture of lime and rubble. In 1793 the house was purchased for use as a courthouse, making it the oldest surviving public building west of the Alleghenies, and the first court sessions and the first elections in Illinois were held there. The building was moved several times and is now reconstructed on its original foundation. The Church of the Holy Family, built in Cahokia in 1799, is believed to be the oldest church in Illinois. Also constructed in the *poteaux* style, it is one of the very few eighteenth-century French churches surviving in the United States or Canada. In 1776 Wisconsin's oldest extant house was erected by the fur trader Joseph Roi, one of the first permanent white settlers at Green Bay. Judge Joseph Porlier later held probate court at the house, which served as British military headquarters during the War of 1812. In 1850 the property was purchased by Nils Otto Tank, who hoped to establish a Moravian colony for Norwegian immigrants. He enlarged the clapboard cottage by adding wings to either side. The center section with its original wattle-and-daub walls—willow branches interwoven on an upright frame, packed with mud, and generally faced with rough boards—is an index of the building means of frontier America.

Roi-Porlier-Tank House, Green Bay, Wis. (1776; 1850)

Pierre Menard House, Fort Kaskaskia State Park, near Chester, Ill. (1802)

The French colonial house on the site of Fort Kaskaskia was built in 1802 by Pierre Menard, presiding officer of the first territorial legislature and the first lieutenant governor of Illinois. Even though France lost all territory east of the Mississippi to England following the Treaty of Paris in 1763, French cultural influence continued for many years. The Menard House, with its basement floor of masonry and its first floor exterior of oak protected by a porch on three sides, is a fine example of the lingering French vernacular. The sandstone and slate mansion in Chillicothe built by Thomas Worthington, sixth governor of Ohio, was designed by Benjamin Henry Latrobe. The house and gardens represent an impressive achievement for this early period in the old Northwest Territory.

OVERLEAF: *Lincoln's New Salem State Park, Petersburg, Ill. (as of 1830's)*. The country village where Abraham Lincoln lived as a young man (1831–37) has been meticulously reconstructed to reflect backwoods life and shelter in Illinois in the 1830's. The only surviving original structure is the Onstot Cooper Shop, where young Lincoln studied by firelight, as depicted in numerous nostalgic reconstructions of the scene.

Adena (Thomas Worthington House), Chillicothe, Ohio (1807). Benjamin Henry Latrobe, architect

Gristmill, Spring Mill Village, Spring Mill State Park, Mitchell, Ind. (1817)

Two midwestern villages established in the early years of the nineteenth century have been restored to give a good insight into living conditions in the frontier states that were once the old Northwest Territory. Spring Mill Village, Indiana, is dominated by the three-story stone gristmill with its waterwheel, twenty-four feet in diameter, and its elevated flume. The mill machinery has been restored to working condition to grind out corn for those who visit the mill museum of early Indiana history. Also in the village, which became a ghost town in the 1870's when it was bypassed by the railroad, are shops, a tavern, a distillery, and a mill office, all restored or reconstructed to their earlier appearance. Many of the residences, even when built of wood, are enclosed by low stone walls around house and garden to keep out animals. In 1817 in Zoar, Ohio, members of a German pietist sect established a village that became an exemplary communal enterprise. Most of the early individual houses are log-based and the restored tinsmith shop is a good example of half-timber construction as it was traditionally practiced in the Black Forest. By 1852 the self-contained village, made up of hard-working peasant stock, had a brickyard, iron foundry, and woolen mill among its industries, as well as a great central garden to sustain its primarily agricultural economy. By 1898 the community ceased to exist, but the physical nucleus remains.

Zoar Village Restoration, Zoar, Ohio (1817-98)

Sibley House, St. Paul, Minn. (1835)

Situated at the confluence of the Minnesota and Mississippi rivers, Mendota (now St. Paul)—the oldest permanent settlement in Minnesota—was a trading village for the American Fur Company in the 1820's and 1830's. Henry Hastings Sibley, who became Minnesota's first governor, built a relatively sophisticated stone dwelling at the outpost to serve as home and office in 1835 when he was a factor for the fur company. The Joseph Smith Mansion was the second Illinois residence of the Mormon leader when Nauvoo flourished as headquarters for the Church of Jesus Christ of Latter-day Saints from 1839 to 1846. The white wooden Congregational church was built in Tallmadge, near Akron, Ohio, by no mere accident, for that section of Ohio was part of the famous Western Reserve, land that Connecticut set aside for emigrants from that state after relinquishing the rest of her western claims to the federal government.

Joseph Smith Mansion, Nauvoo, Ill. (1844)

First Congregational Church, Tallmadge, Ohio (1825). Lemuel Porter, architect

Cotton House, Green Bay, Wis. (1840)

Taft House Museum, Cincinnati, Ohio (about 1820)

In 1820 Martin Baum, one of Cincinnati's prominent early citizens, who introduced viticulture to the region, built an elegant residence of white-painted wood in the Greek Revival style, with a two-story central block, a handsome portico, and an unusual play of oval window lights. It was subsequently the home of Charles Phelps Taft, whose half-brother, William Howard Taft, accepted the presidential nomination from the porch. With its inset porch, two-story Doric columns, and flanking wings, the handsome house built by Captain John Winslow Cotton at Green Bay, Wisconsin, is in the Greek Revival style. In Dayton, Ohio, the august courthouse, also Greek Revival in style, with

its tawny limestone walls and unfluted Ionic columns, is now serving as a museum of local history. It has a temple front, pilastered sides, and a coffered Roman dome over the old courtroom.

OVERLEAF: *Amana Village, Iowa (1855)*. A German religious sect resettled from western New York to Iowa and founded a group of seven villages, the most successful of the utopian communities that flourished in America in the mid-nineteenth century. The industrious, God-fearing Amana settlers shared communitive living in plain houses and farm buildings that reflected their dedication to strict principles.

Old Courthouse, Dayton, Ohio (1850). Howard Daniels, architect

State Capitol, Columbus, Ohio (1839-61). Henry Walter and Alexander Jackson Davis, principal architects

The weather-beaten sandstone temple at Springfield, which served as Illinois' fifth state house from 1840 to 1869, and thereafter as the Sangamon County Courthouse, is linked to the political careers of Abraham Lincoln, Stephen A. Douglas, and Ulysses S. Grant. Lincoln sat in the state legislature here (1840-41) and in 1858 accepted the Republican nomination for the United States Senate and made his famous "house divided" speech in the structure. Its Greek Revival design, with two Doric porticoes and with a lantern surmounted by a dome, was undoubtedly the work of the eastern architects Town & Davis, and John Rague may have acted as superintendent. The two-story limestone classical revival building in Columbus, Ohio, is one of our state capitols of great distinction. The design—a solid rectangle with recessed porches on all four sides, a triangular pediment above the entry, and a cylindrical drum above—required the services of seven architects over a period of twenty-two years.

Old State Capitol, Springfield, Ill. (1840). Town & Davis, architects; John F. Rague, associate

Hillforest, Aurora, Ind. (1856)

Honolulu House, Marshall, Mich. (1860)

The houses on these pages reflect the remarkable eclecticism that was so pervasive in architecture as well as in the decorative arts during the middle years of the nineteenth century. In 1856 a leading Ohio Valley skipper and industrialist, Thomas Gaff, built his mansion on a green-carpeted hill in Aurora, Indiana. Although semi-Italianate in style, it is sometimes called the "steamboat mansion" because its verandahs and wrought-iron balconies offer views of the Ohio River and its cylindrical cupola resembles a riverboat pilothouse. The lavish limestone Tuscan villa designed for James Burbank in St. Paul, Minnesota, has bracketed eaves running around the roof edges and an elaborate belvedere. A later owner, Mary Livingston Griggs, added a wing in the 1920's and then imported ten complete period rooms of European antiques which are now on display in this Victorian mansion. In Marshall, Michigan, stands an exotic house that Abner Pratt built as a replica of his residence in Honolulu, when he was United States consul to the Sandwich (Hawaiian) Islands. It is dominated by a high gallery which rises into a central tower and is set off by triple-scrolled brackets on the porch and around the eaves.

Burbank-Livingston-Griggs House, St. Paul, Minn. (1865; 1920's). Otis E. Wheelock, architect

The Culbertson mansion at New Albany, Indiana, overlooking the Ohio River and Louisville, Kentucky, across the way, is an inspired Victorian dwelling that has been restored to pristine condition. With its unusual balustrade topping a dark, shingled mansard roof, its variety of arched windows and doors, and its light yellow exterior walls, the house presents a façade that is both an attractive and colorful statement of its age. That age is even more extravagantly expressed in Terrace Hill, built a year later in Des Moines. This is one of the most representative examples of high Victorian architecture in the country, even though it was built when Des Moines had a population of but seventy-five hundred persons. The architect was the same William Boyington who designed Chicago's beloved Old Water Tower, a credential that gives the structure special interest. It was originally commissioned by Benjamin Franklin Allen, Iowa's first millionaire, and for a long time it was occupied by the successive presidents of the Equitable Life Assurance Society of Iowa.

Culbertson House, New Albany, Ind. (1868)

Terrace Hill, Des Moines, Iowa (1869). William W. Boyington, architect

The Old Water Tower in Chicago remains the city's only public building to have survived the Great Fire of 1871. Because of its interest as a historic relic and its endearing Gothic Revival fancifulness it has been called a structure "as sacred as a religious symbol." It was built to contain a standpipe 138 feet high and three feet in diameter, providing a hydrostatic head to equalize the pulsation of the pump and thereby achieve a continuous flow of water drawn from a spot several miles offshore in Lake Michigan. The tower has not been needed for years but it has long been regarded with affection by local citizens. Another sturdy suspension bridge designed and engineered by John Augustus Roebling crosses the Ohio River at Cincinnati. More than one thousand feet in length, it was the longest such span in the world at the time—as each of Roebling's bridges were as he built them in succession with increasing scale, until his final achievement with the Brooklyn Bridge at New York. The Cincinnati example combines suspension cables with Howe trusses for strengthening. By the time he designed the Brooklyn Bridge Roebling had refined his suspension techniques and dispensed with such trusses.

Bridge, Cincinnati, Ohio (1856-67).
John Augustus Roebling, engineer

Old Water Tower, Chicago, Ill. (1869).
William W. Boyington, architect

Iowa's fourth state capitol, here illustrated, is a many-domed building. The scale of the central vault, rising to a height of 275 feet and covered with gold leaf, is emphasized by similar but smaller domes at each of the structure's four corners. In an open competition New Hampshire-born John C. Cochrane along with French-born Alfred H. Piquenard won first place and were awarded the commission to undertake construction of their unusual variation on classical themes. About the same time, in Bellville, Ohio, some inspired soul designed what may well be the most engaging village bandstand that remains in the United States. It is a gem of Victorian fancifulness, and a nostalgic reminder of a time when musical entertainment came from the community itself, not to the community over the air waves from sources far distant from the village green or local park.

Bandstand, Bellville, Ohio (1879)

State Capitol, Des Moines, Iowa (1871-84). Cochrane & Piquenard, architects

Isaac M. Wise Temple, Cincinnati, Ohio (1866). James K. Wilson, architect

The Isaac M. Wise Temple, a synagogue that ornaments Plum Street in Cincinnati with its two minarets and other elements of Saracenic design, stands directly opposite the Roman Catholic Cathedral of St. Peter in Chains, "one of the handsomest and most monumental of Greek Revival churches in the United States," a corner of which can be seen in the above illustration, in a fascinating confrontation. The interior of the temple presents an extraordinary mixture of architectural motifs derived from Middle Eastern and Gothic sources, combined with disciplined judgment. It is one of America's outstanding religious monuments, inside and out.

Two of the most ebullient office structures of the 1870's and 1880's, the Mitchell Building and the Mackie Building, stand cheek by jowl in downtown Milwaukee. Their unabashed architectural hedonism was achieved with knowing talent and without timidity by a designer with invincible trust in the taste of his day, and an indulgent budget. In McLeansboro, Illinois, the People's National Bank goes even farther, incorporating in one structure half the architectural motifs known to architects in the latter part of the last century (plus metal awnings of the twentieth century). Its banded columns, roundheaded windows, outward-splaying chimneys, mansard roof, topped by a square dome, which is in turn surmounted by filigreed ironwork, are just a few of the elements that have been brought together in a colorful combination of red brick and white stone.

People's National Bank, McLeansboro, Ill. (1881)

Mitchell Building (1876) and Mackie Building (1879-81), Milwaukee, Wis. Edward Townsend Mix, architect

Vanderburgh County Courthouse, Evansville, Ind. (1891). Henry Wolters, architect

The courthouses of Indiana, especially those of the 1880's and 1890's, comprise one of the most astonishing arrays of municipal buildings in the United States. No other state in the nation can equal their determined ostentation. During the course of the nineteenth century, it has been said, all ninety-two Indiana counties built at least two and several as many as five courthouses in a span of less than ninety years. Some smaller towns splurged on such structures in the hope of being named the county seat. In all cases they bear witness to extravagant demonstrations of civic pride.

Lake County Courthouse, Crown Point, Ind. (1879). John C. Cochrane, architect

Tippecanoe County Courthouse, Lafayette, Ind. (1884). James F. Alexander and Elias Max, principal architects

The published guide to the courthouse at Fort Wayne alleges with apparent reason that the building is "the largest, most beautiful, costly, safe, and the most splendid structure designed for County uses, of any in Indiana, or indeed, the entire West." It is, as the guide further attests, "a combination of the Renaissance, Roman and Grecian, in architecture." The exterior of the structure, built of the famous Indiana limestone, is hardly less imposing than the Vanderburgh Courthouse, just noted; but the interior is unrivaled in its splendor. The dome and its pendentives and arched supports blaze with a whirling kaleidoscope of colored glass and bright murals of allegorical interest or depictions of various aspects of regional history.

Allen County Courthouse, Fort Wayne, Ind. (1900). Brentwood S. Tolan, architect

Courthouse, Bowling Green, Ohio (1895). Yost & Packard, architects

Glessner House, Chicago, Ill. (1887). H. H. Richardson, architect

Mabel Tainter Memorial Building, Menomonie, Wis. (1889). Harvey Ellis, architect

The pervasive influence of H. H. Richardson's designs in the Romanesque manner toward the end of the last century can be seen over much of the northern areas of the country. He himself was responsible for the Glessner House in Chicago, all but a granite arsenal in its robust solidity, with its small-windowed halls and service quarters on the street side and family rooms opening onto a garden court within, away from noise and dirt. At Bowling Green, Ohio, the turreted stone courthouse pays its heavy debt to Richardson's models, albeit in a distinctive manner. Richardson has been called the "godfather" of the Mabel Tainter Memorial in Menomonie, Wisconsin. With its paneled arch entry and massive, rugged stone façade, the building, which serves as a library, does ample credit to his formulas.

With its great cage of glass and iron serving as a lobby, among other important distinctions, the Rookery is one of the outstanding achievements of the Chicago architectural firm of Burnham & Root. In 1906 Frank Lloyd Wright renovated the lobby with a staircase and landing of marble and gold leaf. In 1895 Burnham's company finished construction of the sixteen-story Reliance Building, which many feel is the most advanced skyscraper of the Chicago School. During the 1880's and 1890's, that outburst of advanced architectural creativity, by the influence of the precedents it established, changed the face of most large cities of the world. Most of the prototypes of the new skyscraper technology are present in the Reliance Building—skeletal steel construction with internal wind bracing, spacious glass panes, and curtain walling (here a narrow band of terra cotta). It was a direct precursor of the glass-sheathed, thirty-story skyscraper projected by Mies van der Rohe a quarter of a century later. The new skyscrapers on nearby Dearborn Street are lineal descendants of the Reliance Building. Only three years earlier Burnham & Root had raised the Monadnock Building, also sixteen stories high and the last of the skyscrapers to be built of wall-bearing masonry rather than a skeleton of iron or steel. Its outer walls are more than six feet thick at the base, a necessarily stout support for the heavy load above. The architects did their best to lighten the appearance of this bulk by creating a lively alternation of windows and bays and by keeping to a pared simplicity.

Monadnock Building, Chicago, Ill. (1892). Burnham & Root, architects

Reliance Building, Chicago, Ill. (1895).
Daniel H. Burnham & Company, architects

The Rookery, Chicago, Ill. (1885).
Burnham & Root, architects

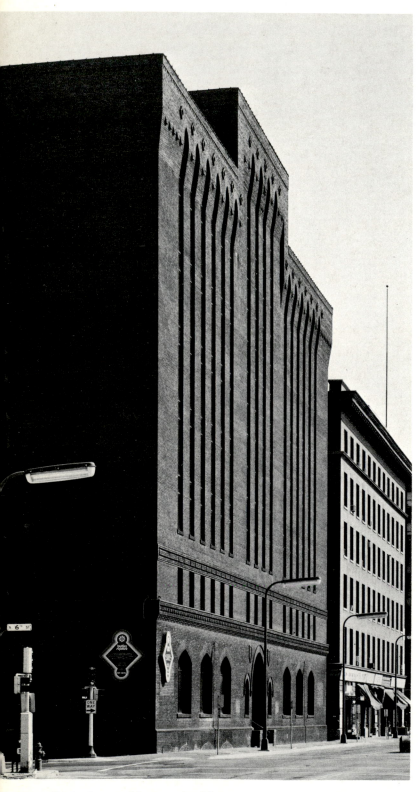

Early in the nineteenth century, skylighted arcades (as opposed to covered sidewalks) began to grace Paris, London, Milan, and Naples as smart meeting and shopping locales—so successfully, it might be added, that many of them are still preserved and actively used for their original purposes. The arcade at Cleveland, built almost ninety years ago, is America's unparalleled example of this highly agreeable and convenient urban form. Not only does it provide a protected pedestrian link between two downtown thoroughfares, it transacts the change in level between them, and it does both things within a light, superbly and daringly engineered enclosure of cast and wrought iron. The engineering problems were such that only a bridge-building firm—the Detroit Bridge Company—would undertake it. A success from its opening day, the Cleveland arcade is still a highly significant urban achievement. It is 290 feet long, 60 feet wide, and 110 feet high. One engaging aspect of its design is that no floor level is treated precisely like the one above or below. As the arcade rises it steps backward in the second level, admitting a maximum of daylight from the skylight-capped roof. The Butler Building (now known as Butler Square), an impressively scaled structure reminiscent of both Italian Renaissance designs and those of H. H. Richardson, was erected in 1906 as a warehouse. It had been vacant for a decade when, in 1975, the firm of Miller, Hanson, Westerbeck, Bell, carefully preserving the essence of its exterior, transformed it into an up-to-date office building and thus preserved an architectural ornament of the Minneapolis scene.

OVERLEAF: *Carson, Pirie, Scott & Company Store (detail), Chicago, Ill. (1904). Louis H. Sullivan, architect.* To give relief to the basic plainness of his Schlesinger and Mayer Department Store (now the Carson, Pirie, Scott & Company store) and to entice customers into it, Louis Sullivan traced out and his associate George G. Elmslie detailed an incredible filigree of cast-iron ornament which comes to full bloom over the corner entrance. It is doubtful that we will ever again see such inventiveness in design and such skilled craftsmanship in American architecture.

Butler Square, Minneapolis, Minn. (1906; 1975). Harry W. Jones, architect (1906); Miller, Hanson, Westerbeck, Bell, architects (1975)

Arcade, Cleveland, Ohio (1890). George H. Smith, architect; John M. Eisenmann, engineer

Carson, Pirie, Scott & Company Store, Chicago, Ill. (1904). Louis H. Sullivan, architect

In addition to the skyscraper and Wright's open-plan "prairie house," Chicago gave the world a special kind of window, the "Chicago window," with enormous central, fixed-glass pane and smaller double-hung sash for ventilation on one or both sides, as demonstrated in the Carson, Pirie, Scott & Company store. Despite his misfortunes in the years following the dissolution of his partnership with Dankmar Adler, Sullivan continued to produce occasional masterpieces, among them an exceptional series of banks for small midwestern communities. The finest of this group is in Owatonna, Minnesota, and consists of a nearly cubic block ornamented with bands of leaves and acorns and with brilliant glass mosaic.

Security Bank and Trust Company, Owatonna, Minn. (1908). Louis H. Sullivan, architect

Merchants National Bank, Winona, Minn. (1911). Purcell, Feick & Elmslie, architects

476

The three architects William L. Steele, George Grant Elmslie, and William G. Purcell had all worked together in Sullivan's Chicago office, and all fell under the master's benign influence. Elmslie was at one time Sullivan's right-hand associate and often personally drafted his intricate ornamental designs. In 1909 he set up a separate shop with Purcell as his principal associate. Two years later they completed the Merchants National Bank at Winona, Minnesota— their finest nondomestic work and one that has been beautifully preserved and thoroughly restored. The two architects both favored broad, plain wall surfaces highlighted by decorative accents of powerful and colorful design, as here seen. In the center of the façade, between sharply cut lower windows, the entry is surmounted by an exquisitely designed and executed ornamental motif—"the play work in the architect's day, his hour of refreshment," as Elmslie wrote. It is one of Minnesota's great buildings. In 1916 Steele was commissioned to produce the Woodbury County Courthouse at Sioux City, Iowa, and he at once got Elmslie to collaborate with him and to take charge of the overall design. The result was one of the finest public buildings of the time in this country. An artificially lit glass dome illuminates the interior, with its extravagance of terra-cotta decoration. Genre paintings on the wall panels contribute to the period flavor of the building—as does the unusual sculptured group at the entrance.

Woodbury County Courthouse, Sioux City, Iowa (1918).
William L. Steel and Purcell & Elmslie, architects

National Cash Register Company, Dayton, Ohio (1888–1906). Frank M. Andrews, architect

Carl Schurz High School, Chicago, Ill. (1909). Dwight H. Perkins, architect

In the years just before and after the turn of the century certain buildings in the public and industrial sectors showed some of the innovations that became commonplace in twentieth-century architecture, while others continued to look to the past for inspiration. The late-nineteenth- and early-twentieth-century buildings in Dayton, Ohio, designed for the National Cash Register Company were pioneers in industrial design. The architect, Frank Andrews, encouraged by an enlightened management, created a comfortable working environment, with a maximum amount of cross ventilation and glass, for the assembly of high-precision machinery. The double-hung windows fill four fifths of most of the walls, which are constructed of reinforced concrete. The Carl Schurz High School in Chicago exhibits a dignified play of angles and planes that has worn well since it was constructed in 1909. High-pitched roofs with deep overhangs suddenly stop the rising verticals of the brick walls. In 1917 with the limestone Marion County Public Library, Paul Philippe Cret produced a superb building in the Greek Revival manner.

Marion County Public Library, Indianapolis, Ind. (1917). Paul P. Cret, architect

Following the Columbian Exposition at Chicago in 1893, neoclassicism became a prevailing style in architecture, particularly in public buildings over the next several decades. Just after the turn of the century two impressive edifices arose in St. Paul, Minnesota, that were in the best classical tradition. A young Minnesota-educated architect, Cass Gilbert—who later gained national prominence for the Woolworth Building in New York City and the Supreme Court Building in Washington, D.C.—won the national competition to design a new Minnesota State Capitol. The white marble building in the Renaissance style boasts a dome that is a scaled-down copy of Michelangelo's dome atop St. Peter's Cathedral in the Vatican. Inside, the grand stairways and upper halls recall the splendor of imperial Rome. In 1906 Emanuel L. Masqueray, a Frenchman from the École des Beaux-Arts in Paris, designed the Cathedral of St. Paul in a triumphantly Beaux-Arts manner. A monumental arch frames a central rose window over the main entry. The Greek cross plan is crowned by a great dome 175 feet high and 96 feet in diameter.

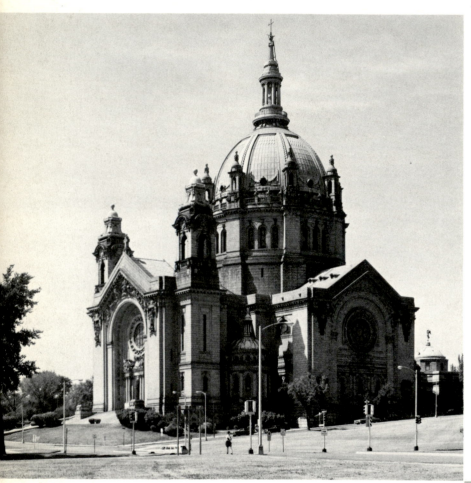

Cathedral of St. Paul, St. Paul, Minn. (1915).
Emanuel L. Masqueray, architect

State Capitol, St. Paul, Minn. (1902).
Cass Gilbert, architect

481

Frank Lloyd Wright's design for Unity Temple, built in 1906, was a revolutionary step in religious architecture of the twentieth century. Wright evolved the Unitarian Universalist church with almost no historical reference to past ecclesiastical structures. Its monumental exterior—solid concrete walls of a textured surface with a band of glass windows set high above the street to screen out noise—encloses a great square sanctuary within. Four massive piers in the corners, with balconies woven between, support the roof slab of poured concrete. Tinted skylights allow daylight to flood the auditorium. In 1909 Wright made his strongest statement in domestic design. He believed that architecture belonging to the prairie must stress the horizontal line—that the house must be considered an extension of the plain. The Robie House in Chicago, his most famous prairie-style example, extends its living-dining room wall in one long axis bound to the earth by its central fireplace. On the exterior, unbroken, horizontal bands of brick with limestone cappings alternating with continuous strips of windows are topped by a low hip roof. The interior is a remarkable design of fluid spaces with every major area having access to a porch or balcony, thus interrelating indoors with outdoors. It has been called one of the most brilliant designs in the history of architecture.

Robie House, Chicago, Ill. (1909). Frank Lloyd Wright, architect   OVERLEAF: *Robie House (detail)*

Unity Temple, Oak Park, Ill. (1906). Frank Lloyd Wright, architect

S. C. Johnson Offices (1939) and Research and Development Tower (1950), Racine, Wis. Frank Lloyd Wright, architect

Some thirty-seven years after its completion, the administration building of the Johnson Wax Company in Racine, Wisconsin, can still claim to have one of the great interior spaces in U.S. corporate architecture. For the central office area Frank Lloyd Wright used fifty-four slender dendriform columns—suggestive of those in King Minos' palace in Crete—to uphold this two-story (128-by-228-foot) room. The concrete columns increase in diameter as they rise and spread into eighteen-foot-wide lily-pad tops. From between these flowerlike circles comes natural light through glass tube skylights. The adjacent fourteen-story Research and Development Tower, with bands of red brick alternating with glass tubing to provide light, is a welcome vertical accent to the low units about it.

OVERLEAF: *Ceiling (detail), S. C. Johnson Offices*

Mount Zion Temple and Center, St. Paul, Minn. (1954). Erich Mendelsohn, architect

Christ Church Lutheran, Minneapolis, Minn. (1950). Eliel Saarinen, architect

Paul Tillich, prominent twentieth-century American theologian and educator, once asserted that space is our most valid symbol of God. On these pages and on the ones that follow are some of the forms employed since World War II to achieve architectural space of symbolic power. Erich Mendelsohn, after escaping from Nazi Germany, designed his finest American synagogue in St. Paul. Mount Zion Temple consists of a large sanctuary and smaller chapel—both copper-clad, almost windowless boxes—in exquisite relation to one another. In Christ Church Lutheran at Minneapolis, Eliel Saarinen's last work, the light-beige brick walls of the nave provide a warm and intimate setting for worship. The most startling feature of St. Jude Church in Grand Rapids is the boldly cantilevered, copper-covered baldachin, or canopy, projecting over the altar.

St. Jude Church, Grand Rapids, Mich. (1963). Progressive Design Associates, architects

Chapel, Concordia Senior College, Fort Wayne, Ind. (1958). Eero Saarinen & Associates, architects

Abbey Church, St. John's University, Collegeville, Minn. (1961).
Marcel Breuer, architect; Hamilton Smith, associate

The triangular chapel and its slender bell tower, resting on a terraced podium at the head of a large lake, is the visual and spiritual center of the Lutheran Concordia College. The church's sharp roof is covered with dark gray tiles as are the roofs of all the secular buildings on the campus, recalling a northern European village. The focus of the St. John's Abbey Church is the stupendous bell banner, some hundred feet wide and slightly higher, resting on four sculpted supports that straddle the entry to the church. The trapezoidal banner is pierced by a horizontal rectangle for bells and above it a vertical opening for a cross. Sun from the southern quadrants picks up facets of bells and cross and bounces from the bell banner to the honeycombed concrete and glass façade of the church rising behind.

When Frank Lloyd Wright designed the Greek Orthodox church at Wauwatosa, Wisconsin, he turned to the mother Byzantine church, Hagia Sophia in Istanbul, for reference. The dome of the Wauwatosa church is 104 feet in diameter, just three feet smaller than the one topping Hagia Sophia, even though it is much shallower. Wright employed a lunette motif on the eaves' edge and repeated it in larger size in the band of windows, and designed an even larger lunette at the entry. This interlocked circular and semicircular geometry is echoed in the interior. Marcel Breuer and Herbert Beckhard created a Roman Catholic church at Muskegon, Michigan, of almost brutal strength. The warped concrete walls rise virtually windowless, while roof skylights provide effective interior illumination.

Annunciation Greek Orthodox Church, Wauwatosa, Wis. (1959).
Frank Lloyd Wright, architect

St. Francis de Sales Church, Muskegon, Mich. (1966). Marcel Breuer and Herbert Beckhard, architects

Cummins Engine Company Technical Center, Columbus, Ind. (1967). Harry Weese & Associates, architects

The south central Indiana town of Columbus, population 28,000, has the most extraordinary building program of any city of any size in the country. Through the enlightened generosity of the Cummins Engine Foundation, the company being the largest manufacturer of diesel engines in the world, and the chairman of its board, Columbus-born J. Irwin Miller, some of the nation's most noted architects have been commissioned to design local buildings. The architects are chosen by the citizens from a panel recommended by outside experts and the foundation pays the architects' fees. The result has been an outstanding parade of fine structures, only a few of which can be illustrated here and on the next two pages. The First Baptist Church and Chapel dramatically cap the brow of their hill; their steeply pitched roofs and semicircular ends set up a geometric interplay. The North Christian Church by Eero Saarinen is in the form of an oblate hexagon whose steel roof ribs continue into a tall spire. A square, six-story administration building and a research and testing unit of prefabricated concrete panels house the Cummins Technical Center.

North Christian Church, Columbus, Ind. (1964). Eero Saarinen & Associates, architects

First Baptist Church and Chapel, Columbus, Ind. (1965). Harry Weese & Associates, architects

The county library, shown below, forms one of the harmonious components of an urban plaza set off by a magnificent walk-through "Large Arch" by Henry Moore. The plaza is paved in red brick which steps up to make a low podium for the library and then rises vertically to form the walls. The planar white metal exterior of the Fodrea School, which functions as an elementary school and community facility, wraps around an open inner court planted with grass and trees. Inside the junior high school just southeast of town, an inner court illuminated by daylight from overhead provides a lively meeting place for students.

OVERLEAF: *Roofless Church, New Harmony, Ind. (1960). Philip Johnson, architect.* One of the most profound religious constructions in the country today stands behind a twelve-foot brick wall set off by living trees and open to the sky. The fifty-foot-high, softly undulating sanctuary, covered with cedar shingles over a wooden arch frame, hovers over a bronze Virgin in the center, sculpted by Jacques Lipchitz, who also created a gilded ceremonial gate at the east end of this unusual building.

Cleo Rogers Memorial County Library, Columbus, Ind. (1968). I. M. Pei & Partners, architects; Henry Moore, sculptor

Southside Junior High School, Columbus, Ind. (1969). Eliot Noyes, architect

Fodrea Community School, Columbus, Ind. (1973). Caudill, Rowlett, Scott, architects

A meticulous analysis of urban educational needs for commuting students and the proper architectural expression of those needs was made before any building was undertaken at the Circle Campus of the University of Illinois in Chicago. It was decided to group facilities by function rather than by discipline: that is, one cluster of rooms for lectures (no matter what the subject), all laboratories·together (whatever the science), and a separate office building for professors (as opposed to departmental buildings). The highlight of the campus is the roof-top agora above the cluster of lecture halls, which comprise one enormous rectangle. This ample piazza, or court concourse, shown below, lies at the confluence of elevated granite walks. Four inward-oriented "exedras" stand near its corners. In the center, twin flights of curved steps march down to the lecture room level in the form of a split amphitheater. This elevated core is one of the great spaces in college architectural planning. The campus is so named for the adjacent Congress Circle Interchange. Cars are allowed only on peripheral parking lots.

Circle Campus, University of Illinois, Chicago, Ill. (1972). Skidmore, Owings & Merrill, chief architects and planners

Assembly Hall, University of Illinois, Urbana, Ill. (1963). Harrison & Abramovitz, architects; Ammann & Whitney, engineers

The assembly hall at Urbana rests lightly on the horizon like some gigantic space ship. In the simplest terms, the structure consists of two domes, the one serving as a roof resting on the upturned base, creating an interior completely free of columns. It represents magnificent coordination between architect and engineer. St. John's Preparatory School consists of terraces of classrooms that step down a hillside, with space allowed for full windows at each level looking over the next lower level to a pine-edged lake beyond. The McGregor Memorial Conference Center is dominated by its full-height central hall and lounge, which bisects the mass of the building, and is topped by a translucent ceiling that, with the glass end walls, suffuses the interior with radiant natural light. This architectural gem is set in an immaculate garden that enhances its luster.

St. John's Preparatory School, Collegeville, Minn. (1962). Hanson & Michelson, architects

McGregor Memorial Conference Center, Wayne State University, Detroit, Mich. (1958). Minoru Yamasaki, architect

Triple Water Tank, Southern Illinois University,
Carbondale, Ill. (1965). Paul O. Hall &
Associates, consulting engineers

Water tanks have commonly been necessary but ungainly features of the landscape.
With its three conjoined spheroid reservoirs
raised on as many stilts, the structure at Carbondale, Illinois, becomes as much sculpture
as container, unmatched in its sensuous
design, which may have been influenced by
advanced examples in Sweden and Finland.
Another three-legged structure, here of
stainless steel, at the General Motors Technical Center near Detroit, graces a handsomely landscaped industrial complex. The
tower rises before playing fountains designed as a computerized "ballet" by the
famed American sculptor Alexander Calder.

OVERLEAF: *John Deere Administration Build-*
ing, Moline, Ill. (1964). Eero Saarinen & Asso-
ciates, architects; Sasaki, Walker & Associ-
ates, landscape architects. This seven-story
building extends 330 feet (there are eleven
bays each thirty feet wide) across a pleasant
valley with a masterfully landscaped approach to the structure itself. One of the two
lakes included in that foreground cools the
water for the air-conditioning system. This is
one of the greatest of America's modern
buildings, and perhaps Eero Saarinen's most
brilliant achievement. Tailored to the
client's request for an "iron building"—actually it is made of self-rusting, self-preserv-
ing steel—it is a consummate expression of a
headquarters for a farm-machinery manufacturer, boldly conceived in a rough, tough
material for a firm dealing with the rough,
tough earth of the world. It represents the
antithesis of the frangible, shiny glass box of
so much contemporary construction. The
placement of beam on beam and beam on col-
umn that frame its exterior balconies
suggests the exquisite simplicity of the finest
joinery in Japanese wooden temples, but
here logically expressed in welded steel.
Four days after the building contract had
been signed and before the ground had been
broken Eero Saarinen died, never to see this
brilliant new masterpiece.

General Motors Technical Center, Warren, Mich. (1956).
Eero Saarinen & Associates, architects

College Life Insurance Company of America, near Indianapolis, Ind. (1972). Kevin Roche, John Dinkeloo & Associates, architects

The hard-edge, geometric, sculptural approach to architecture has probably reached a climax in the three startling structures (there will eventually be six) of the College Life Insurance Company of America on the plains of Indiana northwest of Indianapolis. Vertical, but splayed, walls of solid concrete form two sides of each structure; sloping, right-angled walls of bluish mirror glass form the other two. The interiors are all interconnected by bridging, and bands of windows overlook the countryside, which includes the group's own pool and landscaped surroundings.

The Blossom Music Center is situated on an ample site covering 526 acres. Under a great pavilion, partially open on two sides and completely so across the front, are some 4,500 seats, an orchestra pit for 110 musicians, and a stage accommodating 200 performers. The structure is based on a large inclined parabolic arch supported by ten inclined exposed steel columns, which together form a structural spine that is stable in all directions. This auditorium looks outward and upward to a bowl-shaped hillside where ten to twelve thousand additional listeners can sit on the grass under the stars of a summer night. The E. J. Thomas Performing Arts Hall, the first phase of an ambitious cultural complex, lies just across the bridge from downtown Akron. A multiterraced, thoughtfully landscaped area leads to this bold, provocatively angled concrete structure. The capacious lobbies have twenty-seven stainless steel cylinders which serve as counterweights for the adjustable ceiling of this highly flexible auditorium.

Blossom Music Center, near Akron, Ohio (1968). Schafer, Flynn & Van Dijk, architects; R. M. Gensert Associates, structural engineers

*E. J. Thomas Performing Arts Hall, University of Akron, Akron, Ohio (1973).
Caudill, Rowlett, Scott; and Dalton, Van Dijk, Johnson, architects*

Orchestra Hall in Minneapolis is one of the most remarkable interiors of its kind. Its excellent acoustics are controlled by a startling arrangement of relief surfacing of plaster cubic shapes that begin at the rear wall behind the orchestra and proceed across the ceiling to the rear of the auditorium in a precise pattern. At first sight these sound-reflecting geometric forms seem to encroach on the visual setting of the hall, but they are soon accepted as an intrinsic part of the over-all design. Also in Minneapolis, the exterior of the Tyrone Guthrie Theater, with its inviting large areas of glass, encloses an intimate interior. Although it accommodates 1,437 persons, no one of them sits more than fifty-four feet from the stage. The spectators in the orchestra seats virtually surround the players on the theater's projecting stage, a variation on the ancient Greek theme in which steeply banked seats fan out approximately 200 degrees about a central stage, reminiscent of the fourth-century-B.C. theater at Epidaurus designed by Polyclitus the Younger.

Tyrone Guthrie Theater, Minneapolis, Minn. (1963). Ralph R. Rapson, architect

Orchestra Hall, Minneapolis, Minn. (1974). Hardy Holzman Pfeiffer and Hammel Green & Abrahamson, architects; Dr. Cyril M. Harris, acoustical consultant

The Hennepin County Government Center is housed in two parallel office blocks—according to the function of courts and municipal offices. These nearly identical units are sheathed in reddish South Dakota granite and are separated by a sixty-foot-wide atrium which is glazed at the ends, X-braced for stability, and roofed with glass to make a covered garden concourse. The resulting inner space, which rises through most of the height of the building, is breathtaking. The nearby Crystal Court (see following page) is another brilliantly airy example of the new architectural trends changing the face of downtown Minneapolis. Directly across the street from Hennepin Center the turreted and beautifully preserved City-County Building (1905) is a fine reminder of the best of the past.

Hennepin County Government Center, Minneapolis, Minn. (1975).
John Carl Warnecke & Associates, architects

Interior Atrium (detail), Hennepin County Government Center

Ceiling (detail), Crystal Court

The IDS complex is comprised of a fifty-seven-floor skyscraper and its enclosed mall, the Crystal Court. Vertical setbacks at the corners, seven uniform notches, soften the profile of the tower, which is wrapped in a greenish-blue glass. The lower section contains the multilevel Crystal Court, a spirited mid-city crossroads of shops and cafés embellished by plantings and banners; a glazed roof floods the interior with sunlight.

OVERLEAF: *Federal Reserve Bank, Minneapolis, Minn. (1973). Gunnar Birkerts & Associates, architects.* The façade of the bank is attached to cables which are slung from the tops of two great piers ten stories high, creating a column-free basement floor so that armored cars could have free access to the gold bullion stored below. On the carefully landscaped terrace are several fine pieces of contemporary sculpture.

Interior (detail), Crystal Court

IDS Building and Crystal Court, Minneapolis, Minn. (1972). Philip Johnson and John Burgee, architects

MOBY
DICK'S

MOBY
DICK'S
BAR

"A WHALE
OF A DRINK"

SCHOOL
BUSINESS

Federal Center, Chicago, Ill. (1964-74). Ludwig Mies van der Rohe, chief architect; Schmidt, Garden, and Erikson; C. F. Murphy Associates; and A. Epstein and Sons, associates

S. R. Crown Hall, Illinois Institute of Technology, Chicago, Ill. (1956). Ludwig Mies van der Rohe, architect

In the building boom following World War II, master architect Mies van der Rohe enjoyed a series of major commissions in Chicago that are impressive examples of his genius. The two identical apartment buildings facing Lake Michigan at 860-80 Lake Shore Drive have been cited by the Landmarks Commission for expressing the potentialities of steel and glass in architectural design. The one-story glass-walled Crown Hall, on the campus of Illinois Institute of Technology, represents the epitome of steel construction, a masterpiece of pure geometric form. Four mammoth steel trusses carry the weight of the roof, freeing the breathtaking interior from the need for supports. The Federal Center, started in 1964, is comprised of three units around an open plaza—a thirty-story federal courthouse, a forty-two-story office building, and a one-story glass-walled post office.

OVERLEAF: *Wrigley Building (1921), Graham, Anderson, Probst and White, architects, and Tribune Tower (1925·), Hood and Howells, architects, both Chicago, Ill.* Among the prominent features of the Chicago skyline two skyscrapers from the twenties add their distinctive silhouettes—the terra-cotta-sheathed Wrigley Building (left) and the Gothic Revival Tribune Tower (right).

860-80 Lake Shore Drive, Chicago, Ill. (1952). Ludwig Mies van der Rohe, architect

The sixty-story twin towers of Marina City, strategically situated at the edge of the Chicago River within a few hundred yards of Lake Michigan, form a microcosm of a city where one can live and work, find recreation and exercise, shop and dine, and park a car or boat without leaving the premises. The circular towers are constructed on a central core of reinforced concrete about which the apartments and their semicircular balconies fan out. The seventy-story Lake Point Tower at the Navy Pier promontory of Lake Michigan is a masterpiece of design. The concrete frame—the highest concrete building in the world when built—is sheathed in bronze-tinted glass set in a framework of bronze-colored aluminum. The architects, once students of Mies van der Rohe and members of his office staff, were influenced by the trefoil shape of the tower on a drawing the master had created in 1921 in Berlin.

Marina City, Chicago, Ill. (1962). Bertrand Goldberg Associates, architects

Lake Point Tower, Chicago, Ill. (1968). G. D. Schipporeit and John C. Heinrich, architects

Civic Center, Chicago, Ill. (1966). C. F. Murphy Associates, architects; Skidmore, Owings & Merrill; and Loebl, Schlossman and Bennett & Dart, associates; Pablo Picasso, sculptor

The Chicago Civic Center is comprised of a thirty-one story skyscraper containing a new courthouse, one venerable old (1906) courthouse, and a polished plaza (345 by 220 feet). The design of the tower, clad in Cor-Ten steel and complemented by bronze-colored plate glass, was dictated by the need of an unusually large bay size (free floor area) to accommodate the numerous courtrooms and was accomplished by the use of large columns to frame these bays and support the building. The central feature of the granite plaza, alive with the interplay of fountain jets and rustling trees, is the fifty-foot-high Picasso sculpture "Woman," made of the same Cor-Ten steel as the building. It was given by the artist to the citizens of Chicago.

Like the pioneering Marina City, the hundred-story John Hancock Center is a microcity, with shops, restaurants, parking areas, skating rink and pool, offices, television and radio stations, and apartments from the forty-sixth to ninety-second floors. Skidmore, Owings & Merrill created the steel-framed, tapered form of "Big John"—all four walls incline inward from the large base—in response to the heavy wind load from the lake. The prominent exterior diagonals, each pair extending across eighteen floors, provide bracing against the wind and form the strongly visual exoskeleton. The 110-story Sears Tower, also designed by Skidmore, Owings & Merrill, is the tallest building in the world. The technically ingenious structure consists of nine independent units strapped together—the units on the corners terminate at different levels, producing the notched profile of the exterior. The steel frame is clad in black aluminum and sixteen thousand bronze-tinted windows.

John Hancock Center, Chicago, Ill. (1970).
Skidmore, Owings & Merrill, architects

Sears Tower, Chicago, Ill. (1974). Skidmore, Owings & Merrill, architects

SOUTHWEST

ARIZONA
ARKANSAS
LOUISIANA
NEW MEXICO
OKLAHOMA
TEXAS

The six southerly states that range from the western bank of the Mississippi River to the borders of California and Nevada contain some of the oldest habitations in the United States, as well as some of the nation's oldest public buildings and oldest cities. Long before the white man appeared in the Americas, the natives in what is now New Mexico, Colorado, and Arizona, ancestors of the present-day Pueblo Indians, had developed a unique type of architecture culminating, almost a millennium ago, in large apartment-house complexes, some with hundreds of rooms and capable of accommodating as many as a thousand persons. In New Mexico's Chaco Canyon alone are the ruins of twelve such multistoried masonry developments, one of them the largest ever uncovered on the continent.

At about the time of the Norman conquest of England, the Chaco area was a lively community of about seven thousand inhabitants. Although these natives knew nothing of writing, the wheel, or elementary metallurgy, they had the advantages of a network of surfaced roads and an elaborate system of irrigation. They had domesticated corn and beans, and their farming methods provided the surplus that sustained their civilization. Here there are no special apartments or buildings for an elite. Almost all rooms are of the same size, as in modern low-cost housing, indicating an egalitarian society that flourished some seven centuries before the Declaration of Independence was signed in Philadelphia, far across the continent.

It was not until the sixteenth century that the first Europeans found their way into this American Southwest, Spanish conquistadores bent on epochal discoveries that would make their fortunes and redound to the glory of Spain and of Christianity. Actually, the expedition of the first of them, Álvar Núñez Cabeza de Vaca, came of an accident that resulted in one of the most remarkable adventures in the annals of exploration. Although the details remain vague, it is evident that this intrepid pioneer along with several companions was shipwrecked off the coast of Texas in 1528 and was enslaved for some years by the local Indians. With his companions he escaped and after much wandering through the Southwest came safely to Mexico City eight years after his shipwreck. (According to one account they arrived stark naked, their clothing having shredded away.)

Almost certainly these were the first white men to see the buffalo, those "wild hunch back cows" that were the very substance of life for the natives of the West and whose incredible numbers blackened the illimitable prairies far beyond reach of the eye. Less probable were stories about the Pueblo Indians, which gave rise to the legend of the Seven Cities of Cibola, famed for immense wealth; a legend that grew more fabulous with retelling and inspired a vast treasure hunt. Within less than a decade Francisco Vasquez de Coronado had wandered as far north as Kansas and as far west as the Grand Canyon, the land where Montezuma's proven wealth was said to be equaled in yet undiscovered hoardings. Coronado's search revealed only humble native pueblos. But years later Spaniards were still hoping and looking for riches north of the Rio Grande. Meanwhile, they were spreading a thin web of empire over that great area. All this wandering and searching took place many years before the English laid serious claim to any part of North America; and before that did happen, it seemed likely that the Spanish might possess the entire continent. When the Spanish ambassador at London learned from a spy about the first Virginia colony, he reported the news to his king, adding, "I hope that you will give orders to have these insolent people quickly annihilated."

In 1609 La Villa Real de la Santa Fe de San Francisco—Santa Fe, in short—was grafted onto an Indian pueblo as a frontier outpost. The next year, Governor Pedro de Peralta constructed at Santa Fe the Royal Houses (Casas Reales) as the center of the new settlement. The principal building, the adobe and timber Palace of the Governors, served as the seat of the government of New Mexico for more than two hundred years to come (except for a brief interim when rebellious Indians took over). It still stands, the oldest structure built by white men in this country and America's oldest public building. It is almost a full century older than the Governor's Palace at Williamsburg, Virginia. Had the expected wealth been there, Santa Fe would probably have become a new center of Spanish power for a vast inland region. As it was, the little village survived the feuds of civil and ecclesiastical factions, Indian uprisings from within, and Apache raids from without, to stand as one of the oldest cities in the United States, a community established a mere two years after the early French settlement at Quebec and the English colony at Jamestown.

Along the far-flung borders of the land she claimed in North America, Spain felt an increasing pressure from nations who had learned from Spain herself the promise of New World empire. France was boldly asserting conflicting claims to the American West. In 1684 La Salle, searching vainly for the mouth of the Mississippi, arrived at Matagorda Bay in what is now Texas to reinforce France's right of possession of all that lay beyond, of, as the American historian Francis Parkman described it, "the fertile plains of Texas, the vast basin of the Mississippi from its frozen northern springs to the sultry borders of the Gulf, from the woody ridges of the Alleghenies to the bare peaks of the Rocky Mountains—a region of savannas and forests, sun-cracked deserts and grassy prairies, watered by a thousand rivers, ranged by a thousand war-like tribes...." Shortly thereafter La Salle fell victim to a shot from one of his disgruntled followers. The New World had lost one of its most inspired pioneers.

In 1718 the Spaniards established a border outpost at and about San Antonio in Texas to guard the western world it had discovered from intrusion by alien forces. Five missions and a presidial garrison of forty-three men were posted at that remote edge of empire. However, the religious and military leaders were ever at odds over the exploitation of the natives, and the Indians themselves were unresponsive to the conflicting demands of their European overseers. In 1730 fifteen families were imported from the Canary Islands to invigorate the community, and although it did not flourish mightily, San Antonio became the most important Spanish settlement in Texas. Here a picturesque civilization combining Spanish and Indian cultures was maintained until, years later, it was infused with fresh admixtures of people—American frontiersmen, Davy Crockett with his famous rifle "Betsy," Jim Bowie with his equally famous knife, and others who would make history at the Alamo.

The Spanish builders of the early Southwest could not flatly impose their pre-existing ideas on a land where their relative sophistication had much to learn from aboriginal experience, a land which had a topography and a climate peculiarly its own and which yielded some materials at once and others only in time. Wherever the sword of Spain advanced, there went also the cross of the Church in a missionary effort that was unmatched in fervor and magnitude. All through the Southwest, from Texas to

California, the landscape is dotted with the missions that were established more than two centuries ago by steadfast and courageous fathers intent on bringing the true faith to a heathen world. The buildings they constructed with the help of native labor endowed that raw world with some of its most distinguished "new" architecture and its most interesting historic structures. Because of the scarcity of wood in these arid regions, most of the missions were built of adobe, varying in style and elaboration according to circumstances, from the simplest constructions to highly ornamented churches that recall, however distantly, the great baroque cathedrals of Spain itself. At their best the missions of the Southwest were a magnificent fusion of the traditions the Spaniard brought with him and what he found in the New World to work with. Earnest padres and attendant craftsmen taught the Indians to carve architectural ornament, to sculpture figures of saints and other votive objects, to paint altarpieces in tempera on wooden panels covered with gesso in the European manner, none of which subjects or techniques were familiar to native tradition and all of which were translated into a local idiom—spare, colorful, and often ambiguous in its imagery—by what remained essentially pagan artisans.

In spite of La Salle's ill-fated venture of 1682, France by no means gave up her claims to authority in the Southwest. In 1718, the same year as the establishment of San Antonio by the Spanish, the city of New Orleans was founded as a trading center for New France by the French governor of Louisiana, Jean Baptiste le Moyne, Sieur de Bienville, who platted the nascent city into eighty rectilinear blocks—what was to become known as the Vieux Carré, or "old square." However, as a consequence of European wars and treaties, in 1762 Louisiana west of the Mississippi and the Isle of Orleans were ceded to Spain, and the remainder of Louisiana was surrendered to England the following year. It was another consequence of Anglo-French hostilities that in 1755, by an act of extreme severity, French Acadians from Nova Scotia were uprooted from their homes and dispersed elsewhere, many coming to Louisiana, as immortalized in Longfellow's "Evangeline," to settle west of New Orleans in an area that became known as "Cajun Country." Since then these unwilling refugees have remained physically isolated from the main current of American life, clinging to their traditional ways and remaining one of the least assimilated peoples in the United States. St. Martinville, on Bayou Teche, enjoyed a brief period of glamour and prosperity when refugees from the French Revolution made it "a pretty little village . . . full of barons, marquises, counts and countesses," but in the middle of the nineteenth century a combination of circumstances brought about a decline of this "little Paris."

Architectural evidence of the early French occupation of New Orleans is almost nonexistent. The first hastily built houses of cypress slabs were soon replaced by low-roofed, story-and-a-half brick structures, many combining shop and residence like the equivalent buildings in European towns. Two disastrous fires wiped out most of those first permanent structures late in the eighteenth century. All that remain today are the Ursuline Convent, begun in 1727, and a small house now known as Madame John's Legacy, built about the same time. There are more impressive remains from the days of the Spanish occupation, notably St. Louis Cathedral on the Place d'Armes built in 1794 and, facing the same central plaza, now known as Jackson Square, the Cabildo built the next year as the seat of the administrative and legislative council for Spanish Louisiana.

For a period of forty years the Spanish flag flew over the Place d'Armes, a period that witnessed an agreeable blending of French and Spanish cultures. The natives of

European descent were termed Creoles, and the Creole aristocracy of New Orleans formed a cosmopolitan society, whose elegant diversions amidst the surrounding lush tropical wilderness are legendary. The international confusion that attended the American and French revolutions kept alive the prospect that Louisiana might rejoin France. During the American Revolution, France and Spain were allies against the British and some help reached the rebellious colonists from New Orleans. Then, at the dawn of the nineteenth century, as Napoleon completely disturbed the European balance of power, in rapid succession Louisiana was ceded back to France and France quickly thereafter, in 1803, surprisingly sold this unimaginably vast territory to the United States. It was one of the most portentous real-estate transactions in history.

The inhabitants of New Orleans were hardly enthusiastic over the prospect of dominion by Americans, whom they knew largely as the coarse and boisterous rivermen who for some years past had descended upon them out of the northern wilderness in flatboats and keelboats by the thousands, with their miscellaneous freight. Until the canals and railroads diverted much of this traffic in other directions, New Orleans remained the gateway for the vast inland trade of the continent. In the first six months of 1803, it was reported to Jefferson, 173 ships of all nations had entered the Mississippi with cargoes valued in the millions of dollars.

American dominion affected the architecture of the old section of New Orleans but little. The great fires of 1788 and 1794 had destroyed most of the early buildings of the city, but those that were built as replacements clung to the traditions of Spanish and French origins. As late as 1828 Mrs. Trollope likened New Orleans to "a French Ville de Provence." For the most part the vernacular architecture of the old city consisted of patio, or courtyard, dwellings, built two stories high and flush with the line of the sidewalk on the exterior, often with a weblike pattern of ironwork galleries gracing the upper story—all concealing an inner court reached through a gate usually constructed of thick planks and opening onto a passageway wide enough to admit the family carriage. In the countryside, from New Orleans far up the Mississippi River Valley, locally developed French traditions revealed themselves in houses with raised ground floors and with encircling porches that served as protection from humidity and heat. Stylistically, neither of these types of dwellings was of notable distinction, but as sensible adaptations to local conditions they could hardly have been improved upon.

The advent of the steamboat on the Mississippi and the proliferation of cotton plantations combined to magnify the wealth of Louisiana. It was in the decades preceding the Civil War that this growing affluence was expressed in mansions built in southern adaptations of the Greek Revival style, like those in Mississippi and neighboring states as already discussed. As the scale of life expanded, houses became bigger and grander. Such was Belle Grove near White Castle, designed by Henry Howard for John Andrews, Jr., a wealthy planter, in 1857. (Some authorities have claimed that James Gallier, Jr., was the architect.) This two-story mansion, with its gabled portico supported by full-length Corinthian columns, and its central hall and great stair, boasted that it could accommodate fifty guests at a time in its seventy rooms. (It was completely destroyed by fire in 1952, after having fallen into ruin.)

The purchase of the Louisiana Territory gave new impetus to the westward movement. Americans, reported one observer from New Orleans, were spreading out like "oil upon a cloth." However, west of Louisiana, the territory under Spanish rule was not altogether hospitable to foreign intruders—as the American explorer Zebulon Pike learned when, in 1806, he reached the Rio Grande after enduring severe hardships, and was arrested for trespassing. But Pike returned from this adventure to tell of a ready market for American goods in the Spanish Southwest if the area could be reached in any practical manner. When Mexico proclaimed its independence in 1821 a flood of Yankee traders found their way to Santa Fe with unerring instinct. The trip to that slumbering little city by horse and mule train and later by caravan through barren, torrid country harassed by savages was an ordeal for man and beast alike. Sante Fe was hardly the golden city Coronado had hopefully looked for two hundred years earlier. But the first northern salesmen found there all the trading prospects Pike had visualized. In short order they opened a highly profitable traffic in furs, mules, calicoes, ribbons, scissors, tacks, and all manner of "notions" which were common to Yankee store shelves but which no one would have dreamed of carting up from Veracruz. And the way was opening for a swarm of westering Americans.

Through the annexation of Texas and the treaties that concluded the victorious war with Mexico that followed not long after (1846-48), by around mid-century the continental United States had virtually assumed its present dimensions, stretching from coast to coast. Now followed the familiar American experience of settlers from easterly sections of the country and from overseas swarming into the newly opened western lands, bringing with them the different local traditions associated with their earlier surroundings. Actually, there was an Anglo-American community in Texas as early as 1821. Overcoming Spanish apprehensions, Moses Austin (a Connecticut Yankee who went west via Virginia and Missouri) had secured a grant from the authorities permitting him, as an *empresario*, to bring American settlers into the territory, a maneuver completed after his death that same year by his son Stephen Austin (often called the "Father of Texas"). Conducting his affairs from a log cabin, the latter brought perhaps eight thousand colonists into the region in and about the settlement of San Felipe de Austin. Other *empresarios* brought in more. During the next fifteen years the total approached thirty thousand.

Parenthetically, some years earlier, in 1817, a contingent of anti-Bonapartists, equipped like a plundering expedition, attempted to establish a military colony, the Champ d'Asile, on the plains of Texas. It was a short-lived experiment in New World colonization, but its failure was significant. Along with the military discipline which the leaders of the group felt was necessary, the rigors of frontier life and the hostility of the Indians and the Mexicans caused the early abandonment of the project. Once again experience made clear that pioneering in the western wilderness was a highly specialized business and might better be left to the native breed who by heritage and training were experts at it. In spite of the fiasco at Champ d'Asile, by chance, what may be the oldest dwelling now standing in Austin was built there in 1841, in the style of a French provincial cottage, by the French government to house its legation to Texas when it was still an independent republic. Built of hand-hewn lumber with imported French doors and hardware, it has been restored in late years.

In the 1840's a society in Germany popularly known as the *Mainzer Adelsverein* was formed for the professed purpose of peopling Texas with Germans. A good deal of unfortunate confusion attended this venture, although a settlement was established at a frontier station named New Braunfels. The quixotic German prince Carl Zu Solms-Braunfels arrived at this outpost with a retinue of velvet-clad courtiers and soldiers who wore brilliant plumes in their cocked hats. However, his preconceived notions of life in Texas were not confirmed by his experience there, and he soon returned to enjoy the traditional amenities of his native land. A considerable number of emigrants did not survive the hardships they had to endure. Nevertheless, twenty-five thousand Germans settled at New Braunfels, at Fredericksburg, and elsewhere in Texas during a single decade. The Ferdinand Lindheimer House at New Braunfels, built in 1852, remains a fine example of German half-timber construction as adapted to Texas cedar and limestone. With its thick-walled limestone houses lined up close to the street, their steep-pitched roofs high in front and slanting toward the rear to cover shed rooms, Fredericksburg still retains the architectural flavor of an Old World community—a flavor intensified by the devotion of its inhabitants to old German traditions. By 1843 enough Germans had already settled in Texas to cause the fledgling republic's Congress to stipulate that the laws be published in the German language as well as in English. Within a decade Germans constituted a substantial minority of the populations of Galveston, Houston, and San Antonio. Indeed, San Antonio has had its German "first families" for more than a century.

Buildings of every description were being constructed in various parts of Texas at one and the same time during the middle years of the last century, according to the different circumstances that prevailed here and there in this enormous area—frontier forts, log cabins (including a typical Swedish example), handsome Greek Revival plantation mansions and city houses, as well as other types that reflected the architectural fashions that had developed in Louisiana and other southern states and more remote parts of the country. The landscape architect Frederick Law Oldmsted stopped overnight at a plantation house which, he reported, was but "a small square log cabin, with a broad open shed or piazza in front, and a chimney, made of sticks and mud, leaning against one end. A smaller detached cabin, twenty feet in the rear, was used for a kitchen. A cistern under a roof, and collecting from three roofs, stood between. . . . Three hundred yards from the house was a gin house and a stable, and in the interval between were two rows of comfortable negro cabins. . . . The [plantation] house had but one door and no window, nor was there a pane of glass on the plantation."

But the soil was immensely productive. In the beginning, better buildings could wait while the land was seeded and the crops harvested. Here in Texas was the fateful boundary of the Cotton Kingdom. Cotton, it was firmly believed, could not move on to a farther West, its limits being set by soil and climate. Largely because of its slaveholding planter class attracted there in great numbers by inexpensive land in the pre-Civil War period, Texas sided with the Confederacy and seceded from the Union in 1861.

A large part of the Southwest remained relatively undeveloped until after the Civil War—until the coming of the railroad. New Mexico and Arizona continued to be troubled by hostile Indians until the fabled Geronimo laid down his arms in 1886. It was plagued also by wars and altercations between whites with conflicting interests, who often expressed their differences without benefit of law and order. Homesteaders, squatters, farmers, and cattlemen, all vying for land and water rights, had in turn to contend with thieves, gamblers, murderers, and rustlers who found the raw frontier a natural theater for their unscrupulous ways. In retrospect, it was a rousing and violent spectacle. The stage was not prepared, however, for any refinements or advances in the art of building, although in the 1880's even such a riotous town as Tombstone, Arizona, boasted an opera house and the first Protestant church in the territory, along with its saloons and gambling casinos—so well known to men like Billy the Kid and Wyatt Earp.

As was ultimately revealed, there was more wealth in and beneath the soil of the Southwest than Coronado could ever have imagined. But it took industrial enterprise he could also not have imagined to unearth and exploit it. The discovery of oil, gas, and other natural resources, combined with the magic touch of the railroads, brought booming economic progress to what had earlier been, often enough, unproductive wasteland. Arizona alone produces more than half the nation's supply of copper; Arkansas more than 90 per cent of the country's supply of bauxite ore, from which aluminum is extracted, as well as oil. New Mexico holds more than two thirds of the country's known uranium reserves. Two of the world's foremost petrochemical and gas centers are in Oklahoma, at Tulsa and Oklahoma City. Texas leads all other states in the value of its annual mineral production. All of which makes no mention of the cattle business and large-scale agriculture, both of which were spurred by the proliferation of railroads late in the last century and early in our own.

Inevitably, results of these truly explosive developments can be read in the architectural landscape of the Southwest, as the illustrations on the following pages make abundantly clear. Especially in the decades initiated by World War II, throughout the area industrial structures, museums, theaters, churches, libraries, and of course private dwellings all bear testimony to the use of a regional culture completely abreast of the most advanced and successful contemporary trends in building designs and techniques. As an early harbinger of these accomplishments, in 1938 near Phoenix, Arizona, Frank Lloyd Wright designed the desert home and studio which he called Taliesin West and where he "gathered his family and apprentices about him like some Apache chief." It was his ideal—and his last abode. He died there in 1959.

OVERLEAF: *San Xavier del Bac, near Tucson, Ariz. (1783-97)*. This elaborate baroque structure is celebrated as the most beautiful as well as the best-preserved example of mission architecture in the Spanish Southwest. In 1692 the Tyrolean-born Jesuit missionary-explorer Father Eusebio Francisco Kino (or Chini) came upon a Pima Indian village in southern Arizona near the site of present-day Tucson. Here, in 1700, he established a mission that he named after his patron saint, Francis Xavier, and introduced cattle ranching to the community. After Father Kino's death in 1711, the original chapel he had built slowly disintegrated and was finally destroyed by the Apaches. In 1783 the Franciscans, who had replaced the suppressed Jesuits, undertook construction of a new church, which was completed fourteen years later. The two blindingly white square towers with octagonal belfries guard the ornately scrolled central portal. Today the restored church is a thriving parish on the San Xavier Indian Reservation.

The migratory tribes of Indians that once roamed over the Great Plains constructed simple shelters of natural materials found in the area. At Anadarko, Oklahoma, villages representing a cross section of Indian dwelling types have been reconstructed to demonstrate the variety prevalent in the plains locale. Dwellings include an Apache wickiup, a Navaho hogan, a Kiowa tepee, a Caddo wattle-and-daub house, a Pawnee earth house, a Pueblo adobe, and a Wichita grass house. The only Indians north of the Rio Grande given to urban-style living were corn-raising tribes who built multiple dwellings in the present-day Four Corners area of New Mexico, Arizona, Utah, and Colorado. When European explorers discovered the large, pre-Columbian community built by ancestors of the Pueblo Indians along the Animas River of New Mexico, they erroneously called it Aztec. By the early 1100's Indian farmers had congregated in large, geometrically planned, multistoried masonry structures facing plazas and focused on a Great Kiva. As restored, this ceremonial room for the men measures over forty-eight feet in diameter and projects half aboveground. It is one of the few evidences of interior space on a large scale, as realized by the Indians in America.

Indian City U.S.A., near Anadarko, Okla.

Aztec Ruins National Monument,
Aztec, N.M. (1100-1300)

Great Kiva, Aztec Ruins National Monument

White House, Canyon de Chelly National Monument, Chinle, Ariz. (1066-1275)

Pueblo Bonito, Chaco Canyon National Monument,
near Bloomfield, N.M. (about 1100)

Chaco Canyon was the center of a Pueblo Indian culture that reached its peak between A.D. 1000 and 1300. The earliest inhabitants of this semiarid region built circular pit houses in Chaco Canyon as early as A.D. 600. By 900 the pit houses had given way to multifamily dwellings, erected aboveground in rows or clusters of rectangular rooms with solid masonry walls—a style borrowed by their neighbors at Aztec (see preceding pages). The largest of these great apartment houses, with a floor plan exceeding three acres, was Pueblo Bonito, rising five stories high, and with eight hundred rooms able to accommodate over a thousand persons. Today, remains of eleven other great pueblos and four hundred smaller ruins are preserved in Chaco Canyon. In Arizona, at the Canyon de Chelly, are ruins of several hundred Pueblo Indian villages built between A.D. 350 and 1300 directly into or nestled at the base of the sheer red sandstone cliffs. From about 700 the Pueblos occupied the area in large apartment-style cliff houses of stone masonry —one of which is the White House, so named because it was covered with plaster, as may be seen in a remaining section. Late in the thirteenth century a severe drought in the region caused the Pueblos to abandon the apartments here as well as in Chaco Canyon and Aztec. Hopi Indians later occupied Canyon de Chelly and were in turn replaced by the Navajos, who still summer there in their hogans—circular structures of poles and logs.

San Ildefonso Pueblo, N.M. (about 1300)

Palace of the Governors, Santa Fe, N.M. (1612)

With the severe drought of 1276-99 in the Southwest, many of the Pueblo Indians abandoned their cliff dwellings and began to move to other adobe communities. These so-called pueblos are large, terraced community houses, with walls of adobe and roofs supported by projecting vigas, or heavy beams. They are entered through the upper story by ladders. At San Ildefonso Pueblo, on the east bank of the Rio Grande, one- and two-story buildings accented by dome-shaped, outside ovens frame the main plaza. In 1609 Santa Fe was founded as the capital of the Spanish Southwest, and the next year work began on the Palace of the Governors on Santa Fe Plaza. The low, viga-punctured, adobe structure, with its shaded passageway across the front and a patio behind, is a graceful blend of Indian and Spanish architectural styles.

Set against the harsh landscape of an upland mesa, a new cultural center-restaurant-motel complex accommodates those seeking to explore the vast Hopi Reservation.

OVERLEAF: *Taos Pueblo, Taos, N.M. (rebuilt about 1700)*. Nestled against New Mexico's high Taos Mountains, the communal dwellings of Taos Pueblo—the tallest in the Southwest—are little changed from those described by Spanish explorers as early as 1540. The several units of the still-occupied pueblo echo the hills beyond with cube piled upon cube in abstract geometric forms. The solid adobe walls—doors and windows were added only in the nineteenth century—contrast with the wooden outrigging of several storage shelters, and with ladders arranged to reach the upper terraces.

Hopi Cultural Center, Oraibi, Ariz. (1971). Gonzales Associates, architects

San Francisco de Asis, Ranchos de Taos, N.M. (about 1772)

By the early seventeenth century, churches and missions had been installed in most of the Pueblo Indian villages, adding to the Indians' resentment of Spanish rule. In 1680 they revolted in an armed protest that forced the Spanish to retreat to the El Paso area of Texas; they did not reconquer New Mexico until 1692. The ancient mission of San Geronimo, first built about 1598 near the entrance to Taos Pueblo, was rebuilt after 1694 and continued to operate until 1847 when it was reduced to ruins by American troops. About four miles southwest of Taos the venerable church of San Francisco de Asis still stands at Ranchos de Taos. The exterior, with its two belfries and Gothic-style pointed arch door, is wrapped around by a low adobe wall. The buttresses which cluster about the base of the apse and lend lateral support to the adobe walls are the remarkable and much photographed feature of San Francisco. Differing from the sophisticated flying buttresses of the medieval cathedrals of Europe, these bulky supports were at times reinforced because of weathering. Apart from their structural function, they appeal as abstract architectural sculpture.

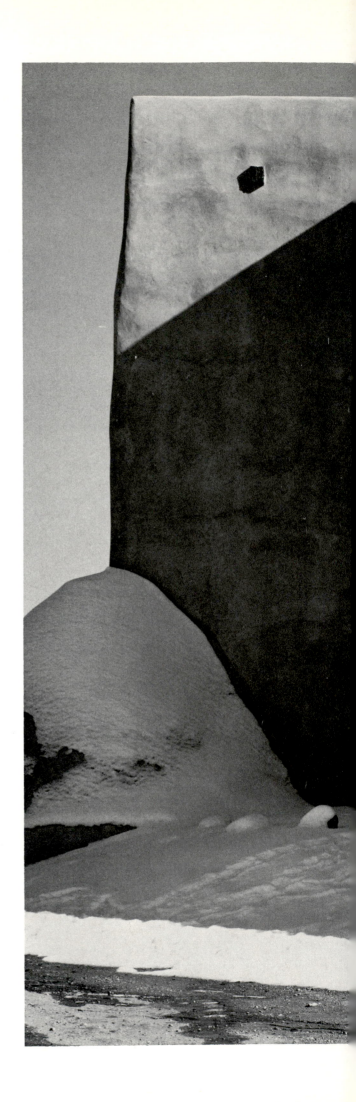

Occupying the heights of a sandstone mesa some 357 feet above the plain, Ácoma Pueblo, established about 1300, claims to be the oldest continuously occupied settlement in the nation. From their aerie, the Indians of Ácoma successfully resisted the Spanish conquistadores for nearly a century, until 1629, when the Franciscans founded the San Estévan del Rey Mission at Ácoma. Materials of the mission's original church, so painstakingly hand-carried to the mesa top, are undoubtedly incorporated in the one built about 1640, which is still in use today. San Estévan epitomizes the thick-walled, narrow, flat-roofed churches with few windows built under Spanish religious influence in New Mexico with Indian labor. The interior illustrates the simple post-and-lintel construction—the supporting vigas of the roof placed atop the stone and adobe walls and braced by corbels often fancifully painted. The chapel at Laguna, New Mexico, is notable for its energetic wall decorations— boldly primitive wainscoting painted to represent the elements. In comparison to these primitive New Mexican examples is the startlingly ambitious church of San Xavier del Bac in Arizona—the high point of Spanish baroque architecture and sculpture in America. The vaulted and domed interior is dominated by its elaborately carved brick and polychromed stucco *retablos* behind the altar, flanked by richly treated transepts.

San Estévan del Rey, Ácoma, N.M. (about 1640)

San José de Laguna, Laguna, N.M. (1706)

San Xavier del Bac, near Tucson, Ariz. (1783-97)

552

San José y San Miguel de Aguayo, San Antonio, Tex. (1768-78)

During the eighteenth century San José y San Miguel de Aguayo was one of the most important missions on the northern frontier of New Spain. Founded in 1720 by Captain Juan Valdez, lieutenant general of the province of Texas, San José was a thriving community by mid-century with some two thousand Indian converts caring for three thousand head of livestock and producing three thousand bushels of corn annually. The mission formed a large, walled compound composed of living quarters for the Indians and soldiers, a granary, and the church itself. After 1824, when the missions were secularized by the Mexicans, San José gradually fell into disuse and started to collapse, but it has now been restored. The façade of the church, started in 1768, is one of the glories of the Spanish contribution to architecture in this country. The main entrance sparkles with its Spanish baroque richness of ornament set off against the simple stuccoed walls of its semi-Moorish façade. Originally most of the building was covered with stucco decorated in brightly colored geometric patterns, a small sample of which remains near a lower corner of the tower. The highly accomplished carvings of the church's façade and of the rose window on the south wall were the work of Pedro Huizar of Aguascalientes, Mexico.

Nuestra Señora de la Purísima Concepción de Acuna, San Antonio, Tex. (1731-55)

San José de Laguna, Laguna, N.M. (1706)

The three structures illustrated here show the contrast between the stone churches of the relatively sophisticated missions of Texas and the simpler adobe churches of New Mexico. Nuestra Señora de la Purísima Concepción de Acuna was relocated to its present site on the San Antonio River in 1731. For more than twenty years Franciscan fathers and Indians labored to erect the massive stone church with walls almost four feet thick, twin bell towers, and pedimented doorway. The charming adobe church of San José de Gracia is the focus of its tiny village set high in the Sangre de Cristo Mountains of New Mexico. The softly molded, white stuccoed façade of San José de Laguna with its twin bells recalls similar churches of the Spanish Mediterranean area.

San José de Gracia, Las Trampas, N.M. (about 1760)

El Santuario de Chimayo, Chimayo, N.M. (1816)

In 1699 Jesuit Father Eusebio Francisco Kino converted the Pima Indians of Tumacácori village and introduced ranching to the area. After the Pima rebellion of 1751 the settlement was moved to its present site, where a small mission was erected. When the Franciscans took over the Sonora mission chain in 1768, San José de Tumacácori became the most important mission in the region. The present baroque adobe church—with its semicircular gable end, arched doorway, pilasters, attached baptistry with belfry on top—was built between 1796 and the end of Spanish rule in the region. The devout Indian converts abandoned it in 1848 and today the ruins of the church remain as a sturdy symbol of the mission period. A little-altered example of a Spanish village church stands at Chimayo village in New Mexico. El Santuario is currently a pilgrims' shrine.

San José de Tumacácori, near Nogales, Ariz. (1796–1806)

Spanish Governor's Palace, San Antonio, Tex. (1749)

The so-called "palace" at San Antonio was completed in 1749 as housing for commandants of the presidio of Béxar, and in 1772 it became the headquarters of the Spanish government in Texas. It was here that Moses Austin came in 1820 to secure the privilege of settling Anglo-Americans in Texas. The last governor left the next year, when Mexico proclaimed its independence from Spain. The Cabildo in New Orleans, with its massive arches and wrought-iron balconies, was built in 1795 of stuccoed brick as the seat of the administrative and legislative council for Spanish Louisiana. After the French returned to rule Louisiana for twenty short days in 1803, the sovereignty of Louisiana was ceremoniously transferred to the United States in this structure.

Cabildo, New Orleans, La. (1795)

Built during the early days of French colonization, Parlange is a fine example of the early Louisiana type of farmhouse in what is known as the "raised cottage style." Its ground floor is built of stuccoed brick as protection from water and dampness, with circular columns also of brick to help support the galleries that surround most of the house. The upper part was constructed of cypress and moss packed together with clay, topped by a steep-pitched roof in the French tradition. It has been lived in by eight successive generations of descendants of the early owners. The Acadian House was built in similar fashion by an early French commandant at Poste des Atakapas, later to be known as St. Martinville. This part of the state was settled by French Acadians who came there when they were forced from Nova Scotia in the middle of the eighteenth century because they would not swear allegiance to the British who had conquered their homeland. Their French-speaking descendants, the Cajuns, remain a group apart to this day.

Parlange, near New Roads, La. (about 1750)

Acadian House, St. Martinville, La. (1765)

Madame John's Legacy, New Orleans, La.

In the late 1720's a French sea captain, Jean Pascal, from Provence, built a country-style raised cottage in New Orleans' Vieux Carré. The house did not survive the great fire of 1788, but it was immediately rebuilt using the original plan and some materials salvaged from the burnt-out structure. Thus, the dwelling that stands today is almost precisely like the earlier one, although the verandah originally went around three sides, including that facing the essential patio. The house represents a rare and excellent souvenir of the intriguing but little-known French period of the city's architecture. (The dormer windows may be later additions.) In his romantic tales of old New Orleans, *Old Creole Days*, published in 1879, the author George Washington Cable dubbed the house "Madame John's Legacy," a name that has stuck to it over the years since. Madame John's Legacy stands just around the corner from Jackson Square, the heart of old New Orleans and long known as the Place d'Armes or, in Spanish, the Plaza de Armas, the most historic spot in Louisiana. (It was renamed Jackson Square in 1851 for Andrew Jackson, the hero of the battle of New Orleans during the War of 1812.) On the north side of the square stands the St. Louis Cathedral, built in 1794, adjacent to the Cabildo. It is the third church to have been raised on the site and christened with the name of the patron saint of Bourbon France.

Cabildo (1795) and St. Louis Cathedral (1794), New Orleans, La.

Fort Smith was established in 1817 to keep peace between the Osage Indians and the Cherokees. Starting in 1839, the original log structures were replaced by a new, more substantial fort built of stone. Ten years later it was observed that the "public buildings for Military purposes at this place are the finest, largest, and best buildings on the Western frontier." The Pentagon Barracks consist of four identical, angled structures built of brick painted pink with white Doric columns supporting galleries on both sides. They constitute a handsome example of military architecture. A fort had been built near this site by the French in 1719. Eight years later the British threw up a redoubt to ward off approaching Spaniards. In 1966 the American barracks, built between 1819 and 1829, were restored and remodeled on the interior to serve as very desirable apartments.

Old Fort Museum, Fort Smith, Ark. (1839)

Pentagon Barracks, Baton Rouge, La. (1829; 1966)

Shadows-on-the-Teche, New Iberia, La. (1834)

Rosedown Plantation, St. Francisville, La. (1835; 1844)

The surviving white-columned mansions of ante-bellum Louisiana are standing symbols of the affluent and suave society they so handsomely served. Shadows-on-the-Teche, facing the street rather than the bayou behind it, was commissioned by the planter David Weeks as a town house at New Iberia. The owner unfortunately died just after he moved in. During the Civil War, General Nathaniel P. Banks made his headquarters here. With its justly celebrated gardens, Rosedown Plantation covers ten acres of land. Six Doric columns support the gallery along the façade, and an identical set above supports the gabled roof. Side wings were added in 1844.

RIGHT *and* OVERLEAF: *Oak Alley, Vacherie, La. (1839).* One of the greatest of the plantation houses, Oak Alley is covered by an enormous hip roof supported by twenty-eight two-story Tuscan columns. Its double galleries are so wide that windows can be kept open virtually all the time, the interior remaining protected from a merciless sun or pelting rain; in clement weather each verandah serves as an open-living room. Thus did the southern adaptations of the Greek Revival style logically and effectively respond to the needs of a specific environment. The plantation derives its name from the twenty-eight almost unbelievably magnificent oak trees that, spaced exactly eighty feet apart, stretch in an *allée* down to the Mississippi.

Porch (detail), Oak Alley

Houmas House, Burnside, La. (1840)

Kellum-Noble House, Houston, Tex. (1847)

In 1834 the highly accomplished Irish-born architect James Gallier, Sr., came to New Orleans at the age of thirty-six, after having been associated for a time with the well-known northern architects Town and Davis, and with Minard Lafever. Among other distinguished contributions to architecture in the New Orleans area, in 1841 he designed Ashland-Belle Hélène near the banks of the Mississippi River. This four-square plantation house, surrounded by a peristyle of twenty-eight massive piers and with an "invisible" roof, has in the past suffered from neglect, but has several times been aided in its fight for survival by Hollywood, which has repaired part of the structure to serve as a set for motion pictures. It is now being gradually restored. Houmas House, named for a tribe of local Indians with a reputation for bravery, was built for John Smith Preston. In 1857 it was sold to John Burnside, who developed the plantation into the nation's leading producer of sugar. The Kellum-Noble House, built by Nathaniel Kellum in 1847 at Houston, Texas, is believed to be the oldest brick house in that city. (Kellum operated a brick kiln.) Completely surrounded by double galleries, it is topped by a low-pitched roof. During the 1850's a Mrs. Z. M. Noble conducted one of Houston's first private schools in the house, which was occupied by the Noble family until 1898, when the city purchased it.

Ashland-Belle Hélène, near Geismar, La. (1841). James Gallier, Sr., architect

San Francisco, Reserve, La. (1850)

Obviously influenced by the design of Mississippi river-boats that once steamed past its front door (the river was then without a levee), San Francisco is a maverick among Louisiana plantation houses. Its style has been variously described as "surrogate Greek Revival gone Victorian" and as an "improbable assemblage of Gothic, Classic and miscellaneous Victorian architectural elements ... Louisiana's best known fantasy in architecture." The top floor is set back, largely camouflaged by a dominating cornice which surmounts the second-floor gallery. Within, the cornice and the cypress ceiling of the drawing room are exquisitely painted by Dominique Canova (nephew of the famous Antonio Canova), an Italian apparently influenced by wall paintings at Pompeii dating from the first century B.C.

Le Prète House, New Orleans, La. (1835)

The Le Prète House, noted for the beauty of the cast-iron ornament that embroiders its many balconies, is a landmark of the Vieux Carré. It was built by Dr. Joseph Coulon Gardette, a Philadelphia dentist who came to New Orleans during Spanish rule and created a flourishing practice here. In 1839 it was purchased by Jean Baptiste Le Prète, a prominent local merchant. James Gallier, Jr., was brought to this country at the age of five and, following in the footsteps of his father, recently mentioned, became a leading architect of Louisiana. In 1860 he completed his own residence on Royal Street in New Orleans, next to an earlier, commercial building. Each of these structures has the distinctive New Orleans balcony on the street façade, here upheld with the slenderest of cast-iron columns burgeoning into a fantasy of cast-iron grillwork at the balcony level and eave. When continued in adjacent buildings, the verandahs create a passage providing shade in the sunshine and an umbrella during a rain.

Gallier House, New Orleans, La. (1857–60). James Gallier, Jr., architect

St. Louis Cemetery #1, New Orleans, La.

Small Houses, Vieux Carré, New Orleans, La.

At first glance the St. Louis Cemetery appears to be a domestic annex to the Vieux Carré. Packed together along the *allées* of the burial ground, the vaults of its infinitely varied tombs are raised several feet above the ground and the underlying water table. These picturesque "homes of the dead" often resemble the houses of the living. Some of them are the work of such highly qualified architects as James Gallier, Benjamin Latrobe, and others. Parts of the Vieux Carré retain its early character, one which was fashioned long ago by local cultures and was shaped in part by the local climate and molded of local materials.

The Old State House at Little Rock was designed by Gideon Shryock, who had recently completed the Kentucky capitol at Frankfort, as earlier described. It ranks among the freshest examples of Greek Revival style in the country and is rightfully the pride of Arkansas. (The triple-tiered fountain in front was brought down from the Philadelphia Centennial Exposition.) In remarkable contrast, the Old State Capitol at Baton Rouge, built in 1850 and restored in 1882, presents a stiffly symmetrical block with octagonal turrets and a machicolated cornice outlining the roof line. The original design was by James Dakin, who for several years had been a member of the New York firm of Town and Davis, largely famous for their Greek Revival structures.

OVERLEAF: *Interior, Old State Capitol, Baton Rouge.* As part of the rebuilding of the old structure in 1882, a magnificent dome was added to the capitol, which had been gutted by fire twenty years earlier during the Civil War.

Old State Capitol, Baton Rouge, La. (1850; 1882). James H. Dakin, architect

Old State House, Little Rock, Ark. (1842). Gideon Shryock, architect

So long as they moved through timbered wilderness, pioneering Americans continued to find log cabins their most practical type of shelter, at least until which time something better could be built. It was not until they reached the sea of grass of the Great Plains that they ran out of timber and turned to sod for their building material. In the Ozark Mountains of northwest Arkansas a collection of mid-nineteenth-century log structures has been gathered at Prairie Grove, the site of a Civil War battle in 1862. The oldest units in the village are the restored F. F. Latta House and its barn, both of extremely simple notched-log construction. Another log cabin village of the same vintage has been assembled in Fort Worth and gives an insight into living conditions on the Texas frontier. Connecting the rooms of the Isaac Parker cabin is a typical "dog trot," a breezeway providing an open-air work space covered over by the roof.

Latta House, Vineyard Village, Prairie Grove, Ark. (1834)

Parker House, Log Cabin Village, Fort Worth, Tex. (1848)

Winedale Inn, near Round Top, Tex. (1834; 1850's)

Fort Davis, founded in 1854 to protect travelers on the San Antonio–El Paso road, played a major role in the defense system of western Texas. Federal troops garrisoned here patrolled the area, escorted stagecoaches and wagon trains, and pursued raiding Comanches and Apaches. In 1861, during the Civil War, Fort Davis was occupied by Confederate troops, who evacuated the post in the next year. It was subsequently destroyed by Apaches and in 1867 was rebuilt by federal forces, who protected the region from outlaws and hostile Indians for the next two decades. The fort was finally abandoned in 1891, and today the National Park Service has restored many of the fifty adobe and red-stone buildings of the western military outpost. The first part of the eight-room Winedale Inn, of native Texas cedar with its log outbuildings of cedar and oak, was built in 1834 by early settlers in the rolling countryside between the Brazos and Colorado rivers. It was subsequently added to and served as a stagecoach inn during the 1850's.

Fort Davis National Historic Site, Fort Davis, Tex. (1854; 1867)

U.S. Courthouse and Federal Building, Galveston, Tex. (1861). Ammi B. Young, probable architect

The former custom house at Galveston established a surprisingly sophisticated classic revival beachhead at this western site, a building which more than a century of hurricanes and man-made batterings has not diminished. The north and south façades are distinguished by inset columned porches on both floors, the whole suggestive of Inigo Jones' early-seventeenth-century Queen's House in Greenwich, England. At Tombstone, the courthouse where frontier justice was sometimes meted out is a surprisingly capable brick structure whose stone quoins, columned entry, and venturesome cupola recall influences from much farther east. At the time it was erected, the "Town Too Tough To Die" was earning an unparalleled reputation for lawlessness and violence.

Courthouse Museum, Tombstone, Ariz. (1882)

The 475-foot-long suspension bridge over the Brazos River at Waco, Texas, was opened to traffic a good ten years before New York's Brooklyn Bridge but some twenty years after the one at Wheeling, West Virginia, both earlier described. Cables for the Texas span, supplied by the Roebling Company, the firm responsible for the two other bridges, were hauled by oxen from Galveston. Almost three million locally made bricks were used in the construction of its four stalwart piers. Built privately, the Waco bridge was sold to the county in 1889 and thereafter has been operated as a free public thoroughfare. Fredericksburg, Texas, named ambitiously after Frederick the Great of Prussia, still reflects the Continental inheritance its early German settlers brought with them in 1846 and translated into central Texas yellow limestone. In 1847 these emigrants signed a treaty with the Comanche Indians, which brought their colony a peace that endured.

Old St. Mary's Church, Fredericksburg, Tex. (1863).
Father Gallus, architect

Suspension Bridge, Waco, Tex. (1870). Thomas M. Griffith, supervising engineer

Bishop's Palace (Gresham House), Galveston, Tex. (1893). Nicholas J. Clayton, architect

Hill County Courthouse, Hillsboro, Tex. (1890). W. C. Dodson, architect

Texas can boast of some of the most unrestrainedly exuberant buildings of the late nineteenth century. In 1885 Walter Gresham commissioned his architect-neighbor, Nicholas Clayton, to build him the most elaborate house in the state, a task that was undertaken with unflinching confidence at the cost of a quarter of a million dollars. The exterior unfolds a catalog of virtually every conceivable architectural motif. With its combination of turrets and gables, roof lines of changing character, wrought-iron railings and brackets, and chimneys of assorted designs, the profile of the house reveals a thoroughly restless imagination. Since 1923 the house has served as the residence of the bishop of the Galveston-Houston Roman Catholic diocese. Somewhat less fanciful, the Ellis County Courthouse is still conglomerate in appearance, with its towers, turrets, and terra-cotta embellishments. The Hill County Courthouse is a foursquare, three-story structure of tawny limestone, topped by a dazzlingly white, triple-tiered metal tower above its Mansard roof.

Ellis County Courthouse, Waxahachie, Tex. (1897). J. Reilly Gordon, architect

591

Santa Fe Railroad Station, Shawnee, Okla. (1901)

From 1877 to 1889 the Santa Fe Railroad developed from a prairie grain and cattle carrier extending a little more than 780 miles to a great transcontinental system reaching from Chicago to the Pacific and the Gulf of Mexico. In 1901 a new station was built at Shawnee, Oklahoma, with stepped gables and a staunchly turreted tower—a somewhat vagrant western outpost of H. H. Richardson's far-reaching influence. When it was completed in 1929, the Boston Avenue Methodist Church in Tulsa attracted international attention as a notable example of modern ecclesiastical architecture. The walls of the four-story-high main building, constructed of massive limestone, terminate in cubistic forms in the shape of praying hands. An illuminated central tower, rising 290 feet above the doorways, suggests the same symbolic imagery. The doorways themselves have pointed arches and are embellished with terra-cotta and bas-relief figures of memorable pioneers. Bruce Goff was the principal designer.

Boston Avenue Methodist Church, Tulsa, Okla. (1929). Rush & Endicott, architects

Meandering through the heart of the oldest city of Texas, San Antonio, with its wealth of historic landmarks—the missions of San José y San Miguel de Aguayo and Purísima Concepción, the Spanish Governor's Palace, and the Alamo—is a delightful river walk. The Paseo del Rio, lying some twenty to twenty-five feet below street level, winds for about three miles in a horseshoe shape through the downtown area. Pedestrians may stroll along footpaths or avail themselves of paddle boats or sightseeing barges on the waters. The Paseo, lined with diverting shops, cafés, and restaurants, and with its flowing water and attractive landscaping, offers a welcome respite from the noises, traffic, and concrete of the city above. An elegant tower originally designed for the San Antonio Hemis-Fair of 1968 is now a prominent part of the city's skyline. The 750-foot tower is anchored by fifty-five piers sunk more than sixty feet down to form a foundation base. External elevators move up and down the twelve-sided poured-concrete shaft of the tower; stairwells are within the hollow core. The steel-frame Top House contains a revolving restaurant, a stationary one, and an observation deck.

Tower of the Americas, San Antonio, Tex. (1968). Ford, Powell & Carson, architects

Paseo del Rio, San Antonio, Tex. (restoration begun 1939)

Price Tower, Bartlesville, Okla. (1955).
Frank Lloyd Wright, architect

Taliesin West, Scottsdale, Ariz. (1938-59). Frank Lloyd Wright, architect

Frank Lloyd Wright described the Arizona setting of his desert home and studio, Taliesin West, as "a grand garden the like of which in sheer beauty of space and pattern does not exist, I think, in the world." Over a period of twenty years Wright designed a series of structures interacting with the hauntingly beautiful landscape of the Maricopa Mesa. For the sloping wall surfaces, indigenous rocks were carefully chosen and placed in concrete to form a mosaic pattern reflecting the surrounding rugged mountains. The angled roof of the famous drafting room was originally of canvas but was replaced by translucent plastic panels after a fire. The master's only sky-scraper, the H. C. Price Tower, adapted from 1929 plans, is based on an X-shaped structural spine from which the floors boldly cantilever. Copper-colored louvers and gold-tinted glass add to the lively effect of the façade.

Kalita Humphreys Theater, Dallas, Tex. (1959). Frank Lloyd Wright, architect

*Outdoor Theater, Institute of American Indian Art,
Santa Fe, N.M. (1970). Paolo Soleri, architect;
Pacheco & Graham, associates*

*Alley Theater, Houston, Tex. (1968).
Ulrich Franzen & Associates, architects*

In the years following World War II the performing arts enjoyed renewed popularity across the nation and new theaters were commissioned to house dramatic presentations. At Dallas, Texas, Frank Lloyd Wright designed his first professional theater. The Kalita Humphreys Theater presents a spirited exterior with its play of curves, and the auditorium radiating around an apron stage achieves an admirable intimacy between actors and spectators. The Outdoor Theater at Santa Fe, New Mexico, is one of the few designs of visionary architect Paolo Soleri that actually have been built (see also pages 602–03). Earth and concrete have been sculpted in sympathetic echo of the mountain background to produce a flexible amphitheater which serves for traditional Indian ceremonies as well as outdoor commencements. The fortresslike contours of the Alley Theater in Houston house two separate stages for fine repertory performances.

OVERLEAF: *New Mummers Theater, Oklahoma City, Okla. (1970). John M. Johansen, architect.* An exciting new building has been designed for the three theater units of this adjunct of the Oklahoma Theater Company. Mechanical and circulatory functions are exposed on top of these units; their brightly colored ramps, stairs, and bridges connect the components.

Cosanti Foundation Workshop, Paradise Valley, Ariz. (1962–70). Paolo Soleri, architect

Paolo Soleri, a gifted Italian-born architect, has spent years in the Arizona desert drafting what he calls "guidelines toward a new option" for modern man, the city dweller. Soleri has designed ideal possible cities that he calls "arcologies," a combination of architecture and ecology in new basic patterns of life for vast populations. In Soleri's visionary cities people are concentrated in elaborate, multileveled structures within small areas. These cities have definite boundaries, beyond which lay an unspoiled countryside within easy reach of the urban dweller. The hand-built desert workshop (left) in Paradise Valley, not far from Scottsdale, Arizona, serves as a gathering place for Soleri's disciples. Here, with spontaneous improvisation, the master and his dedicated student-apprentices have fashioned their "earth colony"—a workshop, living quarters, and small museum—mostly of concrete cast in desert silt. The structures, some below ground and cavelike, abound in circles, arcs, and apses and are enlivened by Soleri's famous ceramic wind bells, the sale of which helps support the foundation. At Arcosanti (below), about seventy miles north of his present headquarters, Soleri and his disciples are constructing the first application of his principles for the new utopia.

Arcosanti, near Dugas, Ariz. (1972-   ). Paolo Soleri, architect

Hopewell Baptist Church, Edmond, Okla. (1953). Bruce Goff, architect

The space requirements for three very different types of enterprises have been successfully met by three very creative architects. Buckminster Fuller's largest geodesic dome yet built, with an unobstructed interior diameter of over 375 feet, services tank cars near Baton Rouge, Louisiana. The all-welded-steel dome is made up of bright yellow hexagonal units supported by an exoskeleton of blue-pipe framing. Philip Johnson designed a beautifully landscaped, below ground-level library for Hendrix College in Arkansas. The roof deck on top of the library and the sunken plaza in front of it provide a gathering place for students; library functions are accommodated below. For a church in Oklahoma, Bruce Goff employed architectural symbolism to tie the religious activities of the parishioners to their working life. The supporting trusses of the twelve-sided church are of pipes ordinarily used in the rigging of oil wells.

Bailey Library, Hendrix College, Conway, Ark. (1967). Philip Johnson, architect

Union Tank Car Repair Facility, Baton Rouge, La. (1958). Synergetics, Inc., dome engineers; Battey & Childs, architects

605

St. Patrick's Church, Oklahoma City, Okla. (1962). Murray-Jones-Murray, architects

A bold and unusual plan distinguishes St. Patrick's Church in Oklahoma City. Thirty-foot-high concrete walls around the church create a religious palisade to shut out the distractions of the urban environment. The inner face of the peripheral wall is decorated by a continuous band of angels with upraised arms, designed by Frank Kacmarcik. The church itself is a great glass box with a concrete roof whose wide overhang shelters an ambulatory completely encircling the church. Daylight floods the sanctuary within, which is marked behind the altar by a freestanding gold-leaf screen designed by Joseph Albers.

BELOW *and* OVERLEAF: *Chapel of the Holy Cross, Sedona, Ariz. (1956). Anshen & Allen, architects.* An evocative memorial chapel is set against the towering red sandstone cliffs of central Arizona. The reinforced concrete walls rise from two rock outcroppings, and a ninety-foot-high cross projects from one of the glass ends. The dramatic cliffside chapel is approached by a sinuous footpath leading up from a parking area which is located below.

Chapel of the Holy Cross

The thirty-three-story Tenneco Building in Houston, Texas, ranks among a handful of great postwar skyscrapers in America. The outer walls are inset five feet from the peripheral structure to provide for sun and weather control by means of clever louvers and for window-washing platforms. This also provides the building with a subtly pierced profile. The ground floor is inset on four sides, creating a sheltered, fifty-foot-high galleria. Also in Houston, the Jesse H. Jones Hall for the Performing Arts is wrapped in Italian travertine. The theater-concert hall is surrounded by a peristyle of slender piers upholding a great sheltering roof. The peristyle is brilliantly illuminated at night and the marble facing is carried right into the lobby, inviting the theatergoer into the foyer. The auditorium itself, accommodating an audience of 3,001 persons, is a chamber whose electronically controlled acoustical devices and imaginative "theater mechanics" contribute to the structure's reputation as "the most sophisticated building of its kind anywhere in the world."

Jesse H. Jones Hall for the Performing Arts, Houston, Tex. (1966). Caudill, Rowlett, Scott, architects

Tenneco Building, Houston, Tex. (1963). Skidmore, Owings & Merrill, architects

Philip Johnson has described his memorial to John F. Kennedy as a "pair of magnets about to clamp together." The design forms an enclosure of two U-shapes, understated to the point of starkness and curiously unsettling in its emotional impact: The Dallas memorial is situated a few hundred yards from the spot where the late President was gunned down and suggests in contemporary architectural terms the inexorable turns of fate. Construction is of simple precast concrete slabs lightly elevated above the ground on short supports. In Houston a nondenominational chapel and meditation center commemorates two great twentieth-century American artists—Mark Rothko and Barnett Newman. A memorial to Dr. Martin Luther King, Jr., by Newman, a twenty-six-foot-high self-rusting steel "Broken Obelisk," points its shattered finger skyward and is reflected in a pool in the courtyard. In the chapel-gallery are fourteen enormous, almost solid-color canvases by Rothko, who died before the chapel was opened.

John F. Kennedy Memorial, Dallas, Tex. (1970). Philip Johnson, architect

Kimbell Art Museum, Fort Worth, Tex. (1972). Louis I. Kahn, architect;
Dr. August E. Komendant, structural engineer

"Structure is the giver of light," wrote the late architect Louis I. Kahn, de-signer of the Kimbell Art Museum, and here light and life are fused throughout the structure. It has one of the country's greatest museum in-teriors. Although the Texas sun furnishes by far the greater part of the illumination, no direct rays strike the art on the walls; the lighting is all in-direct. This is achieved by running continuous skylights down the center of fourteen of the sixteen cycloidal vaults that form the building's distinc-tive roof. Finely pierced metal screens, suspended directly beneath the skylights, reflect and disperse the light over the soffits of the vaults and thence onto the works of art. The vaults, the two forward of which form entry porches, are supported only at their ends. They measure 104 feet long and twenty-three feet wide and are separated by concrete channels containing air-conditioning outlets and electrical conduits.

Amon Carter Museum, Fort Worth, Tex. (1961). Philip Johnson, architect

The two very different Texas art museums (right, top and bottom) were both designed by Philip Johnson. The Fort Worth museum was planned as a showcase to display the late Amon Carter's superb collection of sculpture and paintings by the western artists Frederick Remington and Charles M. Russell. Stepped terraces, defined by low walls of shellstone, lead up a gentle slope to a formal building whose façade is marked by natural fossil-shell stone arches. The main gallery on the first floor is double height with teak walls; there are also four smaller galleries to display Mr. Carter's original collection and later acquisitions. The smartly angled and curved Art Museum of South Texas suggests the Mediterranean in its dazzlingly white reinforced concrete contours overlooking Corpus Christi Bay. The all-white interior is planned almost like a village square, with different elements—auditorium, library, walled sculpture garden, and galleries—enframing the central exhibition hall. Natural light from skylights illuminates the major galleries of the museum.

Art Museum of South Texas, Corpus Christi, Tex. (1972). Philip Johnson, architect; John Burgee, associate

616

BELOW *and* OVERLEAF: *Robert R. McMath Solar Telescope, Kitt Peak Observatory, Kitt Peak, Ariz. (1962). Skidmore, Owings & Merrill, architects.* The McMath structure houses the largest solar telescope in the world. This fixed instrument is five hundred feet long (most of it underground), angled at 32 degrees into its mountain base. At the top, 110 feet above the level of the earth, a heliostat eighty inches in diameter, supported on a substantial concrete shaft and driven with incredible precision, follows the arc of the sun. This reflects the solar image down the long optical tunnel (oriented along a north polar axis) to a sixty-inch mirror at the bottom, which returns the image to another mirror, forty-eight inches in diameter, near the spot where the casing enters the earth. This last shoots the sun's image into the observation room with its vacuum spectrographs for analysis.

Robert R. McMath Solar Telescope,
Kitt Peak Observatory

617

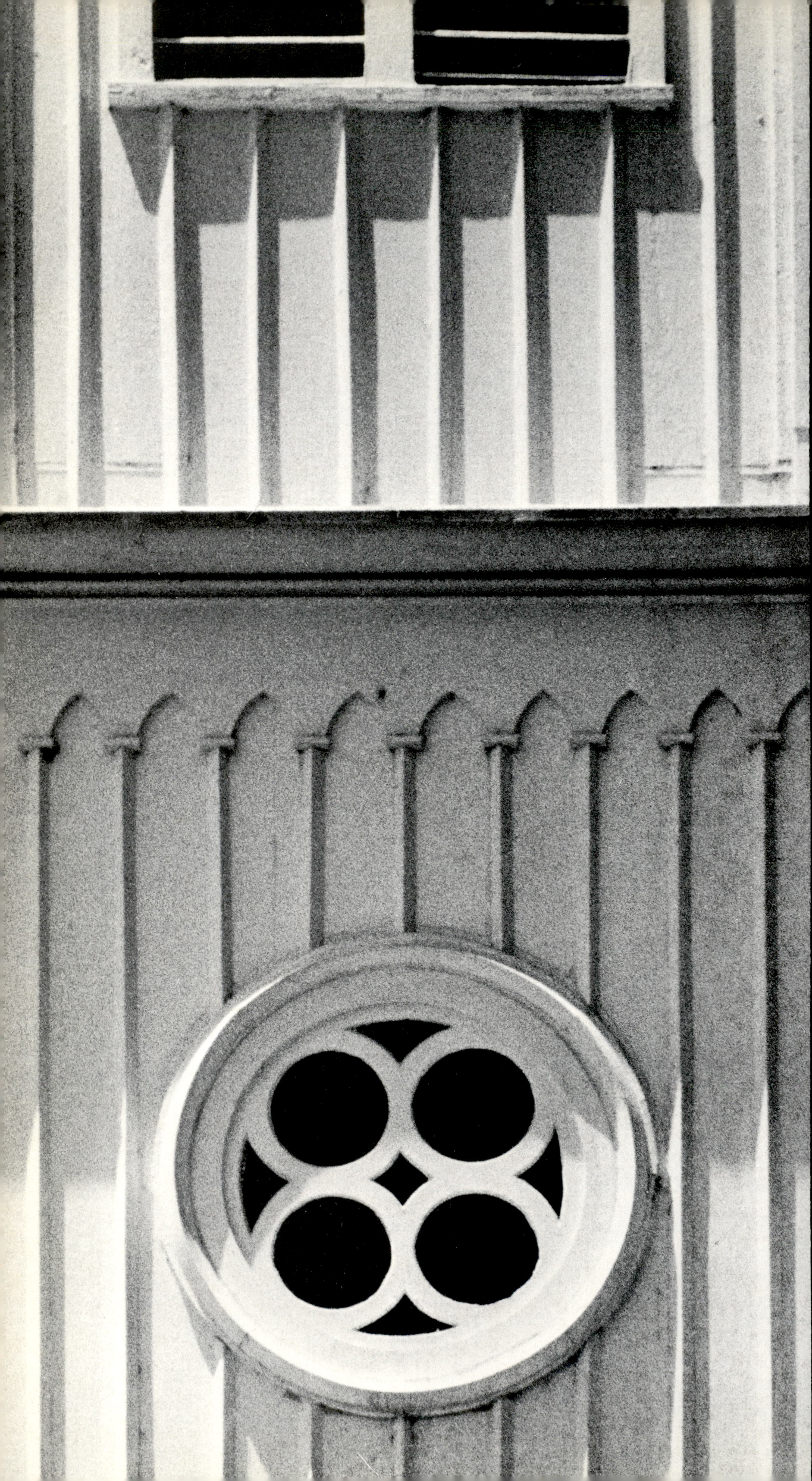

PLAINS & ROCKIES

COLORADO

IDAHO

KANSAS

MISSOURI

MONTANA

NEBRASKA

NORTH DAKOTA

SOUTH DAKOTA

UTAH

WYOMING

In the eighteenth century Benjamin Franklin, a major prophet and apostle of American expansion, grossly miscalculated that it would take ages to fill the North American continent. For once this very sage old man did not know what he was talking about. His younger contemporary Thomas Jefferson was hardly more prescient when, surveying the West of his day, he saw there "room enough for our descendants to the hundredth and thousandth generation." There was no sensible way of making sounder judgments, since at the time no one was sure what did lie to the west. From the East it looked at first like an interminable, dense, and dreary forest that the most determined and expert axmen might never be able to clear to let the sunlight in. Someone judged that squirrels might have hopped from tree to tree for a thousand miles without touching the ground and scarcely seeing the daylight. To travel weeks on end through that thick gloom among trees a hundred feet high was oppressive beyond the imagination of those who had not experienced it.

Beyond that, as reports by Lewis and Clark and other explorers revealed early in the nineteenth century, were the prairies and the plains, "a world of unexplored deserts and thickets," as the French traveler Constantin Volney wrote at the time of the Louisiana Purchase. And beyond that barren prospect rose the Rocky Mountains, standing "like a Chinese Wall," as one Congressman put it in 1828. For some years yet to come the territory between the Mississippi and the Missouri rivers and the Rockies continued to be labeled on maps as the "Great American Desert," a dry and treeless immensity fit for nomads but not for settlers. That "desert" today includes large parts of states discussed in this and the preceding chapter—land as productive in agriculture and in mineral wealth as any comparable area in the world. In some justification of Franklin's and Jefferson's predictions much of this territory does remain as open, relatively unoccupied land. However, as early as 1890 the Superintendent of the Census reported that to all intents the old frontier was closed. Geronimo had only recently been captured, a few straggling remnants of the once immense herds of buffalo remained on the plains, and several territories still awaited statehood. But the good free land to the west was largely staked out. The "interminable" forests were so far on their way to destruction that in 1891 President Theodore Roosevelt signed a Forest Reserve Act in an effort to save what remained. Lands "forever" set aside for the Indians by government regulation had been invaded from all directions; lands that were "impassable" had been crossed and recrossed by fortune hunters of one sort or another; land that was "uninhabited" had been opened for settlement.

As elsewhere on the continent, the big, open, western country had long been familiar to Indians before the earliest intrusions of the white men. There were Indians of many tribes, speaking various languages and following different ways of life. Along the eastern edge of this expanse were villages of farmer-hunter natives. Farther west were nomadic tribesmen who lived by hunting alone. An early legend told of a mysterious nation of white-skinned, Welsh-speaking Indians somewhere in the upper Missouri River Valley, who would become identified as the Mandans. The first white man to visit these people, in 1738 near what is today Bismarck, North Dakota, found them handsome, genial, hospitable, some of whom were indeed light-skinned but none of whom spoke Welsh. He was amazed by one Mandan village where he found hundreds of acres of tilled fields and a virtually impregnable palisaded fort. Within this compound he counted 130 "cabins," ranged along streets so uniform that he and his companions would lose their way trying to get about. What he called cabins were well-lit, spacious lodges, ranging from forty to ninety feet in diameter at the base, with a domed earthen roof supported by heavy cottonwood pillars and with sturdy crossbeams. These natives were carrying on a profitable trade in European goods and raising bumper crops, whose surplus they sold to other tribes. Then, just short of a century after their first contact with the white man, they suddenly vanished from the scene. A smallpox epidemic virtually wiped them out overnight.

Other distinctive Indian cultures have disappeared even more completely. On a bitterly cold and snowy day in 1888 two cowboys searching for stray cattle in the wild canyons of southwestern Colorado rode to the top of a mesa for a look about the countryside. Through a clearing in the junipers and piñon brush they suddenly saw what appeared to be the substantial remains of a whole city nestled in the opposite wall of the canyon. Finding their way to the site they there discovered several skeletons, clay pots, a stone ax, and other objects that gave indications of a hasty departure and that had lain there untouched by the weather and undisturbed by human intrusion for six centuries past. What fate had befallen the departed inhabitants was not apparent.

Others had earlier known of the existence of this site. In 1776 it was named Mesa Verde by a priestly Spanish explorer who, however, did not pause to investigate what he had seen in passing. The Utes in the region were awed by those "cities of the dead," and kept their distance. A United States government surveying party had also noted some such ruins, but without pursuing the matter. It was not until the two cowboys went there that the significance of the site was suspected.

These remains are, obviously, representative of the same prehistoric native culture as the neighboring cliff-dweller ruins in New Mexico discussed in the preceding chapter. What these people called themselves can never be known for they left no written records. The Navajos referred to these earlier people as "Anasazi," the "Ancient Ones," and, lacking a better designation, so they are called today by scholars who are trying to probe the mysteries of this complex and long-vanished civilization—a civilization whose influence apparently spread across the entire Southwest and into Texas and Nevada, and whose cliffside constructions remain to our wonderment.

Long before adventurers from the eastern United States had wandered so far in any numbers, French explorers, traders, and trappers had combed much of the land beyond the Mississippi and Missouri rivers. On their epic journey in the late seventeenth century the young priest Jacques Marquette and his companion Louis Jolliet reported seeing "prairies extending farther than the eye can see," covered by a sea of grass spangled with myriad flowers—a land, as one of the group wrote, "that somewhat resembles an earthly Paradise in beauty." "A settler would not there spend ten years cutting down and burning trees," wrote Jolliet; "on the very day of his arrival, he could put his plough into the ground." La Salle had written that this land of "vast meadows" was the best in the world—so the farther West seemed, at least, to the wondering eyes of these pioneers who journeyed down from Canada in the North.

However, after cutting and hewing his way through a thousand miles of forested land, the American farmer viewed the treeless expanse that lay beyond with some suspicion. It was true that such land needed no girdling and grubbing, but there was a scarcity of good water and little enough timber for fuel and building material. A land that grew no trees might not be rich enough to support crops of grain, vegetables, or fruit.

There were no nuts to feed the pigs. To break the thick and tough prairie soil was in itself a formidable challenge for the first plows to try it. The sticky, heavily root-matted earth did not yield easily to customary tools and methods. How to build houses and farms without available timber was another problem to be faced, along with the presence of inhospitable aborigines.

As the agricultural frontier paused temporarily before such obstacles, plainsmen and mountain men swarmed over this western expanse. They were men who came to know the wilderness beyond the wide Missouri more keenly and sensitively than the Indians and wild beasts which they had to outwit if they were to survive and make a living. When their heyday was over, the land had yielded both its precious furs, so prized in distant markets, from Leipzig to Canton, and most of its geographical secrets, and lay ready for the invasion of immigrants who would follow.

The town of St. Louis was born as a fur-trading post in the winter of 1763-64 when Pierre Laclède Liguest and a company of followers operating from that site obtained a monopoly of the trade with the Indians who hunted and trapped the plains and the Rockies before the white men had reached out first to plunder and then to settle those areas. Long after the Louisiana Purchase, the streets of that village swarmed with the frontiersmen who ventured to deal and compete with the natives in the more distant borderlands. St. Louis was soon celebrated as the gateway to the West, a city of proud buildings, which conspicuously included a cathedral along with extensive limestone warehouses along the river's edge and an abundant display of public and private structures typical of a flourishing community.

Few of those buildings survived a disastrous fire which swept through most of the waterfront area in 1849. One that did was the courthouse, which had been designed in the Greek Revival style a decade earlier. It was here that Thomas Hart Benton advocated a transcontinental railroad and that Dred Scott sued for his freedom. Another survivor, Old Rock House, for a while served as a warehouse for the great company with which John Jacob Astor hoped to win complete control over the western fur trade.

Following the conclusion of the War of 1812 the War Department had set up a series of garrisons to guard the extreme limits of the farmer's advance into the West. For some years to come these forts remained the most impressive buildings on the wide horizon. As early as 1819 Fort Snelling had been put up at the head of navigation on the Mississippi to dominate the northwestern wilderness. "It is built of stone," wrote Captain Marryat in 1839, "and may be considered as impregnable to any attempt which the Indians might make, provided that it has a sufficient garrison. Behind it is a splendid prairie, running back for many miles. . . ." Close by that remote outpost of civilization, St. Paul and Minneapolis grew up in another generation, but by then the farmers had advanced far beyond. (The fort's round tower, part of the original structure, is believed to be the oldest building in Minnesota.)

Such redoubts were not only fortifications; they became natural gathering places for fur traders, red and white, and for emigrants passing by. They served as social centers for a wide neighborhood, and not all were built by the government. Three miles above the mouth of the Yellowstone River, in what is now North Dakota, Fort Union was built by Astor's company in 1829 as a permanent trading post and as a depot for others farther out in the wilderness (hence its name). Palisaded with poplar logs and stone bastions, with towered blockhouses twenty-four feet square, it was the company's greatest fort and attracted a variety of curious visitors, from postgraduates of Europe's salons and studios eager for adventure and study to the roughest of hunters and Indians in from the surrounding prairie to swap their season's catch for tobacco, alcohol, firearms, or whatever seemed most appealing or necessary at the moment. Periodic balls were held at which the Indian wives of the factors appeared bedecked in the latest fashions that had reached the outpost via St. Louis from New York and Europe.

For thirty years, Fort Laramie, in what is now Wyoming, eight hundred miles northwest of St. Louis, remained a strategic point in the center of the Sioux country. The original quadrangle was built as a private fur-trading post in 1834, taken over by Astor's company, rebuilt in adobe, and sold to the government as a military post in 1849; new structures were then added. Lumber for the officers' clubhouse was hauled eight hundred miles by wagon from Fort Leavenworth in Kansas. One visitor was entertained in a room which he described as resembling the barroom of an eastern hotel. However, cannon were always at the ready to discourage marauders from the surrounding plains. Emigrants on their way to the farther West were expected to register here, as Francis Parkman did on his celebrated journey along the Oregon Trail to the Pacific coast. During the first six months of 1850, in the feverish rush to the gold fields, 37,570 men, 825 women, 1,126 children, 9,101 wagons, 31,502 oxen, 22,878 horses, 7,650 mules, and 5,754 cows were checked in at the post, and that apparently did not account for all the travelers and their equipment and beasts.

Once he had passed the limits of the eastern forests the settler was faced with unwonted building problems. He could hardly afford to freight in timber (it had cost between $60,000 and $85,000 to haul the lumber used for the officers' club at Fort Laramie), and in large areas stone was not available in any quantity and there were few masons to work it in any case. Under such circumstances his most sensible option was to use the earth itself for his building material. Western Kansas, for example, sprouted with sod houses—"soddies," as they have been called—built of heavy slabs of topsoil bound together by roots of growing buffalo grass. These elementary structures effectively served generations of Kansans.

In Utah and elsewhere adobe clay was shaped into sun-hardened bricks which were widely used in constructions of various sorts. Although not as durable as modern fired bricks, those made of adobe were easy and cheap to produce, they provided good insulation, and adequately protected with a coat of stucco or plaster, they were long-lasting enough for most practical purposes, as so many surviving and still-functioning early structures made of them in various parts of the West give evidence.

In 1834 Congress had forbidden any white person without a special license to set foot in Indian country beyond Missouri, an edict that as already indicated had become virtually a dead letter as soon as it was issued. By the 1840's the trails to Oregon and Santa Fe were deeply rutted by the passage of emigrants and traders; by 1849 the great rush was on to the California gold mines. In the summer of 1847 with Brigham Young in the lead, the first body of Mormons pushed westward to choose the site of a new state beyond reach of persecution by those who disagreed with their special religious beliefs—and, indeed, beyond reach of the restrictive laws of the United States. With directions from Jim Bridger, that almost legendary mountain man, Young found his way to the Great Salt Lake Valley, which he determined was the Promised Land of his people. Some of his followers thought that it was rather a blistering and interminable wasteland of sagebrush. However, within a month of their arrival the well-regimented brethren had, in the words of one of them, "broke, watered, planted and sowed upwards of 100 acres with various kinds of seeds, nearly stockaded with adobes one public square (ten acres)," and built cabins to live in. Two years later, visitors found there a city of eight thousand inhabitants, laid out on a magnificent scale, needing only trees to make it a "Diamond of the Desert." The first Mormon Tabernacle was raised in the city in 1851. Within two years after that, work was undertaken on Salt Lake's great Mormon Temple, to be built of granite hauled over twenty miles to the site by ox teams. That monumental structure, designed by the noted pioneer architect Truman O. Angell, took forty years to complete. In the meantime, a huge tabernacle boasting the world's largest domed roof was finished in 1868. (Ironically, Brigham Young's hope to escape any government but his own was almost immediately thwarted when the United States took over the entire area that is now Utah as part of the territory it claimed at the conclusion of the Mexican War.)

Throughout much of the West the coming of the railroad had a profound effect on architectural developments. Portable houses could be shipped in and quickly thrown up as a new settlement sprouted. If the community flourished, sometimes entire blocks of such provisional structures were set afire and destroyed to be replaced by more substantial buildings. And in the wake of the railroad came eastern fashions in domestic and public architecture, more or less undigested or sophisticated, according to varying circumstances. Virtually all the styles of the later nineteenth and early twentieth centuries that have been discussed in the opening chapters of this book took their turns. In the eighties and nineties it was not uncommon for county commissioners to buy plans for courthouses, mostly showing the influence of Richardson's Romanesque designs, from salesmen whose illustrated folders represented samplings.

At terminal points, wherever the railroad lines started or ended, they gave rise to colorful and prosperous communities. After a few short years of railroad activity, Omaha, Nebraska, which had been chosen as the starting point for the transcontinental Union Pacific, sprang from a small frontier settlement to what one early visitor described as "the liveliest city in the United States." Cheyenne, the site chosen by the Union Pacific as a division point in 1867, was soon made the capital of the Wyoming Territory and in good time developed into the largest city in the state. Elsewhere, as the tracks were pushed forward, provisional terminals that had supplied the "front" of operations and that briefly provided all the raucous, brawling excitement rude men of action could contrive, gave up their streets and rickety false-fronted buildings to wolves and coyotes that wandered in from the surrounding wilderness.

During the 1860's–80's, successive reports of rich mine discoveries in Utah, Montana, Wyoming, Idaho, and Nevada kept the whole mountain area of the West in an almost constant ferment. In these parts the wandering prospector replaced the frontiersman and the farmer as the first tester of the unsettled land. Unlike the gradual, continuous advance of the frontier east of the Mississippi and into the plains, the early rush into the mountains was explosive and erratic. Men and women of every sort and from all points of the compass joined the quest for sudden wealth and gave the upland wilderness a cosmopolitan cast. In one mining gulch a reporter from Connecticut met an old Boston merchant successfully running a quartz mill and a Presbyterian deacon from Kansas retailing whiskey and selling pies on Sundays. At another site the inveterate traveler Bayard Taylor met a Norwegian merchant he had last seen in the arctic wastes of Lapland. A German miner from San Francisco devised a new system for getting at the precious ore, and intrigued experts from many countries came to examine this engineering achievement.

Some of the communities born of these gatherings of adventurers grew into enduring, thriving cities. Denver, for example, soon became the capital of a large region, and Last Chance Gulch matured into Helena, Montana. It was with the great, nearby silver strikes of the late 1870's and 1880's that Denver boomed into its permanent prominence. Earlier discoveries of gold had brought treasure hunters to the area, and for some years the fortune of the little city fluctuated with the alternating hopes and disappointments of those mining adventurers. Early in the game, in 1859, Horace Greeley, on his way to the diggings, paused at Denver to lecture on temperance and reported that he found there "more brawls, more pistol shots with criminal intent in this log city of 150 dwellings, not three-fourths of them completed, nor two-thirds of them inhabited, nor one-third fit to be, than in any community of equal numbers on earth." The future of the place seemed dubious to all but confirmed boosters.

However, when in the 1880's the bonanza kings, silver-rich, moved from the mountains to Denver, they vied with the wealthy cattle barons to raise mansions that would testify to their material worth and their individual importance. "The distinguishing charm of Denver architecture," observed one visitor of that time, "is its endless variety. Everyone is ambitious to build a house unlike his neighbor, and is more desirous that it shall have some novel feature than that it shall be surpassingly beautiful." One of the great early architectural monuments to western progress is the Brown Palace Hotel that was opened in Denver during the summer of 1892 and that still claims admiration for both its character as a building and its distinction as a hostelry. Built of native red sandstone, with onyx from Mexico used for paneling, and with its central rotunda rising for nine stories, the Brown Palace deserves its old, established reputation and remains a highly popular stopping place for travelers.

In other towns of the mining districts, life flickered on and off over the years as prospects flowered and faded. Still others became ghost towns without having lived a human generation, leaving buildings that remain the shells of old hopes—ghost towns, like the railroad camps that had been passed by.

The quest for precious and useful metals in the mountains continues unabated. From time to time important new finds are made, while the exploitation of earlier-revealed sites of enduring yields continues. At Lead, South Dakota, the Homestake Mining Company, organized in 1877, operates what remains the largest gold mine in the Western Hemisphere. Kennecott Copper Corporation's Bingham Canyon open pits in Utah, an immense excavation measuring two miles across and one-half mile deep, is one of the richest mines of any kind in the world. Since 1864 Montana has produced about five billion dollars worth of metals of various kinds, much of it from Butte Hill, called the "richest hill on earth," just off the Continental Divide. Idaho has yielded vast amounts of silver and lead; and so on. In recent years the new uses in advanced technology found for such metallic elements as uranium, vanadium, and molybdenum set in motion a fresh swarm of private and corporate treasure hunters sheltered, modern-style, in house trailers and tents.

In widespread arid and semiarid reaches of the West, water could be more precious than gold, the ultimate treasure for the farmer, for the urban dweller, and for industry. To tap the water that drains down from the Continental Divide in various river systems, to control it, store it, and distribute it would be to make the desert green, to encourage the rise of cities, and to encourage the growth of industrial plants. Thus, shortly after arriving at their pioneer settlement at Salt Lake, Brigham Young and his followers began tapping City Creek to water their fields, and over the ensuing years they developed an irrigation system that enabled them to survive and flourish in that otherwise inhospitable land. With that example in mind, other irrigation projects were undertaken around Denver, enabling that miners' headquarters rapidly to earn the title "Queen City of the Plains." In recent times the promise of an abundant water supply influenced the choice of Colorado Springs as the site of the new Air Force Academy with its remarkable architectural complex.

The monumental symbols of this reclamation and conservation are the gigantic dams that have risen by the hundreds in all parts of the West during the last generation. In 1857 a government report concluded that the "lone and majestic way" of the Colorado River seemed "intended by Nature to remain forever unvisited and unmolested." Each spring it ran wild, ruining the land in its path. In another season it went dry, the land about it parched. Then, in 1931, the Secretary of the Interior awarded the largest labor contract ever let by the United States government for the construction of a dam—the Hoover Dam—across that awesome and erratic channel; a structure that would impound a reservoir of 10,500 billion gallons of water. Seven states and Mexico were included in the plan to control floods, provide water for irrigation and for domestic and industrial purposes, improve navigation, and provide a recreational area and a wildlife refuge. About two million acres of irrigable land are within reach of the water of the huge artificial lake backed up behind it. However, this is but one prominent item among related works that have been established over a widespread region.

The American West includes some of the most dramatically beautiful landscape in the world. Spellbinding rock formations, vast canyons, rugged peaks, magnificent vistas, lure the eye and the imagination with their spectacular variety and the immensity of their setting. This magnificent natural architecture has presented a stern challenge to men who would match its spirit appropriately with their own architecture and in the spirit of our own times. However, as the later illustrations of this chapter indicate, quite aside from the monumental dam constructions, this they have successfully done in a good number of instances. The Red Rocks Amphitheater at Denver and the Air Force Academy buildings at Colorado Springs are fine examples.

OVERLEAF: *Cliff Dwellings, Mesa Verde National Park, near Cortez, Colo. (about 1200-1300).* Prehistoric cave and cliff dwellings are to be found in many parts of the world—in France, Spain, Italy, Turkey, and China, for example. (In some regions modern man is still living, and quite comfortably, in such shelters.) But nowhere do habitations of this nature exhibit a more architectural character, more of the creative option of placing stone on stone, than in the hundreds of cliff dwellings along the precipitous bluffs in the southwest corner of Colorado. Some are tiny affairs seemingly glued to the escarpment and capacious enough for only one agile brave and his limited possessions; others are virtually of village size. The Mesa Verde ("green table"), which presents such a spectacular assortment of these primitive accommodations along its cliffsides, rises from 1,300 to 2,000 feet above the surrounding plains—to a maximum height of 8,572 feet above sea level. Practically immune from attack, the inhabitants of these sanctuaries could still commute to their working fields on the top of the butte by means of footholds and ladders.

Spruce Tree House is one of three majestic cliff dwellings constructed by Anasazi Indians at Mesa Verde in the thirteenth century. (The other two are Cliff Palace and Square Tower House.) By then, possibly because of raids by covetous nomads, the Indians had retreated from their well-constructed stone pueblo apartment houses on the mesa top to the greater security of the cliff dwellings built in yawning caves just beneath the mesa rim. Each of these villages was comprised of a vast assembly of rooms, towers, kivas, courtyards, and terraced paths. The architectural features of Spruce Tree House are generally similar to other Anasazi cliff dwellings in the area: small rectangular doorways constructed well above ground level; thin slabs of sandstone for doors; roofs set on stout logs; masonry walls generally plastered inside; and small windows for light and air. These tiny chambers served exclusively as sleeping quarters and for storage. The kiva, the subterranean ceremonial chamber and men's gathering place, may be visited at Spruce Tree via a ladder through a small hole in its roof on the courtyard.

Entrance to Kiva, Spruce Tree House

Spruce Tree House, Mesa Verde National Park, near Cortez, Colo. (1200-1300)

Explorers Lewis and Clark spent the first winter (1804–05) of their epic-making journey to the Pacific on the Upper Missouri River near the earth-mound villages of the Mandan tribe. These handsome, hospitable Plains Indians and their distinctive domed dwellings were captured for posterity by George Catlin on a canvas, "The Bull Society Dance," in 1832. Five years later the Mandans suddenly vanished, obliterated by a smallpox epidemic. At Fort Abraham Lincoln State Park in North Dakota, five Mandan earth mounds have been reconstructed on the excavated sites of the originals. The inner framework consists of four stout tree trunks set in a square and braced at the top by horizontal crossbeams. Willow branches were laid on top of the angled roof rafters and then were packed with earth to create the domical effect. The central section was excavated to form a row of built-in seats around the fire. An engraving by the Swiss artist Charles Bodmer reveals the interior of a Mandan lodge as a commodious, well-lit, and seemingly comfortable place.

Slant Indian Village, Fort Abraham Lincoln State Park, near Mandan, N.D. (as of 1750)

Interior detail,
Mandan Earth Lodge,
Slant Indian Village

Bolduc House, Ste. Genevieve, Mo. (about 1785)

Ste. Genevieve, the first permanent settlement within the present boundaries of Missouri, was founded in 1732 on the west bank of the Mississippi River by French fur traders and was originally part of the vast French territory of Louisiana. Even after the United States acquired the territory through the Louisiana Purchase in 1803, French influence and culture lingered on through the entire Mississippi Valley from New Orleans to Wisconsin. The Louis Bolduc House, built by a wealthy merchant, is a fine example of the French colonial style, with its oak timbers set upright into a stone foundation—the space between the uprights filled with clay and straw—and its steeply pitched hip roof forming a gallery around the house. The Amoureaux House, an older dwelling, dates from about 1770.

Amoureaux House, Ste. Genevieve, Mo. (about 1770)

Sod House, Pioneer Village, Minden, Nebr. (as of 1860's)

The Homestead Act of 1862 entitled an American citizen to lay claim to 160 acres of unappropriated government land, which became his after he lived on it and cultivated it for five years. At Beatrice, Nebraska, the Homestead National Monument commemorates the legislation, and the story-and-a-half Palmer-Epard log cabin illustrates the simplicity of the lives of the homesteaders. The Pioneer Village in Minden, Nebraska, has reconstructed a typical sod house of the treeless plains. The crude rafters of the soddy's roof were usually covered with earth and planted with grass to reduce erosion. Jacob Hamblin, a Mormon pioneer and Indian missionary in Utah, erected a two-story house of red sandstone roofed with hand-split cedar shingles to shelter his several wives and two dozen children.

Jacob Hamblin House, Santa Clara, Utah (1862)

Palmer-Epard Cabin, Homestead National Monument, near Beatrice, Nebr. (1867)

Coeur d'Alene Mission of the Sacred Heart, Cataldo, Idaho (1853)

In the mid-nineteenth century, Christian missionaries to the Indians of the trans-Mississippi West played an important role in the settlement of that region just as they had in the previous century in the Southwest. In 1838 the Shawnee Methodist Mission, founded in 1830 by the Reverend Thomas Johnson, was moved to its present site in Kansas on the Santa Fe and Oregon trails, near their points of origin. The mission at one time covered more than two thousand acres and had sixteen buildings in which Indian youths were taught English, crafts, and agricultural skills. During the Civil War the mission was used as a barracks; the Kansas State Historical Society has restored the site. In 1848 Jesuit Father Anthony Ravalli drew the plans for the Coeur d'Alene Mission of the Sacred Heart—the oldest building still standing in Idaho—which he and the Indians erected over the next several years. The huge beams and columns were hewn and dressed only by a broadax and were mortised and pegged together without nails. The façade shows some architectural flair with its Greek Revival and baroque elements, and the interior has a carved and painted ceiling and an altar of some note. It has recently been completely restored.

North Building, Shawnee Methodist Mission, Kansas City, Kans. (1845)

As the pioneers pushed westward across the plains, military outposts were established to protect the trails and to keep open the lines of communication. Just after the outbreak of the Black Hawk War in 1867, the Mormons under the leadership of Brigham Young built Old Cove Fort to protect travelers on the Salt Lake–Pioche stage line as well as to guard the newly installed telegraph line. Constructed of local black volcanic rock and rubble, the square fort has six rooms on both the north and south sides with prominent chimneys rising from each room. In the summer of 1874 the Custer expedition to the Black Hills reported the likelihood of a gold strike, and the first group of prospectors, led by John Gordon, arrived the following winter and erected a primitive stockade, shown below in its reconstructed state. During the 1860's and 1870's Fort Larned was the principal guardian of the Kansas segment of the Santa Fe Trail. The buildings around the four-hundred-foot-square parade ground were rebuilt in local yellow sandstone in the years following the Civil War.

Old Cove Fort, near Beaver, Utah (1867)

Gordon Stockade, Custer State Park, Custer, S.D. (as of 1875)

Fort Larned, Larned, Kans. (1860's)

OVERLEAF: *Front Street Reconstruction, Dodge City, Kans. (as of 1870's).* Founded with the coming of the Santa Fe Railroad in 1872, Dodge City soon became a major shipping center for cattle, a rendezvous for cowboys and Indians, gamblers and outlaws, and famous lawmen. The two-block reconstruction of store fronts, guided by old photographs, recalls those wide-open days.

Thomas P. Kennard House, Lincoln, Nebr. (1869). John K. Winchell, architect

Brigham Young Winter Home, St. George, Utah (1869; 1873)

The four different types of domestic architecture illustrated on these pages belonged to some interesting personalities who settled in the Great Plains and Rockies region. The fine Italianate mansion was designed for Thomas Perkins Kennard, one of the three commissioners who selected Lincoln as the Nebraska state capital. The spirited yellow-painted façade with white wood trim and over-windows of terra cotta has other interesting details in the cornice, square cupola, and captain's walk. The Tuscan villa has been meticulously restored as a statehood memorial. A much simpler expression of the Italianate fad is the house where Mormon leader Brigham Young spent his last winters in the milder climate of southwest Utah. In 1873 a two-story north wing was added to the existing structure of adobe brick and ponderosa pine on a lava rock foundation.

Antoine de Vallombrosa, Marquis de Mores, established the town of Medora, North Dakota, as the center of his grandiose scheme for a meat-packing empire. The Marquis purchased cattle, built a packing plant, ran a stagecoach line between Medora and the Black Hills, and even built a Catholic church for his wife, Medora. His twenty-six-room wood-frame "château" was no more than a summer home from which he could supervise his short-lived operations. The château and its French period furnishings survive as a reminder of the European adventurer. Astute showman Buffalo Bill Cody built a frame rancher's dwelling on his Scouts Rest Ranch during the affluent days of his Wild West show. The central tower, stained-glass windows, and gunstock-eave supports add some interest to this example of the western Victorian vernacular.

Château de Mores, Medora, N.D. (1883)

Buffalo Bill Cody House, North Platte, Nebr. (1886)

belfries, the two structures shown here epitomize the small-town, all-wood Victorian Gothic churches which were raised from one end of the country to the other in the last century. Many of them, no doubt, were designed after models illustrated in the usual English and American building manuals and magazines. The present examples have sides of vertical battens and boards painted white. Both are very well preserved ornaments of the western scene. The one at Fairplay was named for a pioneer Presbyterian missionary who, after leaving Colorado, became an energetic champion of Alaskan Indian rights.

Sheldon Jackson Memorial Chapel, Fairplay, Colo. (1874)

St. Paul's Church, Ironton, Mo. (1870)

Mormon Tabernacle, Logan, Utah (1877-1915). Truman O. Angell, architect

Mormon Temple, Manti, Utah (1877-88). William H. Folsom, architect

The Mormon Church has a number of tabernacles and temples. The two structures here illustrated, at Logan and Manti, both in Utah, exemplify the commanding presence of these religious edifices that overlook communities of earnest believers.

OVERLEAF: *Mormon Tabernacle (1868), William H. Folsom and Henry Grow, architects; and Mormon Temple (1853-93), Truman O. Angell, architect; Salt Lake City, Utah.* Most impressive of all such buildings is the great tabernacle at Salt Lake City on Temple Square, a ten-acre walled compound in the heart of the city. Other buildings on the square include the great temple, an assembly hall, and the tiny log Pioneer House.

The Zion Cooperative Mercantile Institution in Salt Lake City was one of the first department stores—if not the first—in the nation. (Wanamaker's in Philadelphia was built the same year). Three sections were built at different times, but the three-story central bay of cast iron, with its Corinthian columns, roundheaded, double-hung windows (lately made solid), and bold pediment, reveals the well-restored original upper façade of 1876. (The ground floor has undergone many remodelings, and only hints of its early appearance remain.) Like so many other cities, St. Louis also went through a phase of cast-iron construction for commercial buildings. In time, efforts to simulate Renaissance designs with this material were abandoned in favor of a light, strong framework which would permit generous-sized windows, as in the Sanger-Peper Building. Energetic urban renewal has wiped out most of the historic sections of Denver. However, a length of Larimer Street, which a century ago was one of the city's main thoroughfares, has fortunately been spared. Much of this is being restored through private enterprise to its pre-1900 condition and appearance.

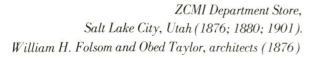

Sanger-Peper Building, St. Louis, Mo. (1874). Frederick Raeder, architect

ZCMI Department Store,
Salt Lake City, Utah (1876; 1880; 1901).
William H. Folsom and Obed Taylor, architects (1876)

Larimer Square, Denver, Colo. (1870's)

Eads Bridge, St. Louis, Mo. (1867-74). James Buchanan Eads, engineer

When it was completed in 1874, the Eads Bridge spanning the Mississippi
River at St. Louis was the longest bridge in the world. With the railways
that it supported, it gave the nation an effective, continuous throughway
from coast to coast, and in so doing hastened the demise of the Mississippi
steamboat of glorious legend. The essential traffic flow of the nation would
soon be from east to west, rather than from north to south along the great
waterways. Although steel was as yet largely untried as a major structural
element, the engineer of the great bridge, James B. Eads, here used it for
the superstructure with signal success. His project has been called "one of
the great calculated risks in engineering history."

Hôtel de Paris, Georgetown, Colo. (1875)

From 1859, when gold was first discovered in Central City, Colorado, a series of boom towns was spawned to support the mining operations extracting gold, silver, lead, copper, and zinc from rich veins in the Rocky Mountains. Here Louis du Puy constructed one of the most celebrated hostelries west of the Mississippi and ran the Hôtel de Paris as though it actually was in Paris. Georgetown also affords glimpses of amusing Victorian domestic vernacular, such as the detail of the doorway and fenestration illustrated at right. The semi ghost-town of Victor boasts a Masonic Hall with three richly treated pediments.

OVERLEAF: *Elkhorn, Mont. (1870's)*. In its boom days, Elkhorn produced about $14 million in gold and silver and provided no less than fourteen saloons for the thirsty miners.

Masonic Hall, Victor, Colo. (1890's)

Domestic Vernacular, Georgetown, Colo. (late 1800's

Situated in Prickly Pear Valley, the capital of Montana, Helena, came into being in 1864 when gold was discovered in Last Chance Gulch. Prospectors and miners, mule-team freight haulers, businessmen and entrepreneurs, camp followers and vigilantes, soon poured into town; and by 1888 Helena was a great mining center and claimed to be the richest city per capita in the United States. At this time some substantial commercial buildings were erected along the main street. Thanks to an urban renewal program, several blocks along Last Chance Gulch are now being preserved as a reminder of the town's heyday. The Novelty Building presents a history of architecture in its façade with its Grecian cornice, a Renaissance window after the Palazzo Riccardi, Gothic ornamental knobs atop classical pilasters, oriel windows from the Second Empire, and Ruskinian color contrasts. The most accomplished building is the Power Block, a six-story block of rusticated granite based on the design of Richardson's Marshall Field Wholesale Store in Chicago. The large windows of the ground-floor shops contrast with the smaller roundheaded ones of the offices above, with an attic band of smaller arched windows.

Power Block, Helena, Mont. (1889).
Shaffer & Read, architects

Last Chance Gulch Restoration, Helena, Mont. (as of 1880's)

Novelty Building, Helena, Mont. (1889). John C. Paulsen, architect

Old Courthouse, St. Louis, Mo. (1845; 1851-63). Henry Singleton, Robert S. Mitchell, and William Rumbold, architects

The Old Courthouse in St. Louis, originally designed by Henry Singleton, was raised in the heyday of the Greek Revival style. Subsequently, it underwent a number of changes and additions at the hands of other architects. Currently, it serves as a museum dedicated to the history of America's westward expansion. The Old Post Office in the same city, a building that also served as a custom house, occupies an entire city block. Its design, realized here with impressive solidity, reflects the styles of the Second Empire in France—appropriate in a city named after a revered French king. It is one of the finest structures of its period in the nation.

Old Post Office, St. Louis, Mo. (1874-82). Alfred B. Mullett, architect

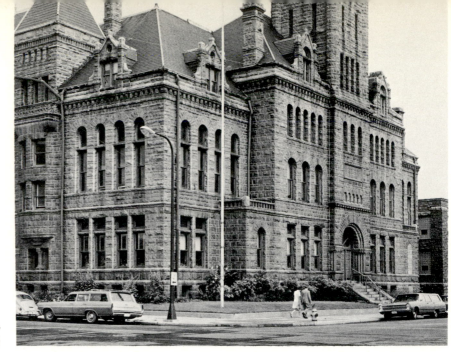

Minnehaha County Courthouse,
Sioux Falls, S.D. (1893)

City and County Building, Salt Lake City, Utah (1894). Proudfoot, Bird & Monheim, architects

County Courthouse, York, Nebr. (1886)

The Minnehaha courthouse was built just a few years after South Dakota entered the Union. This turreted municipal pile was built of quartzite, a rock so hard and expensive to work with that it is rarely used today for building, even with sophisticated modern power tools. The City and County Building at Salt Lake City was built about the same time, serving initially as the territorial capitol, then as the first capitol of the newly designated state of Utah. Both of these structures reveal debts to the wide-ranging influence of H. H. Richardson. The upper floor, the tower, and the roof of the courthouse at York, Nebraska, break out into a medley of pediments, porticoes, corner turrets with pagoda roofs, and a cupola.

State Capitol, Cheyenne, Wyo. (1887). D. W. Gibbs, architect

Anderson Hall, Kansas State University, Manhattan, Kans. (1884). E. T. Carr, architect

The Wyoming capitol at Cheyenne was built a few years before this territory became a state of the Union. Combining both neoclassical and modified Romanesque designs and constructed with considerable technical skill, it expressed a bold confidence in the area's future. Old Main was the first building raised on the campus of the University of Wyoming. Of no particular style, the structure nevertheless has more character than most of the other buildings that grew up around it over the years. (A tower that once rose above it was removed as a safety measure.) It was remodeled as an administration building in 1939. Anderson Hall at Kansas State University, also now serving as an administration building, includes a museum among its various chambers. Native limestone was used for its construction, as it was for the other structures in this attractively landscaped campus. All the buildings follow a modified Gothic Revival style.

Old Main, University of Wyoming, Laramie, Wyo. (1887). Frederick A. Hale, architect

667

Wainwright Tomb, St. Louis, Mo. (1892). Louis H. Sullivan, architect

Standing on a desolate summit on the plains of Wyoming is a rare example of H. H. Richardson's work west of the Mississippi. The sixty-foot-high pyramid commemorates Oakes and Oliver Ames, who opened up this area to settlement when they pushed through the nearby Union Pacific Railroad. Near the top of its angled mass of random ashlar are plaques to the Ames brothers designed by Augustus Saint-Gaudens. Louis Sullivan designed one of the country's most sensitive tombs for Ellis Wainwright in memory of his lovely wife, who died thirty-three years before her husband. The mausoleum, a solid sculptural mass of limestone topped by a dome, is outlined by an exquisite band of Sullivan's delicate incised designs.

OVERLEAF: *Wainwright Building, St. Louis, Mo. (1892). Louis H. Sullivan & Dankmar Adler, architects.* In one of his essays, Louis H. Sullivan, the "father of modern architecture," reflected on the chief characteristic of the tall office building: "it is lofty . . . it must be every inch a proud and soaring thing, rising in sheer exultation that from bottom to top it is a unit. . . ." His nine-story-plus-attic Wainwright Building in St. Louis in its expression of verticality and unity influenced the development of the modern skyscraper. Sullivan achieved this upward thrust with seven-story-high red brick piers between the ranks of windows, the piers set forward and given prominence by their smoothness in contrast to the ornamental red terra-cotta spandrels. The panel designs differ on each floor and follow no historical antecedent; they are a testament to Sullivan's gift for invention.

Ames Monument, Sherman, Wyo. (1879). Henry H. Richardson, architect

Katz Building (Boley Clothing Company), Kansas City, Mo. (1908). Louis S. Curtiss, architect

Brown Palace Hotel, Denver, Colo. (1892). Frank E. Edbrooke & Company, architects

The two buildings illustrated here represent landmarks in the country's architectural development. The little-known pioneer Boley Clothing Company, now the Katz Building, in Kansas City was one of the first expressions of continuous cast-iron–mullioned strip-windows alternating with uninterrupted metal spandrels to form a curtain-wall façade. The venerable Brown Palace Hotel in Denver creates a delightful inner space in its nine-story lobby topped by an enormous stained-glass skylight. Balconies embellished with bronze panels open out on this great interior courtyard. The Guggenheim Museum in New York and the Hyatt Regency Hotel in Atlanta are direct descendants of Denver's spatial masterpiece.

The picturesque façade of Union Station in St. Louis, Missouri, extends over six hundred feet, its turrets romantically suggestive of medieval castles, and its massive pile reminiscent of H. H. Richardson's Romanesque Revival. Within is the grand barrel-vaulted waiting room and behind it stretches the seemingly endless train shed (601 by 700 feet), its width spanned by a five-arch roof. Some fifteen miles north of St. Louis the Missouri River flows into the Mississippi, and this famous union is celebrated by Carl Milles' fountain on the plaza in front of Union Station. Fourteen bronze-sculptured figures, among them a demure bride and serious groom and several gleeful sea scoundrels, are pleasingly grouped among the jets and sprays of water. In Lincoln, Nebraska, a handsome old brick relic, once a Rock Island Railroad station, was imaginatively restored in 1969 for use as a drive-in bank. Old railroad souvenirs and posters and piped-in train sounds add to the nostalgic atmosphere.

City National Bank, Lincoln, Nebr. (1892; 1969). Clark & Enersen, Hamersky, Schlaebitz, Burroughs & Thomsen, architects (1969)

*Aloe Plaza Fountain, St. Louis, Mo.
(1940). Carl Milles, sculptor*

*Union Station, St. Louis, Mo. (1896).
Theodore C. Link, chief architect;
E. A. Cameron, associate;
George H. Pegram, engineer*

675

Civic Center, Helena, Mont. (1920). Link & Haire, architects

The bold state capitol of Nebraska is considered to be the romantic and eclectic architect Bertram Grosvenor Goodhue's greatest building—his other famous commissions include St. Bartholomew's in New York City and the Academy of Sciences in Washington, D.C. Goodhue won the competition for the capitol when he broke with tradition by rejecting the usual Roman dome and designed a lofty tower that would soar over the flat plains landscape. The base of the building is a low mass pierced at mid-points by four entrances—in plan forming a Greek cross—above which the tower rises skyward with its boldly modeled figures, a rare instance of integrated architecture and sculpture. During the Depression the municipality of Helena, Montana, acquired a Shriners temple to house a civic center. With its minaret, domes, horseshoe arch, and geometric ornament, the ambitious structure is based on Islamic prototypes.

In the foothills of the Rocky Mountains the city of Denver maintains a 13,500-acre park system comprised of twenty-seven recreational and scenic areas easily accessible by an extensive highway network. The most outstanding part of the system is the Park of the Red Rocks, with its spectacular monoliths of Pre-Cambrian quartzitic sandstone. Cradled between Creation Rock and Ship Rock, with Stage Rock as a backdrop, is a spectacular outdoor amphitheater that boasts of excellent acoustics from the semienclosure of rocks. Some nine thousand seats have been eased into the wild beauty of this natural bowl shape, whose integrity was preserved where possible by the architect. The retaining walls are of local stone, the seats of natural wood, and the stepped ranks of concrete. The double-decked stage has services concealed on the lower floor; parking facilities are totally out of view. In short, nothing interferes with the grandeur of the natural setting.

OVERLEAF: *Grain Elevators, Topeka, Kans.* The most impressive monuments to the wealth of Kansas, as well as to the wealth of all the other plains states, are to be found housing the source of its income. The great grain elevators around northern Topeka in their unadorned functionalism appear to be gigantic pieces of geometric sculpture.

Red Rocks Amphitheater, near Denver, Colo. (1941). Burnham Hoyt, architect

Annunciation Priory, Bismarck, N.D. (1963). Marcel Breuer, architect; Hamilton P. Smith, associate

The Annunciation Priory of the Sisters of St. Benedict and its nearby affiliate, Mary College, occupy rolling sites on opposite sides of a hill overlooking the Missouri River. The powerful buildings constitute one of the country's best architectural groups concerned with the Roman Catholic religion and education. The priory is marked by a three-dimensional, 100-foot-high bell banner, recalling a similar one by Marcel Breuer at Collegeville, Minnesota (see page 492), that lends a vertical accent to the landscape and to the long, low building mass of the four main units. The circular Priory of St. Mary and St. Louis at Creve Coeur, Missouri, is a skillful exposition of concrete design. The lower tier of twenty-one-foot-high arches is surmounted by a second tier twelve feet high and topped by a thirty-two-foot arched steeple belfry.

Priory of St. Mary and St. Louis, Creve Coeur, Mo. (1962). Hellmuth, Obata & Kassabaum, architects

683

A wondrous web of simple plastic panels and intricate aluminum struts, based on R. Buckminster Fuller's geodesic principles, forms an ideal canopy for the Missouri Botanical Garden in St. Louis. The geodesic dome sheltering a prodigal array of plants is 175 feet in diameter and seventy feet high and forms a low vault that rests on five concrete piers. The exoskeletal framing of the Climatron is composed of hexagonal components of aluminum tubes in two planes connected by aluminum rods. A weather skin of some four thousand triangles of acrylic plastic is hung about a foot below this frame—the Plexiglas is unbreakable and permits photosynthesis. Inside under one partitionless roof, two major meteorological zones ranging from hot tropics to cool uplands are maintained by an ingenious air-conditioning system. A peripheral walk encircles the flourishing gardens on several levels and there is even a waterfall within.

Climatron, St. Louis, Mo. (1961). Murphy & Mackey, architects; Synergetics, Inc., dome engineers

The striking geometric form of the McDonnell Planetarium has made it a landmark since it appeared in St. Louis in the early 1960's. The planetarium dome nestles within the curves of the outer shell and an internal ramp around the half-dome leads to an observation deck on top. In Colorado, against the backdrop of the Rocky Mountains, the buildings of the Air Force Academy stand sharply etched on a partly natural, partly man-made acropolis.

RIGHT *and* OVERLEAF: *Chapel, Air Force Academy, and Exterior (detail), Colorado Springs, Colo. (1956-62). Skidmore, Owings & Merrill, architects.* The heavenward-thrusting spires of the chapel provide the architectural as well as the spiritual focus of the academy. Its dramatic profile has been likened to the folded plane wings on the flight deck of an aircraft carrier. Actually, it is comprised of a technically ingenious geometric steel-tube framing with aluminum panels separated by narrow bands of stained glass.

McDonnell Planetarium, St. Louis, Mo. (1963). Hellmuth, Obata & Kassabaum, architects

Chapel, Air Force Academy

The Fine Arts Center provides a powerful anchor for the eastern edge of the campus of Utah State University at Logan. Constructed of striated natural concrete and red brick, the complex functions as a concert hall, orchestra rehearsal hall, theater, art and ballet school, and staff office. At Billings, Montana, the Fortin Educational Center of Rocky Mountain College houses a complicated series of functions in an expressive architectural setting. An intriguing collection of forms were generated by the space requirements of separate facilities. The gymnasium and pool are eased into the slope on the north side with separate access and parking space. The south side accommodates a smaller gym, an auditorium, classrooms, health clinic, and administrative offices.

Fine Arts Center, Utah State University, Logan, Utah (1968).
Burtch W. Beall, Jr., architect

Fortin Educational Center, Rocky Mountain College, Billings, Mont. (1969). Cushing, Terrell & Associates, architects

Engineering Science Center, University of Colorado, Boulder, Colo. (1965).
Architectural Associates of Colorado, architects: W. C. Muchow, partner in charge

Forest Park Community College, St. Louis, Mo. (1971).
Harry Weese & Associates, architects

The architects of the Engineering Science Center had to fit their complex into the Tuscan hill-town style of the University of Colorado campus, designed by the late Charles Z. Klauder. To harmonize with the older and adjacent buildings, they employed the same red tile roofs and local sandstone for some walls and raw concrete for others. The office tower provides the central focus with the lower lab buildings radiating about it. The major engineering units of the ten-acre center are laid out in a thoughtfully landscaped area of courtyards and fountains. Forest Park Community College in St. Louis is housed in one stretched-out five-story unit for classrooms. The administration block is attached behind the classrooms by a three-tiered open walkway.

National Center for Atmospheric Research, near Boulder, Colo. (1967). I. M. Pei & Partners, architects

Situated on the edge of a mesa south of Boulder, Colorado, a complex of buildings—illustrated on these two and the following two pages—stands dramatically silhouetted against the backdrop of the Rockies and with the flat plains stretching before it.

OVERLEAF: *National Center for Atmospheric Research.* A winding road leads up to the summit and through a sculptured gate to the brownish-pink-colored concrete units—two tall structures connected by a lower base—of the Atmospheric Research Center. The two office and laboratory blocks, rising five stories above ground, flare out at the top like mysterious, hooded sentry posts. Narrow bands of dark windows run up the center of the broad sides of each tower and open up in wide canopied glass horizontals in the top-floor meeting spaces.

Office Complex, Crown Center, Kansas City, Mo. (1967-77).
Edward Larrabee Barnes, architect; Alexander Calder, sculptor

The three office buildings illustrated on these pages, while constructed of different materials, all have a geometric quality in their design. The office complex (top, left) by Edward Larrabee Barnes is part of the Crown Center in Kansas City, Missouri, one of the country's most ambitious and successful mixed-occupancy downtown rehabilitation undertakings. Privately financed by Hallmark Cards, Inc., Crown Center is a $350-million residential and business community comprised of offices, shops, hotel, printing plant, and apartments. The continuous chain of offices—five interlocked units with separate entrances, lobbies, and elevator towers—step up a moderate hill and zigzag at right angles. The precast concrete façade is set off by a bright orange-red sheet-steel stabile by Alexander Calder entitled "Shiva," after the Hindu god of destruction and reproduction. The Park Central complex in Denver, with its three towers of varying heights and its series of structural modules wrapped in a skin of anodized aluminum, presents an imaginative and lively geometric profile. A lofty banking area occupies most of the lobby floor of one of the buildings, with separately defined areas for commercial rental in the tower. Crowning the highest hill in Kansas City, Missouri, the nineteen-story Business Men's Assurance Company Building is one of the country's outstanding recent skyscrapers. The ground floor is not enclosed; the building rests on stilts, allowing the park setting and the distant city to be seen in and around and through the structure. There is a stunning contrast between the structural grid clad in white marble and the dark-tinted glass walls set back six feet from the frame.

Park Central, Denver, Colo. (1974). Muchow Associates, architects

Business Men's Assurance Company Building, Kansas City, Mo. (1963). Skidmore, Owings & Merrill, architects

The United States Corps of Engineers has designed over fifty dams—two of which are illustrated here—thus making it the developer of the largest number of hydroelectric power plants in the country. One of its grandest architectural-engineering achievements is Libby Dam stretching over twenty-nine hundred feet across the rocky cleft gouged by the Kootenai River in northwestern Montana. The 448-mile Kootenai River rises in British Columbia, flows south into Montana, turns northwest through Idaho, and empties into Kootenay Lake in British Columbia. The building of the regal dam prompted a formal diplomatic treaty between the two nations to ensure proper attention to environmental concerns. Garrison Dam extends over eleven thousand feet—one of the world's longest earth-filled dams—across the Missouri River near Riverdale, North Dakota. Like the TVA undertaking, this dam has transformed an entire region, controlling and utilizing the river for irrigation, power, and recreation—the dam created 178-mile-long Lake Sakakawea.

Garrison Dam, Riverdale, N.D. (1959). U. S. Corps of Engineers, engineers; Charles T. Main, Inc., power plant designers

Libby Dam, Libby Mont. (1975). U. S. Corps of Engineers, engineers; Paul Thiry, architect

Base of Gateway Arch (detail)

Soaring 630 feet skyward on the levee of the Mississippi, Eero Saarinen's great stainless steel arch proudly proclaims St. Louis' historic gateway role in the settlement of the West. The nation's tallest man-made monument is situated in a national memorial park commemorating the vast expansion of the United States following Thomas Jefferson's Louisiana Purchase of 1803. Saarinen's catenary arch was raised nearby the famous Eads Bridge, which in 1874, in fact, opened up the trans-Mississippi West to the railroad. The arch is not only a great symbol of history, it is also a unique expression of the ongoing renaissance of downtown St. Louis. In cross section the arch is an equilateral triangle, fifty-four feet wide at the base tapering to seventeen feet at the tip. A capsule transporter in each leg carries visitors to an observation platform at the top, and a Museum of Westward Expansion occupies the underground visitor's center. The arch is a supreme achievement of twentieth-century American architecture, engineering, and sculpture.

Gateway Arch, Jefferson National Expansion Memorial, St. Louis, Mo. (1965).
Eero Saarinen & Associates, architects

FAR WEST & PACIFIC

ALASKA
CALIFORNIA
HAWAII
NEVADA
OREGON
WASHINGTON

West of the tall mountains that once seemed—and were in fact—such formidable barriers to migrants from the East lies the Pacific Coast, the restless edge of American dominion on the continent. During the last several generations, this long, relatively narrow region of the country, long since become easily accessible to easterners, has in many ways become the epitome of changing America. Here, the centuries-old westward movement has since World War II approached a climactic stage. In the course of recent years California has become the most populous state of the Union. Los Angeles has become the third largest city in the nation. As have some other fast-growing, western communities, Portland, Oregon, has even attempted to discourage the influx of new settlers, whose numbers threaten to burden its existing population with unwanted civic and economic problems (much as California tried to exclude the Oakies and the Arkies more than a generation ago during the Great Depression).

The West Coast is a region of many extremes, and of contrasts. In Mount Whitney (14,494 feet) it has the highest peak in the country, except for Alaska; nearby, Death Valley drops to 282 feet below sea level, the lowest point in the United States. There are rain-drenched forests in the north and scorching deserts to the south. In some parts these contrasts are so immediate that it is possible to swim in the ocean within view of snow-capped highlands, or swim in a desert pool overlooked by not-far-distant ski slopes. In spite of such sharp differences, however, there remains a fundamental uniformity that has helped to develop a special quality of life throughout most of the region, a quality of life that is importantly conditioned by the climate. Some years ago in the early autumn it was observed that at a given hour the temperature at Seattle, Portland, San Francisco, Los Angeles, and San Diego—and at Anchorage, Alaska— was at an even 72 degrees. Although that was an unusual phenomenon, it could hardly have happened in any other part of the world over such a wide range of latitude.

The millions of Americans who have settled in the Far West from every other part of the United States have been in good part attracted by this generally benign climate that makes possible a year-round way of life in the open. A large proportion of the populace is composed of fairly recent settlers. Within a very few generations they have produced a society that is in a real sense a synthesis of American society at large, adapted to a distinctive regional environment. Here, too, it is a land of extremes. "In a prosperous country," wrote the adopted California writer Wallace Stegner in 1959, "we are more prosperous than most; in an urban country, more urban than most; in a gadget-happy country, more addicted to gadgets; in a mobile country, more mobile; in a tasteless country, more tasteless; in a creative country, more energetically creative; in an optimistic society, more optimistic; in an anxious society, more anxious. Contribute regionally to the national culture? We *are* the national culture, at its most energetic end."

Long before eastern Americans had any awareness of the West Coast, men of other nations were scouting the possibilities of settlement in and domain over that remote area. In September, 1542, the Spanish explorer Juan Rodríguez Cabrillo landed at San

Diego Bay, the first European to step on California soil. (The name California was derived from that of Calafía, a legendary black Amazon who ruled over a far western island rich in gold.) Cabrillo sailed north, possibly as far as what is now the Oregon border, but returned to California without having found gold anywhere. There he died and was buried, the first European to be buried in California soil. The intrepid Englishman Sir Francis Drake apparently visited the San Francisco Bay area in 1579, after having cruised possibly as far north as the present state of Washington (and finding there only the "most vile, thicke and stinking fogges"), but he paused at that site only to await favorable weather for crossing the Pacific, without entering San Francisco Bay itself.

But it was not until two centuries later that interest in the American Pacific was seriously aroused. Then, during the last decade of the eighteenth century, a number of maritime powers—Britain, France, Holland, and even the infant United States— became aware of the colonial and commercial possibilities in those far western reaches; and Russian fur traders who had gained a solid hold in the Aleutians and Alaska through the discoveries of Vitus Bering, a Danish-born Russian Navy commander, were pushing southward to confront these others. The restored remains of their stockaded settlement at Fort Ross in northern California, built in 1812 and held by the Russians until 1841, may still be seen. Short of cash, Spain met these threats to her extended claims by wielding her most effective instrument of defense, her Sword of the Spirit. Under the inspired direction of Junípero Serra, a lame and aging Franciscan friar who traveled on mule-back, a chain of twenty-one red-tiled adobe missions was stretched up the coastal valleys at intervals of a day's march, with four modest presidios—fortified posts—for their protection. The first California mission was established at San Diego in 1769, the first presidio was founded at Monterey a year later. That same year a party under Gaspar de Portolá exploring the territory farther north by land spotted the majestic harbor that lay within the Golden Gate. In 1775, as other men far across the continent were stirring in rebellion against British rule, Manuel de Ayala took the first ship through the Golden Gate to survey the great untenanted bay within. (Cabrillo, Drake, and others had missed the port completely in their excursions up and down the coast.) The San Francisco presidio was dedicated in the summer of 1776, the unhappy season that saw Washington retreating before the British army.

The effort to settle California strained the resources of the Spanish outposts there. The primitive native Indians offered little resistance to the Spanish advances northward. One eighteenth-century French explorer described the straw huts of these indigenes as "the most miserable one could find anywhere." Father Junípero Serra and his companions baptised thousands of them and taught them the mysteries of farming and of adobe construction, but in the end, aside from the mission compounds, the colonizing efforts of the Spanish in California left very little trace. Nevertheless, ever anxious to affirm Spain's claims to the whole far western region, an expedition was sent to the Northwest in 1789. In 1778, on his tragic last voyage, Captain Cook had explored that area in quest of the Northwest Passage, and succeeded in charting the western coast as far north as the Bering Strait. Among his crew were William Bligh, later master of the *Bounty*, George Vancouver, who was subsequently to make a more detailed survey of the northwestern coast, and the young Connecticut Yankee John Ledyard, a corporal of the Marines who had joined the expedition just before the Declaration of Independence was signed. Ledyard was "painfully afflicted" with nostalgia at the sight of the American coast, he later wrote, although it was "more than 2,000 miles from the nearest part of New England." However, he noted that the Indians of that region, who had never before seen a white man, nevertheless carried European-made knives and bracelets. "No part of America," he concluded, "is without some sort of commercial intercourse, immediate or remote." Ledyard planned to return to the Pacific Northwest one day and make his fortune dealing in the abundance of furs to be had there from the natives in exchange for all but valueless trinkets.

When an expedition from Mexico arrived in those waters they were faced with English trading ships which had already established bases there and which repulsed the Spanish advances. Also present was the brig *Columbia* out of Boston with Captain Robert Gray in command. After garnering a cargo of precious furs for an ordinary chisel apiece, Gray returned to Boston via Hawaii and China, the first American sea captain to sail around the globe. Gray was welcomed at his home port by a "great concourse of citizens assembled on the various wharfs." To their amazement they saw Gray march off to call on Governor Hancock in the company of a Sandwich Islander clad in a feather cloak of golden suns set in flaming scarlet, with a gorgeous feather helmet to cap his elegance. Two years later Gray was back in the Pacific. He found ships of six other nations cruising those newly important waters. After swapping for more pelts at Nootka Sound, at the site of present-day Vancouver, Gray turned southward down the coast, hailing Captain George Vancouver who was on the way up with a commission to reclaim any territory in the Northwest seized earlier by the Spanish. On May 11, 1792, two days after Vancouver had, in passing, advised him that nothing of importance was to be observed to the south, Gray sailed into a "spacious harbor" and up a "fine river" which he named the Columbia, after his ship. He had discovered the great River of the West that had for centuries troubled the dreams of the world's most hopeful adventurers. To all intents the ancient riddle of the Northwest Passage was finally solved by the little brig from Boston. It was by then no anticlimax that its waters did not reach back into the eastern ocean. Gray had planted the flag of empire on the other side of the continent and opened a world-wide dominion for American trade. With the publication of Cook's account of his voyages, in 1784, which was peddled by no less a character than Parson Weems and was, as well, reprinted in the Pennsylvania *Packet*, Ledyard's dreams came back to life in the visions of other Americans. By the turn of the century, as Yankee traders found their way to the Northwest, in the wake of the *Columbia* the fur trade of that region had become an exclusively Boston business.

Just a dozen years later, Captain Meriwether Lewis and William Clark reached the Columbia River after a heroic overland trek and, in November, 1805, came to the coast where they "saw the waves like small mountains" rolling out of the Pacific. A few years after that John Jacob Astor, following John Ledyard's earlier design, launched his plan to drain the northwest country of its furs from both ends. The divide was to be from a post on the Columbia River, sea otters going west into the China Trade, beaver and other furs going to the American and European markets. Slipping in before Russia or England could lay claims to the spot, Astor's agents completed a stockaded fort—Fort Astoria—between the mouth of the Columbia River and Young's Bay. However, two years later the English took over that modest redoubt practically at the point of a frigate's guns, and changed the name to Fort George. At the time, that was too removed a matter for most Americans to worry over. As one representative derisively asked Congress as late as 1828, "What can lead any adventurer to seek the inhospitable regions of Oregon unless, indeed, he wishes to be a savage. . . ." As for Oregon entering the Union as a state, in 1843 congressional spokesmen ridiculed such a notion, pointing out that it would take ten months for representatives from such a remote point to travel to the District of Columbia and back again, which would leave them practically no time at either end of their business. Oregon became a state in 1859.

Nevertheless, the groundwork for the great migration had been laid, a migration which in the 1840's became almost epidemic as thousands of westering Americans crossed nearly two thousand miles of raw country to reach the wooded and well-watered lands of the northwest coast. To Horace Greeley this phenomenal wandering of peoples wore "an aspect of insanity." But by 1846, it was reported, the American Village in Oregon, flourishing under the good management of the Hudson's Bay Company, boasted "two churches, and 100 houses, store houses, etc. all of which has been built in five years." The Oregon Trail had become a national highway. Twenty years later Portland was a budding metropolis of a large region, with "water, gas, and Nicholson pavements; and had more of a solid air and tone, than any city we had seen since leaving the Missouri," as one visitor reported. "Several daily papers, two weekly religious ones, and a fine Mercantile Library, all spoke well for her intelligence and culture, while her Public Schoolbuildings and her Court-House would have been creditable anywhere. . . . Nearer to the Sandwich Islands and China, by several hundred miles, than California, she had already opened up a brisk trade with both, and boasted that she could sell sugars, teas, silks, rice, etc., cheaper than San Francisco." In 1873, Portland opened its New Market Theater, where celebrated artists drew audiences that came as far as two hundred miles to attend performances.

South of Oregon, for years California had hung like a ripe plum at the far end of Spain's vulnerable American empire. Little was changed by Mexico's revolt from Spain in 1821. United States squadrons, eager to improve this nation's opportunities, kept watch on the war vessels habitually maintained in the eastern Pacific by Russia, France, and England. Fired by one incentive or another, by the early 1840's Americans were already filtering into the territory through the mountain passes or by sea, some to settle, some to return home with tales of a fertile land of genial climate, of picturesquely decaying missions, and of tranquil ranches where *mañana* was always the day of action—a land of sunshine, lazy Indians, and gracious Latins. What a land it *could* be, mused Richard Henry Dana in *Two Years Before the Mast*, if it were governed and worked by people with Yankee enterprise. At Monterey and Santa Barbara he discovered that already most of the chief *alcaldes* were Yankees by birth, men who had "left their consciences at Cape Horn" and renounced their Protestantism to enjoy political liberty and trading opportunities in the land of sun-soaked, decaying Catholic missions. Dana had visited Yerba Buena, the future San Francisco, when that peninsula site had nothing to show but a few adobe huts besides its presidio and nearby mission. But, like others before him, he foresaw the ultimate importance of the place with its magnificent harbor rimmed with impressive hills. In a few years the enterprising people Dana looked for were arriving in earnest. By the winter of 1847–48 the little settlement had grown into a modest trading community with about eight hundred people, two small hotels, a few shops, and a sprinkling of private residences.

The most active focus of American interest in California was the semifeudal fort that had been built by John Augustus Sutter, directly in the line of overland travel from the East at a site that would become the present-day Sacramento. When California "revolted" against Mexico, General Vallejo and his brother were imprisoned in that compound, and in July, 1846, the American flag was raised over it. In 1841, the Russians, who had been hunting fur seals and sea otters out of Fort Ross for the past twenty-nine years, had sold their outpost to Sutter for $30,000 in gold and produce. (Their chapel, stockade, and blockhouse have been restored, and the Commander's House, an almost unaltered example of Russian log housing, all may be seen there today.) It was near there a year and a half later that "some kind of mettle was found in the tail race that looks like goald," as a contemporary record announced. Further reports embellished that statement with all but incredible claims, and an unprecedented gold rush was on its way. President Polk solemnly acknowledged that a strike had been made that would make Cortez seem like a smalltime operator.

Men who had never before dreamed of leaving home found themselves swept into one of the great pioneering adventures of the age—or of any other age, for that matter. This great treasure hunt took on something of the fervor of a crusade. Groups went to church to receive blessings before starting out, and sometimes the preacher left his pulpit to join them on their way. Farmers, clerks, doctors, lawyers, mechanics, left their callings and joined men of leisure to head westward to pan and dig for the precious metal. One forty-niner reported that San Francisco attracted "one of the most heterogeneous masses that ever existed since the building of the tower of Babel." Hopeful prospectors came from France, Germany, England, Japan, China, Australia, Peru, Chile, Mexico, as well as from other parts of the United States—men of all nations, creeds, and colors, dressed in every variety of costume, and babbling a medley of tongues. There were "Yankees of every possible variety, native Californians in *sarapes* and sombreros, Chilians, Sonorians, Kanakas from Hawaii, Chinese with long tails, Malays armed with everlasting creeses, and others in whose embrowned and bearded visages it was impossible to recognize any special nationality." Among them, according to one witness, were more well-informed and clever men than might be found in any other community of its size. In 1851 there were 136 lawyers in the city, more than half of them from eastern cities and some from the Midwest; and there were, it was reported, a sprinkling of women, most of whom were "neither maids, wives, nor widows."

For some time to come architectural niceties could wait until at least minimal accommodations could be contrived for the growing and floating populations, be they sheds, tents, or whatever. Houses of one sort or another were going up at the rate of fifteen to thirty a day, without satisfying the demand. Some were imported from Canton to be raised by Chinese carpenters. Others were imported prefabricated from the East and from England. Ships deserted by sailors who had quit their posts to try their luck in the gold fields were pulled up on the beach to serve as lodgings and warehouses. The flimsily built city was burned nearly to the ground half a dozen times during the first few years of its growth, but it shot up again after each disaster to harbor a growing population drawn from every corner of the earth, as happened so dramatically after the devastating fire and earthquake of 1906. By the end of the Civil War it had a population of more than one hundred thousand persons and a history like Alladin's palace. It was accurately reported to be "far more cosmopolitan than any other city except New York." Architecturally, the vigor and the confidence in the city's unlimited possibilities is probably best represented by the colonnaded Palace Hotel, opened in 1875, with its great glass-roofed center courtyard where San Franciscans still dine in splendor. (The hotel, now known as The Sheraton Palace, was destroyed in the fire and earthquake of 1906, but was quickly rebuilt along the original lines.)

Parenthetically, the Boston ships that plied the western waters were as well known in Hawaii. China Traders and whalemen, in fact, made those Pacific islands practically a suburb of Boston and, according to one visiting mariner, almost a facsimile of the New England city in some spots. For years the most conspicuous building in Honolulu, and a landmark for seamen, was the large church built of coral blocks by American missionaries in the image of a New England frame meetinghouse. Looking back on his own adventures in the South Seas, Herman Melville earnestly thought for a while that his countrymen had more to learn from the natives of those parts, cannibals though some of them were, than the natives could learn from the missionaries.

The first white men to visit the islands of Hawaii (then known as the Sandwich Islands) did not come there to conquer the land and subjugate its people. However, the advent of Europeans and, later, Americans inevitably resulted in vital changes in the life of the islanders, some of which were to be good, some bad. Before this intrusion, there were several warring kingdoms in the islands, each with its hereditary nobility. The introduction of firearms enabled one chief, Kamehameha I, to consolidate most of Hawaii into a single kingdom in 1795 with himself as ruler. Ancient religious taboos were gradually discarded, native cultural traditions declined, and, primarily because of the spread of white men's diseases, the population dwindled drastically. On the other hand, thanks to the missionaries' zeal, progress was made in education. In 1889 the then-current king, Kamehameha III, guaranteed religious freedom in the islands, and four years later, in spite of the incursion of whites and peoples of other races, Hawaiian independence was recognized. The increasing presence of American businessmen slowly led to the annexation of the islands in 1898 as a territory of the United States. Statehood finally came in 1959, with more ethnic and cultural groups represented in the population than in any other state.

To return to the mainland: The gold fever that brought such intensive excitement to the San Francisco area had only slowly affected southern California. In 1850, as the population of San Francisco suddenly swelled with newcomers, there were fewer than two thousand inhabitants in Los Angeles County, most of them Mexicans and Indians. When the miners called for more meat, however, and cattle prices started to soar, ranchers of the southern area began to share the boom from a distance. However, the ranching business was hard hit by two successive years of drought in 1862 and 1863. Great herds were stricken by the unrelenting sun. Without water the cattle were converted into baking, rotting carcasses. Large ranches—Mexican land grants—were divided and sold.

As had earlier happened everywhere across the nation, when the railroads arrived in the Far West they sparked fresh activity in every direction. Merchants like Collis P. Huntington, Mark Hopkins, Leland Stanford, and Charles Crocker who financed the Central Pacific Railroad, grew enormously wealthy from that investment, and built their marble palaces atop Nob Hill and in their other favored locations in San Francisco, replacing the fading wooden shanties; palaces that aped in style and grandeur those of their fellow millionaires in the East. (The first through train from Boston to the Pacific in 1870, with eight cars, made the trip in ten days. At the end of the journey the passengers ceremoniously poured a bottle of Boston Harbor water into San Francisco Bay.) San Francisco became a major station linking the Occident and the Orient.

When the rails reached Los Angeles from the East, a whole new chapter opened for that city and its surrounding areas. More than fifty thousand prospective migrants came to California on the Southern Pacific Railroad between 1881 and 1885, and over the years from 1880 to 1887 the population of Los Angeles increased six or seven fold. The most prominent indication of southern California's new importance as a tourist attraction was the Hotel del Coronado, the largest of California's early resort hotels, built in 1888 by the Canadian-born California architects Reid & Reid. In the fourth edition of his guide to the United States Baedeker referred to this great hostelry as "one of the largest, finest, and most comfortable hotels in California . . . delightfully situated close to the ocean. . . . Adjacent are bathing-tanks of salt water, for summer and winter use, while steam-yachts, launches, and boats afford opportunities for excursions by water." It featured electric lights in most of its nearly four hundred guest rooms, and catered to opulent easterners and dignitaries of all ranks, including four presidents of the United States and the king of Hawaii.

Southern California's rapid growth as a vacation and retirement area brought about a population mix that was unprecedented in the nation's history. Communities developed that were composed of well-to-do and educated people who had left behind their accustomed routines and, detached from the familiar European focus, were exposed to the unfamiliar traditions of the Orient. The landscape was exotic, the climate genial, altogether a milieu favorable to architectural innovation of every sort and at every level, from the most sophisticated experiments to lunatic extremes.

It was under those circumstances that in the late nineteenth and early twentieth centuries two brothers, Charles Sumner and Henry Mather Greene, natives of Cincinnati, came to southern California after having completed their architectural education at the Massachusetts Institute of Technology, and created a distinctive style of modern domestic architecture in and about Pasadena. It was almost precisely the same time that Frank Lloyd Wright was developing the "prairie house" in the Midwest. Like Wright in their search for designs suitable to the local climate and terrain, but more obviously, the Greenes were influenced by Japanese building methods and designs. However, in their hands this exotic strain was domesticated into an architecture so well adapted to the American scene, particularly that of the Southwest, so fresh in its interpretations, that its influence spread beyond California to the rest of the country in modified versions that became known as the "California bungalow style"—a forerunner of the modern ranch house. Like Wright also, the Greenes dispensed with all reference to European traditional forms and all the vaunted upper-class iconography of class and status, in their interior as well as their exterior designs, in preference to a hospitable openness of plan with a comfortable scale and a colorful variety of woods even in their most extravagant constructions. (When he returned from Japan for the last time in 1922 Wright went to work for a time in southern California, here as ever originating structures that were his individual solutions to the problems of the terrain, climate, and technical resources of the region, before moving on to his last headquarters at Taliesin West.)

For a time it seemed that such advanced, well-adapted styles of building might be engulfed in California—as was happening elsewhere in the nation—by a tide of eclectic revivalism. When, in 1915, San Francisco celebrated its rebirth after the great fire with the Panama-Pacific International Exposition, the structures that housed the fair were strictly in the classical tradition of the École des Beaux-Arts in Paris. Bernard Maybeck, a graduate of that venerable institution and a transplanted New Yorker, designed the most famous building at the fair, the Palace of Fine Arts. Many easterners made their first transcontinental trip to wonder at the "dream city of cobweb palaces" that recalled the grandeur of ancient Rome, among other things. At the Panama-California Exposition, held at San Diego that same year, the guidance of the elegant architect of the eastern establishment, Bertram Goodhue, abetted by Carlton M. Winslow, led to a revival of the indigenous Spanish colonial styles, freely interpreted and formally dressed up for the ceremonial occasion. This was by no means the earliest example of contemporary architecture that revived the old, provincial Spanish tradition on the West Coast, but the exposition served to spur that revival much as the World's Columbian Exposition had stimulated the revival of the classical styles twenty-two years earlier. The style quickly became a prevailing theme that set about to recapture the spirit of an all-but-legendary past. Featured by red-tiled roofs, relatively plain plastered walls, grilled windows, patios, and other reminiscences of the indigenous provincial houses, it was at its best well-enough adapted to the nature of the land and the climate, although it was hostile to the independent advances made by the Greene brothers. And at its best, it found expression in the creations of the architect George Washington Smith, who worked in the style from 1916 until his death in 1930. Such houses reflected the tranquil life that visitors and immigrants chose to associate with California at its most accommodating best.

Meanwhile, north of California, Oregon and Washington had also been spurred to new growth when a transcontinental railroad reached that area in 1883. In 1870 more persons were living in San Francisco than in Oregon and Washington combined. Then, between 1880 and 1890, the population of Seattle increased more than twelve times over; Tacoma's, more than thirty-six fold in that same decade. Although Portland also grew, it lost its pre-eminence to its northern neighbors.

Still farther north, in 1867 Secretary of State William H. Seward purchased the huge Alaska territory from the Russians for $7,200,000, a bargain which was commonly referred to at the time as "Seward's Folly." (The price paid was less than two cents an acre.) The Russians, who had claimed this land for more than a century past, were at this point—following the Crimean War—eager to strip off their outlying possessions in order to gather strength for a struggle with Great Britain for the control of Asia. They had, moreover, already reaped a colossal harvest of furs from these northern climes. The impress they left on Alaska was picturesque but generally insignificant. All that is left today of their imperial adventure in Alaska are a few unpretentious structures still standing among the colorful totem poles and other artifacts of native origin. Under American administration the pattern of life in Alaska changed little for years to come.

Then in 1897 the S. S. *Excelsior* and the S. S. *Portland* came down from Alaska with a great fortune in gold drawn from the streams and mountains of that farthest North American territory. Seattle became the nation's chief link with Alaska, as several hundred thousand treasure hunters came to the city. By 1910 the population of the state of Washington was twice that of Oregon. Alaska went through its period of rough and lawless mining camps—a period made romantic by the writings of Jack London and Rex Beach. It did not get a territorial representative in Congress until 1906, and even then did not enjoy self-government for another six years. Alaska's greatest boom would come with the approach of World War II, when the area's strategic importance became a matter of national concern and its unfathomable natural resources a matter of growing interest. In 1959 it became the largest state in the Union, some two and a third times as large as Texas.

Throughout its history the Far West has faced the problem of water: too much in a few areas, not enough in by far the greater part of the region. To control and distribute the flow where it was destructive or imbalanced, to introduce it where the supply was otherwise meager or nonexistent, to harness it for power needed throughout the most rapidly growing region of the United States, required heroic measures. Without water supplies contrived by ingenious means and often from far distances, much of southern California would have remained virtually a desert. Hoover Dam, described in the previous chapter, has enabled southern California—along with other regions—to tap the great reserves piled up in Lake Mead by the Colorado River. Shasta Dam, north of Sacramento and at the head of the Central Valley Reclamation Project, stores enough water to serve two million acres of land, the agricultural heartland of California. Another great enterprise, the California Water Project, dwarfs every other water-transfer system in history. Farther north, the Grand Coulee Dam in eastern Washington, the world's most massive concrete dam, is one element of a project that, in all its ramifications, will serve still another empire of land in the Columbia River Basin with its increasing population. On one of the state buildings in Sacramento is inscribed a line from a popular nineteenth-century poem: "Bring me men to match my mountains." Such were the men who envisioned, planned, engineered, and realized these vast constructional schemes—modern pioneers who have opened up new frontiers for their restless fellow countrymen.

The problems and possibilities that contemporary architecture confronts in the states facing the Pacific Ocean are basically the same as they are elsewhere in the country. Here as elsewhere the planner has been freed from the necessity of limiting his project only to locally available materials. The natural materials of the entire world and new synthetic ones are accessible to architects everywhere in developed areas. Technological advances have made human habitation possible in almost any environmental circumstances (including outer space). Communication at the speed of light and transportation faster than sound have made the exchange of ideas, in architecture and engineering as well as in all other matters, virtually instantaneous. However, the tendency of such factors to reduce architectural designs to a universal idiom, as encouraged by the theories and practices of the so-called international school, has been countered by other tendencies that reassert a traditional regionalism in architecture. Frank Lloyd Wright, a modernist if there ever was one, did this by disassociating regionalism from its old dependence on archaic, historic formulas and orienting it towards the living present. Other architects who have worked in the Far West—John Yeon and Pietro Belluschi in the Pacific Northwest and William Wilson Wurster, Harwell Harris, and Gardner Dailey in California, for example—have won international respect for their essentially regional approach to architectural problems. In very recent years a threatened lack of the energy and resources needed to overcome demands of local circumstances by costly expedients has led to more imaginative and innovative accommodations to local climates and local expectations. For various sound and practical, as well as esthetic, reasons, regionalism remains a continuing aspect of American architectural progress.

OVERLEAF: *La Purísima Concepción Mission, Lompoc, Calif. (as of 1818).* Occupying an unspoiled little valley, La Purísima Concepción Mission was first established in 1787 some four miles southwest of its present location. In 1812 it was destroyed by an earthquake. A decision was made the next year to move to the site the mission now occupies on the famous Camino Real. It was the eleventh of the twenty-one Franciscan missions stretching from San Diego to Sonoma, 650 miles to the north. In 1824, three years after Mexican independence from Spain, the local Indians revolted. In 1834 the mission was secularized, and after that the entire establishment began its decline. There were further earthquakes, and vandalism added to the destruction. However, from 1934 to 1939 the mission was carefully rebuilt, and this splendid reconstruction provides a convincing indication of the full cycle of mission life, its functions of housing and converting Indians and of teaching them skills, of the shops and quarters required by such routine activity, of the facilities for accommodating travelers, and, of course, of the chapel used for religious purposes. This was one of the most ambitious reconstructions in the Far West.

San Diego de Alcalá, near San Diego, Calif. (1813)

On July 16, 1769, Father Junípero Serra founded the mission San Diego de Alcalá, the first and "mother mission" of the chain of missions that were subsequently established at intervals up the western coast. Moved in 1774 from its original site on Presidio Hill in what is now Old Town San Diego, the mission seen today is the fourth of its name and the third on this site. The present church, completed in 1813, with its complex of patio, garden, mission school and quarters, is evocative of the mission era in California. San Carlos de Borromeo at Carmel was the second mission in the chain and the final resting place of Father Serra and his successor, Father Fermín Francisco de Lasuén. Completely restored, with its lovely gardened court-yard, the stoutly constructed stone church has an unusual vaulted roof, two towers of unequal size, and a fine baroque star-shaped window over the prominent central doorway.

San Carlos de Borromeo, Carmel, Calif. (1797)

San Gabriel Arcángel, San Gabriel, Calif. (1805)

San Miguel Arcángel, San Miguel, Calif. (1818)

The San Gabriel Arcángel Mission was founded by a band of monks from San Diego. Ten years later, colonists from this site founded the pueblo of Los Angeles. The mission, in the Spanish-Moorish style of architecture with massive buttresses, reflects those the Franciscan fathers recalled from home and repeated in the isolated countryside east of Los Angeles. California's first winery was founded behind the mission, which today has been completely restored. San Miguel Arcángel was founded in 1797 as the sixteenth mission, halfway between San Francisco and Los Angeles. The church, built in 1818, is noted for its mural decorations. The frescoes were executed by Catalan artist Estevan Munras, who with his Indian helpers stenciled and painted most of the interior. The side walls have architectural motifs, and the pulpit is enlivened by a fanciful folk-art design. An unusual arcade, illustrated above, graces the front of the church.

San Luís Rey de Francia, near Oceanside, Calif. (1815)

Known as the "King of the Missions," San Luís Rey was founded in 1798 by Father Lasuén as the eighteenth mission. Sitting atop a comely ridge, this largest and most productive mission for many years was the home for more than three thousand Indians. As was the case with the others, the mission was secularized in 1834 by the Mexicans and the buildings fell into disuse and disrepair, lying virtually deserted. The single-towered church itself, built in 1815, escaped collapse due to its brick-faced adobe walls over six feet thick. In 1893 San Luís Rey was rededicated, and the mission was then totally reconstructed and today serves as a Franciscan seminary and parish church. Inside the church, five bays marked by prominent multidecorated pilasters divide the nave; the sanctuary wall has a Renaissance-inspired altar and *reredos.*

"Queen of the Missions," Santa Barbara was established by Father Serra in 1786. Completed in 1820, the church has a monumental quality enhanced by twin towers, while the arched monastery wing extending alongside contributes fine relief to an otherwise static effect. The interior is decorated with marbleizing and neoprimitive designs.

OVERLEAF: *San Juan Capistrano Mission, San Juan Capistrano, Calif. (1776; 1806).* Father Serra founded the seventh California mission in 1776 and dedicated a small adobe church, now restored, two years later. The tower and roof of the elaborate stone church completed in 1806 came crashing down on the congregation in the earthquake of 1812. The church's ruins with its great sanctuary arch provide a romantic setting for its famed swallows.

Santa Barbara, Santa Barbara, Calif. (1820)

Old Custom House, Monterey, Calif. (1827; 1846)

Larkin House, Monterey, Calif. (1835-37)

722

Although Cabrillo first sighted Monterey Bay in 1542 and Vizcaíno landed there in 1602 and named it, the colonization of Monterey did not begin until 1770 with the establishment of a presidio and mission. As Monterey expanded, it became the capital of Alta California under the Spanish and then Mexican (1822–48) flags. There, in 1827, the Mexican government built a custom house, which is now California's oldest official building; it was expanded from 1841 to 1846. When Commodore Sloat raised the American flag over the Old Custom House on July 7, 1846, it signaled the annexation of the territory, made official two years later. The old adobe and stone structure served for American customs until 1867. The simple hip-roofed adobe house with its encircling two-story verandah is regarded as the pioneer example of the Monterey domestic style that so influenced the subsequent architectural development of California. Built by Thomas Oliver Larkin, U.S. consul to Mexico, the Larkin House combines Spanish colonial (thick adobe walls) and wooden elements of a New England character. Larkin, a native of Massachusetts, spent ten years in North Carolina and was undoubtedly influenced by the double porches of its traditional tidewater dwellings.

Los Cerritos Ranch House,
Long Beach, Calif. (1844)

Both of these two-story adobe ranch houses with balconies have survived more than a century from the period when Mexico held sway over California. The largest adobe house in northern California belonged to General Mariano Guadalupe Vallejo, who grazed thousands of cattle and horses on his 66,000-acre Petaluma Ranch. The L-shaped structure below is the restored section of half the original full-square building that combined the then-developing Monterey domestic vernacular (see the Larkin House on the preceding pages) with the long-established Spanish-Mexican patio layout. The wide overhanging eaves and peripheral balconies provided protection against the elements and permitted circulation to the upstairs rooms. Los Cerritos Ranch House—of adobe brick baked on the grounds and local redwood beams resting on a foundation of fired brick brought around the Horn—was built by Don Juan Temple as headquarters of his vast ranch. It too combines the Monterey style with the Spanish-Mexican plan.

Petaluma Adobe State Historical Monument, Petaluma, Calif. (1836)

The fierce wood-sculptured figures on the preceding pages are representations of the old Hawaiian gods set above the palisades of the restored City of Refuge to warn intruders off the sacred grounds. Situated on a shelf of lava overlooking the Pacific Ocean on the Island of Hawaii, this square sanctuary is protected by a great stone wall laid without mortar about the year 1550 by the ruling chief of Kona. It was the most important of old Hawaii's sacred places of refuge, which offered haven to vanquished warriors, tabu breakers, and all other fugitives. Within the walls are stone platforms, where chiefs' houses stood, a tent-shaped thatched reconstruction of a temple, royal fishponds, and palace grounds. Near the shore, a few hundred yards north of the temple, stand two thatched shelters, one left unfinished to show the intricacies of Polynesian grass construction.

OVERLEAF: *Kailua Village, Hawaii Island, Hawaii.* In 1820 the first Christian missionaries to Hawaii arrived at picturesque Kailua Bay on the western Kona coast. The spire of Mokuaikaua Church, originally built in 1836, can be seen from the palm-fringed bay, as can the two-story balconied Hulihee Palace. It was built of coral mortar, lava rock, and native wood in 1838 for Queen Kaahumanu's brother and became King Kalakaua's summer palace in 1884.

City of Refuge National Historical Park, Honaunau, Hawaii Island, Hawaii

Kawaiahao Church, Honolulu, Oahu Island, Hawaii (1842)

The Congregational Kawaiahao Church and the nearby Frame House commemorate the first contingent of Protestant missionaries who arrived from New England in 1820 and in subsequent years strongly influenced the religion, education, medical practices, and economics of the Hawaiians. The proper New England Frame House, the oldest structure of its kind in the islands, was largely prefabricated in Boston, disassembled and shipped around the Horn, and reassembled on its present site in 1821. Twenty-one years later the Reverend Hiram Bingham replaced a series of thatched churches with a permanent edifice of coral blocks and a Gothic tower. The Old Waioli Church at the former whaling port of Hanalei on Kauai capably solved the occasional wet and windy climate problems with wide skirting about a sturdy clapboard inner structure, the whole topped by a steeply pitched roof. The design of this church developed into a regional Hawaiian style.

Old Waioli Church, Hanalei, Kauai Island, Hawaii (1841)

Frame House, Honolulu, Oahu Island, Hawaii (1821)

734

Iolani Palace, Honolulu, Oahu Island, Hawaii (1882).
T. J. Baker, C. S. Wall, and Isaac Moore, architects

Iolani Palace, the only royal palace in the United States, housed Hawaii's last two monarchs and served as the seat of authority for the provisional government, the republic, the territory, and the state. The Italian Renaissance-style structure, with double porticoes and cast-iron columns on all four sides, was constructed in 1882 by King Kalakaua on the site of an earlier Iolani Palace. It was used as a royal residence by Kalakaua and then by his sister Queen Liliuokalani until the monarchy was overthrown in 1893. Iolani is now a beautifully restored museum with artifacts, particularly in the throne room (above), pertaining to Hawaii's history. Also on the island of Oahu is a white frame house used by Queen Emma, consort of King Kamehameha IV, as a cool summer retreat and social center. With its high ceilings, fluted Tuscan columns, and wide verandah, it bears some resemblance to the contemporary plantation houses in Mississippi and Louisiana.

Queen Emma's Summer Palace, Honolulu, Oahu Island, Hawaii (about 1847)

Russian Blockhouse, Sitka, Alaska (as of about 1805)

The octagonal Russian blockhouse illustrated above commemorates Sitka, Alaska's, early days as a fortified fur-trading post. Old Sitka, founded in 1799 by the manager of the Russian-American Trading Company, Alexander Baranof, was burned in 1802 in a surprise attack by the Tlingit Indians. Baranof subsequently resettled about six miles to the south, and within a short time Sitka became the flourishing capital of Russian America. Eventually the Tlingits returned to Sitka, which remained a thriving fur-trading center for over sixty years. On nearby Castle Hill, which was the site of Baranof's castle, in October of 1867 the Russian flag was lowered and the American flag was raised over Alaska for the first time. The native Alaskan Indians left their cultural imprint on the land in the form of their magnificent totem poles. These painted wood carvings celebrated family history, mythological beliefs, deaths, and tribal events. The Old Witch Totem Pole at left, carved by the Haidas, was moved to Juneau from Prince of Wales Island in southern Alaska.

Old Witch Totem Pole, Juneau, Alaska (about 1860)

The two Russian Orthodox churches illustrated here are vestiges of Russian cultural influences that lingered on in Alaska long after America had purchased the vast northern territory for less than two cents an acre. The Church of the Assumption of the Virgin Mary was built as a mission church about 1894 in Kenai, one of the oldest permanent settlements in Alaska. In 1791 the Russians had established a fortified fur-trading post at the mouth of the Kenai River on Cook Inlet, and seventy-eight years later the U.S. Army built one of its first Alaskan military posts there. The scaled-down domes of the church faintly recall the ancient Byzantine origins of its rites. The small, octagonal St. Nicholas Orthodox Church with its onion dome was built in the 1890's in one of Alaska's newer cities, Juneau, founded in 1881 with the discovery of gold there.

Church of the Assumption of the Virgin Mary, Kenai, Alaska (about 1894)

St. Nicholas Orthodox Church, Juneau, Alaska (1895)

OVERLEAF: *Broadway and its Buildings, Skagway, Alaska (late 1890's).* The buildings on Broadway and others in the historic district constitute the largest unspoiled example of an Alaska frontier mining town. Prior to the discovery of gold in the Klondike region of the Canadian Yukon in 1896, the site of Skagway was marked by a single cabin. But it was strategically located on a direct route into the gold-bearing region via the Chilkoot Trail and White Pass routes. By the winter of 1897-98 Skagway had turned into a thriving city with hotels, saloons, stores, and dance halls for its population of twenty thousand. Today the main thoroughfare is still of gravel with sidewalks of wood under projecting canopies, and its picturesque structures, such as the domed Golden North Hotel (1898), recall the booming Gold Rush days.

Surgeon's Quarters, The Dalles, Oreg. (1857)

Bishop's House, Portland, Oreg. (1879)

The older section of downtown Portland, especially the area near the Willamette River, still has—in spite of fires and demolition—a number of nineteenth-century buildings of considerable architectural and historical merit. Built in 1879 of cast iron and brick, the Bishop's House is a three-story Victorian Gothic structure that, following its sale by the diocese, served various commercial functions. Thoroughly restored outside and in, it now provides attractive office space. Calvary Presbyterian Church, the oldest church in the Portland area, is an energetic example of the Gothic Revival style in wood, with its steeples, gables, brackets, buttresses, tracery, barge boards, all actively deployed about and above its oyster-colored board-and-batten walls and its dark roof. The Surgeon's Quarters is one of the exemplary Gothic-style cottages in the Northwest and the only remnant of Fort Dalles, east of Portland, around which a settlement grew up in the mid-1800's.

Calvary Presbyterian Church, Portland, Oreg. (1883). Warren H. Williams, architect

In their quest for suitable forms and designs for their public buildings, American communities have looked in all directions. With all its classical dignity the Capitol at Washington, D.C., set a precedent for the new nation that could hardly be ignored as regional and local state houses and courthouses were raised across the land. Traces of such classicism, mingling pleasantly enough with Victorian features, can be seen in the state capitol at Carson City, Nevada, built just over a century ago by an architect from California. The roundheaded paired windows, the prominent quoins, and the capably handled hexagonal cupola contribute strong accents to the design of the structure. At Spokane, Washington, on the other hand, the county courthouse owes a recognizable debt to the French châteaux of the Loire Valley. It was built at a time when Richard Morris Hunt was lining Fifth Avenue with fashionable buildings in the châteaux manner. The Pioneer Post Office and Courthouse at Portland, Oregon, is the oldest standing federal structure in the Northwest, a mellow and pleasant reminder of the classical dignity of the faraway National Capitol, built almost a century earlier.

Pioneer Post Office and Courthouse, Portland, Oreg. (1873). Alfred B. Mullett, architect

State Capitol, Carson City, Nev. (1870). Joseph Gosling, architect

County Courthouse, Spokane, Wash. (1895). W. A. Ritchie, architect

New Market Block, Portland, Oreg. (1872). Piper & Burton, architects

Like almost every other city of consequence in the nation, Salem and Portland in Oregon went through a cast-iron phase in the nineteenth century. As everywhere else, the metal fronts of these buildings generally followed formal historical designs, such as had originally been realized in carved stone. Salem's Ladd & Bush branch of the U.S. National Bank was patterned directly after the Ladd & Tilton Bank built in Portland in 1859. The almost identical cast-iron façades of the two buildings were turned out by the Willamette Iron Foundry and are examples of the finest cast-iron work in the country. When the Salem Bank was expanded in 1969 by the architectural firm of Skidmore, Owings & Merrill, carefully preserved sections of the old Portland bank, which had been replaced by a new structure in 1955, were incorporated into the addition. The first floor of Portland's old three-story New Market Block, now used as a garage, presents a startlingly rich mixture of white-painted cast-iron columns and fancifully carved wood cornice.

Ladd & Bush Bank, Salem, Oreg. (1869). John Nestor, architect

Pioneer Square Historic District Redevelopment, Seattle, Wash. (1890's; 1970's)

Spritely in spite of its years, having survived fire, earthquake, semineglect, and even scorn, in a once deteriorating section of downtown Los Angeles, the five-story Bradbury Building remains a treasure of its architectural kind. Lavish use of French-fashioned wrought iron, especially in the open elevator cages, distinguishes its skylit central court. Like an increasing number of other cities, Seattle is awakening to the architectural heritage from its early years. The Pioneer Square area was once the heart of the old city. Among the historic district's attractive features is the glass and cast-iron pavilion, which originally stood over underground municipal rest-rooms and was restored in 1972 to its present use as a bus-stop shelter.

Bradbury Building, Los Angeles, Calif. (1893). George H. Wyman, architect

Bowers Mansion, near Carson City, Nev. (1865)

The sudden wealth unearthed from Nevada's mines in the 1860's and 1870's spawned a variety of private and public buildings, some of which still stand to recall the hectic social circumstances that prevailed in that area at the time. One "Sandy" Bowers, an illiterate teamster who struck it rich, built a pretentious but by no means unseemly "mansion" in Washoe County, importing stonecutters from his wife's native Scotland to put up its meticulously laid granite walls. In Virginia City the red brick Mackay House remains one of the oldest buildings of that bonanza town. After 1875 it became the residence of John W. Mackay, the richest man of the famous Comstock Lode. The Storey County Courthouse speaks for the law and order that countered the turbulence of the frontier community.

OVERLEAF: *Ghost Town, Rhyolite, Nev. (about 1908).* Rhyolite, just east of Death Valley, was once a community of eight thousand persons. The crumbling remnants of its once-proud masonry are a poignant witness to hopes run dry.

Storey County Courthouse, Virginia City, Nev. (1876)

Mackay House, Virginia City, Nev. (1860)

Old State Capitol, Benicia, Calif. (1852)

Founded in 1846, Benicia was briefly the capital of California in 1853-54. The old capitol building, a modified classical temple that was built in three months, still stands. In 1854 the capital was moved to Sacramento, a settlement situated on the Mexican land grant that had belonged to John A. Sutter. Following a limited competition for the design of a new capitol, excavation was begun in 1860 and the cornerstone laid the next year, but the building was not completed until 1874. The final result, a somewhat stylistically confused rendering of classical ingredients, is a substantial pile magnificently enveloped in a semitropical assortment of trees and flowering bushes. For more than three score years, a mansion that was raised in 1878 for a local merchant was used as the governor's residence—a wooden house that displayed all the clichés of Victorian eclecticism.

Governor's Mansion, Sacramento, Calif. (1878). Nathaniel D. Goodell, architect

State Capitol, Sacramento, Calif. (1861-74). Miner F. Butler, chief architect

Haas-Lilienthal House, San Francisco, Calif. (1886). Peter R. Schmidt

Victorian Houses, San Francisco, Calif. (1860-80)

No city this side of Bucharest has a more engaging collection of nineteenth-century wooden houses than San Francisco. The rapid growth of this bayside community and its mounting wealth following the Gold Rush of 1849 coincided with the period that saw the flowering of those domestic architectural styles severally called Victorian, Eastlake, and Queen Anne. Most of the great mansions built by the social leaders of the time with their sizeable fortunes disappeared in the earthquake and fire of 1906, but many modest houses of a frothy exuberance, built on the steep hillsides with their breathtaking views, escaped destruction. It is as streets of such houses, rather than as individual examples, that San Francisco claims its particular character. The bay window may not have been invented in San Francisco, but it is one of the appealing and distinguishing architectural features of this picturesque city scene.

E. J. Baldwin Guest Cottage, Arcadia, Calif. (1881). A. A. Bennett, architect

The Carson Mansion presents what is probably the finest late Victorian exterior in the country, a culmination of profligate fancies haughtily but gloriously dispensed. Built for a highly successful lumber magnate, it now serves as a private club, not open to the public. Seemingly all but engulfed by the surrounding arboretum is the guest cottage built for E. J. Baldwin in 1881, the latest of a cluster of buildings in the early vernacular style of the region that stand in this verdant remainder of what was once a thirteen-thousand-acre working ranch.

William Carson Mansion, Eureka, Calif. (1886). Samuel and Joseph C. Newsom, architects

Hotel del Coronado, Coronado, Calif. (1888). Reid & Reid, architects

After almost a century of service, the Hotel del Coronado, one of the few remaining examples of hotels in what for obscure reasons is referred to as the Queen Anne style, is the *grande dame* of such resorts. Turrets and balconies embellish this wooden behemoth, with, as claimed, two million shingles. The monumental dining room, which seats a thousand persons, and the bars are of a quality any seaside resort might envy. The structure was planned about a large court (150 by 250 feet) filled with a "garden of tropical trees, shrubs, and flowers," with the public rooms overlooking the bay and the ocean; its nearly four hundred guest rooms originally had fireplaces and wall safes and, like the rest of the hotel, electric lights installed by Thomas Edison himself. It was the first hotel provided with such illumination in the country. (Facilities for lighting by gas were also installed but were never needed.) The building has been beautifully maintained over the years, and not substantially changed, except for a few of the public rooms. As observed in the introduction to this chapter, this splendid hostelry has numbered kings and presidents among its distinguished guests.

The thirty-four-story skyscraper built in 1914 in Seattle was for years the tallest north of San Francisco and west of the Mississippi. Conforming to its irregular site with imagination, its windows admit a maximum of light and air, and its design has a minimum of historical trappings. Irving Gill, one of the most brilliant early advocates of the modern movement in America, reflected his love for southern California and the geometry of its Spanish missions in his work. The La Jolla Women's Club possesses a potent simplicity in its multiple arches. Gill devised a very advanced tilt-slab method of construction—the concrete walls were poured on platforms tilted by jacks at a 15-degree angle, metal frames for doors and windows were placed in the forms, and when ready the wall, "smooth finished and complete with window and door openings . . . was raised to perpendicular by means of a single donkey engine."

David B. Gamble House, Pasadena, Calif. (1908). Greene & Greene, architects

Hollyhock (Barnsdall) House, Los Angeles, Calif. (1920). Frank Lloyd Wright, architect

In 1907 Henry Mather Greene and his brother Charles Sumner Greene were commissioned by Mr. and Mrs. David Berry Gamble to design a house for them in Pasadena, California. The Gamble House "will be somewhat Japanese in feeling," reported a local newspaper when plans were announced. The resulting structure remains today the most complete and best preserved of the Greene brothers' "California bungalows." The structural woodwork, inside and out, expresses elements of the composition and design—the rounded and corbeled beams that support the overhanging eaves and porches constitute a decorative pattern that casts shadows across the hand-split cedar shingles of the walls. Hand-finished teak, mahogany, quartered oak, cedar, and other attractive woods were used for the paneling and trim of the interior. Fixtures and furnishings were also designed by the architects as part of the totally integrated scheme. About ten years later Frank Lloyd Wright designed the famous Hollyhock House for Aline Barnsdall, the first of seven of his works in the Los Angeles area. The house suggests a Mayan influence in its plain concrete walls set off by a band of rich decoration, an abstract motif of the hollyhock in the cast concrete on both exterior and interior.

In the early years of the twentieth century architects in California seemed to synthesize avant-garde building techniques with styles and elements of the romantic past to produce widely disparate structures on the landscape. The seven-story Hallidie Building in San Francisco though built in 1917–18 still stands as a monument to the use of boldly scaled glass. Its all-glass façade, with the exception of four fanciful banks of superimposed cast-iron decoration plus fire escapes, makes architect Willis Polk one of the pioneers of the glass curtain-wall method of construction. William Randolph Hearst turned to the Mediterranean for inspiration for his 123-acre estate La Cuesta Encantada, The Enchanted Hill, set on a coastal knoll of the Santa Lucia Mountains. Three palatial guesthouses in Mediterranean Renaissance style were completed before work was begun in 1922 on his fabled La Casa Grande. The Hispano-Moresque castle topped by twin towers was designed by distinguished Berkeley architect Julia Morgan. Constructed of poured reinforced concrete and partially faced with Indiana limestone, the imposing hundred-room mansion serves as a display area for Hearst's vast collection of art and antiques. Among the terraced grounds and exotically landscaped gardens are many pieces of ancient sculpture and art.

Hallidie Building, San Francisco, Calif. (1918). Willis Polk, architect

San Simeon, San Simeon, Calif. (1919-47). Julia Morgan, architect

Mann's (Grauman's) Chinese Theater, Los Angeles, Calif. (1927). Meyer & Holler, architects

Architect Bernard R. Maybeck, even with his Beaux-Arts classical training, was at heart a romantic eclectic. For the Palace of Fine Arts at the Panama-Pacific International Exposition of 1915 in San Francisco, Maybeck sketched a building of vanquished grandeur in the manner of a Piranesi engraving. Comprised of an arc-shaped gallery, an elliptical colonnade, and a circular rotunda, the Palace was constructed of a mixture of plaster of Paris and hemp fiber over a wood frame meant to be demolished after the fair. But as the years passed, the colonnade and rotunda grew dearer to the hearts of San Franciscans, and in 1959 philanthropist Walter S. Johnson donated two million dollars which the state of California matched for its rebuilding in permanent materials. In Santa Barbara the handsome county courthouse epitomizes that area's continuing romance with the Spanish colonial style. And an exotic movie palace has survived from Hollywood's heyday in the twenties. In the forecourt of what was long known as Grauman's (now Mann's) Chinese Theater are impressed in cement hand and foot prints of the famous movie stars.

OVERLEAF: *First Church of Christ, Scientist, Berkeley, Calif. (1910). Bernard R. Maybeck, architect.* Constructed with the most modern industrial materials then available, the Christian Science church combines a Renaissance plan with hints of Gothic tracery, Romanesque columns, Byzantine decoration, and Japanese timberwork in great harmony.

County Courthouse, Santa Barbara, Calif. (1920). William Mooser, architect

Palace of Fine Arts, San Francisco, Calif. (1915; rebuilt 1967). Bernard R. Maybeck, architect

Two great engineering feats completed in the West during the Depression years of the thirties still rank among the monumental landmarks of the century. The 4,200-foot suspension bridge linking San Francisco with Marin County across the Golden Gate entrance to the harbor graces one of nature's incomparable settings. Chief engineer Joseph B. Strauss had to contend with Pacific high winds, swift currents, and dense fogs in the construction of the world's longest suspension bridge when completed in 1937 —it is now surpassed by sixty feet by the Verrazano Narrows Bridge in New York City. The skeins of yard-thick cables holding the road deck are suspended from two red steel-plate pylons some 746 feet above the bay. Hoover Dam, rising approximately 726 feet above the bed of the mighty Colorado River, with its complex of powerhouse and substations, and net of high-tension wires, comprises one of the country's greatest achievements of man harnessing nature. Clamped in the rocky vise of its wild landscape, the dam, with its crest length of 1,282 feet and a bottom thickness of 660 feet of solid concrete, relays an aspect of stunning splendor.

Golden Gate Bridge, San Francisco, Calif. (1937). Joseph B. Strauss, chief engineer; Othmar H. Ammann, Leon S. Moisseiff, and Charles Derleth, Jr., consultants

Hoover Dam, near Boulder City, Nev. (1936). U.S. Bureau of Reclamation, engineers

Each of the four structures below, representing a cross section of building types, opened a new direction and enriched the vocabulary of architecture just before and after the war. Richard J. Neutra's pioneering elementary school changed the traditional enclosed classroom into a light and airy teaching area in direct contact with the outdoors. Edward D. Stone's pharmaceutical plant combined administration and production functions in a beguiling setting of grilles, reflecting pools, fountains, and hanging plants reminiscent of his newly completed U.S. Embassy in New Delhi. Pietro Belluschi designed both the trail-blazing office building and church: Four years before Lever House in New York, his Equitable (now Commonwealth) Building introduced the flush façade—the structural frame, spandrels, and glass all in one plane—and revived the use of color in a high-rise. His First Presbyterian Church relied on no historical precedent but sought sympathetic answers for religion in today's world. And the eldest son of Frank Lloyd Wright sensitively interpreted the tenets of the New Jerusalem sect in an eloquent chapel (right) with glass panes set in a redwood frame on a stone base.

Corona School, Bell, Calif. (1935). Richard J. Neutra, architect

Stuart Company, Pasadena, Calif. (1958). Edward Durell Stone, architect

First Presbyterian Church, Cottage Grove, Oreg. (1951). Pietro Belluschi, architect

Commonwealth (Equitable) Building, Portland, Oreg. (1948). Pietro Belluschi, architect

Wayfarer's Chapel, Palos Verdes, Calif. (1951). Lloyd Wright, architect

The fantastic towers illustrated at left silhouetted against the sky of the Watts district of Los Angeles are the eloquent legacy of an Italian-born laborer to his adopted country. Simon Rodia, a tile setter by trade and a man of few words, justified thirty-three years of labor on his labyrinthine towers with simple logic: "I wanted to do something for the United States because there are nice people in this country." Using only hand tools, Rodia worked with castoff steel reinforcing rods, wire mesh, and concrete; he then incrusted his brilliant cobwebs with shells, glass, tile fragments, and other improbables. In 1959 a committee of Los Angeles citizens battling condemnation proceedings against the celebrated towers called in structural engineers who attested to the stability of this prime example of folk art. In direct contrast is the V. C. Morris Building in San Francisco designed by Frank Lloyd Wright. Its elegant brick façade verging on the monumental recalls H. H. Richardson's structures, and its radiating arch is reminiscent of Louis Sullivan's well-known Transportation Building of the Chicago fair of 1893. However, within the building the spiral ramp is a forerunner of Wright's Guggenheim Museum.

V. C. Morris Building, San Francisco, Calif.
(1949). Frank Lloyd Wright, architect

Rodia (Watts) Towers, Los Angeles, Calif. (1921-54). Simon Rodia, designer and constructor

Ghirardelli Square, San Francisco, Calif. (1863 and 1893–1915; 1970). Wurster, Bernardi & Emmons, architects; Lawrence Halprin & Associates, landscape designers

The Greater San Francisco Chamber of Commerce with federal aid recently made a survey of its old commercial buildings to determine their soundness for rehabilitation. Among others, the three projects here illustrated enrich the urban scene of the bay city. The most imaginative and most successful redevelopment, conceived before the survey, is the transformation of the four-story Ghirardelli chocolate factory of 1915 and a half dozen nondescript loft and residential structures into an engaging multilevel shopping, strolling, and dining center. A lively fountain by Ruth Asawa, landscaped terraces, cheerful lighting, and amusing shops all add to the pleasant experience of Ghirardelli Square. Near Fisherman's Wharf the three-story brick block of the Cannery, once owned by Del Monte, has been sandblasted to its original richness, an arcade placed on the upper floors, and a courtyard added at street level to entice customers into the new boutiques and bars. A glass-enclosed exterior elevator, an escalator, and a broad stairway tend to draw one within. The Ice Houses, two sizeable old cold storage facilities newly connected by an all-glass bridge, are now used as showrooms for the contract furniture and home furnishings trades.

OVERLEAF: *Auditorium Forecourt Fountain, Portland, Oreg. (1970). Lawrence Halprin & Associates, designers.* This block-square fountain, with its terraces and platforms, its cascades and still pools, its flat decks and secret caverns, serves as brilliant urban design and is one of the great attractions of the Portland city scene.

*The Cannery, San Francisco, Calif. (1903; 1968).
Esherick, Homsey, Dodge, and Davis, architects*

*The Ice Houses, San Francisco, Calif. (1914; 1968).
Wurster, Bernardi & Emmons, architects*

Marin County Government Center, San Rafael, Calif. (1962; 1969).
Frank Lloyd Wright, architect (1962); William Wesley Peters and
Taliesin Associated Architects, architects (1969)

The Marin County Government Center is Frank Lloyd Wright's largest creation and the most spectacular civic building in the country. Striding across the landscape for some seven hundred feet over hill and dale, increasing its depth in the valleys and cutting it on the ridges, with its tiers of arches it recalls the famous first-century B.C. Roman Pont du Gard in southern France. Wright's noted solicitude for the landscape has produced a fascinating sociability between structure and site. The building was basically conceived as a long, sky-lit spine lined with a double row of offices. Three tunnels for auto traffic pierce its base. A pylon (with boiler stack within) punctuates the mid-point of the complex.

The keenly designed and engineered Oakland-Alameda County Coliseum comprises a circular earth plinth on which rests a drum framed by thirty-two gigantic (fifty-seven-foot-high) X-members of reinforced concrete that were poured in place, topped by an eave-level compression ring, 420 feet in diameter. From this ring ninety-six cables are slung to the small tension ring at the center, and on this net of cables the roof is laid. A seventy-foot-high wall of gray glass next to the frame, but independent of that structure, encloses an inner area that accommodates as many as fifteen thousand spectators. The San Diego Stadium seats fifty-thousand spectators in armchair comfort and with good views of the proceedings. Facilities for vertical circulation—four cylinders of elevators for top-level seats, high-speed, reversible escalators, and six spiral ramps, each structurally independent—embrace the modified horseshoe arena.

Stadium, San Diego, Calif. (1967). Frank L. Hope & Associates, architects and engineers

Oakland-Alameda County Coliseum, Oakland, Calif. (1966). Skidmore, Owings & Merrill, architects

Sea Ranch, Calif. (1965-   ). Moore, Lyndon, Turnbull & Whitaker, architects of the condominium;
Lawrence Halprin & Associates, planners

Situated a bit more than one hundred miles north of San Francisco, the Sea Ranch enterprise covers a ten-mile stretch of rolling, lovely land rising from the Pacific to meadows and wooded hills. Primarily an area for second homes, it is a remarkably well-planned development, undertaken only after considerable research into environmental problems and possibilities. To ensure maximum freedom of land, "clusters and commons" of houses were grouped together to leave the ground about them open to all property owners; the houses are angled so that none impede the view of those behind. Ten apartments, redwood town houses on a seagirt point, form a small hilltown condominium. After close study of wind patterns, angled or shed roof designs were planned to create tranquil lee-side shelter. The Kukui Garden project on Oahu is one of the finest housing developments undertaken by the Federal Housing Administration in any of the fifty states of the Union. This large complex, which accommodates 820 families, has been compactly but imaginatively planned. Six-story duplex units add variety to the basic three-story row houses. The latter combine a ground-floor flat with a duplex above reached by outside stairs. A community and recreational center acts as the focus of the development, with a fifteen-story tower at one corner reserved for the elderly. There are well-considered housing details, such as jalousie windows for protection from the sun, along with excellent apartment planning. The Portland Center project, with its three rental residence towers and adjacent shopping mall, garage, and related facilities, is a general model for middle- and upper-income urban housing. Located within easy walking distance of the central business district, only a block or so from the civic auditorium, and replacing the substandard structures that had previously stood on the site, this residential and commercial development has lured taxpaying citizens back from the suburbs.

Kukui Garden Housing, Honolulu, Oahu Island, Hawaii (1970). Daniel, Mann, Johnson & Mendenhall, architects

Portland Center, Portland, Oreg. (1968). Skidmore, Owings & Merrill, architects

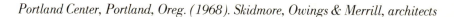

Mauna Kea Beach Hotel, Mauna Kea Beach, Hawaii Island, Hawaii (1965). Skidmore, Owings & Merrill, architects

The main building of the Mauna Kea Beach Hotel contains three levels of bedrooms, half of them facing the ocean, half the mountains, each level stepping back as the structure rises to create tiers of privately screened balconies on both sides. These tiers do not meet at the top of the building, so its center is open to the sky. The planting is so deft that at times it is difficult to tell outside from in, which adds to the hotel's distinction. This unfolding and interweaving of spaces, both vertical and lateral, creates an extraordinary effect. With its roof open to the sun by day and the stars by night, with full-grown palms reaching towards the sky from the center of the building, and with the stepped-back levels that form the inner gallery corridors and overlook the garden courts, this architectural wonderland displays vitality at every turn.

State Capitol, Honolulu, Oahu Island, Hawaii (1969).
John Carl Warnecke & Associates and Belt, Lemmon & Lo, architects

The large central court of Honolulu's state capitol is also open to the sky, and with its sharply delineated contrast of lateral and vertical spaces develops potent architectural forces. This courtyard also imaginatively serves as a platform for viewing the two chambers for the Senate and the House of Representatives, which occupy lower levels on opposite sides and whose end walls are of glass enabling the public to watch proceedings. (There are, of course, interior spectator galleries.) The late Richard Neutra was a transplanted Viennese who added immeasurably to architectural developments in the United States, especially in California where he lived. His work includes some of the finest houses in the country. Among his larger commissions is the excellent Orange County Courthouse at Santa Ana.

Orange County Courthouse, Santa Ana, Calif. (1968). Richard and Dion Neutra
in collaboration with Ramberg & Lowrey, architects

Oakland Museum, Oakland, Calif. (1968). Kevin Roche, John Dinkeloo & Associates, architects; Dan Kiley, landscape architect

University Art Museum, University of California, Berkeley, Calif. (1970).
Mario J. Ciampi, architect; Richard Jorasch and Ronald Wagner, associates

The Oakland Museum—or museums, for there are three that are interconnected —is a highly imaginative architectural complex. Occupying four city blocks, the entire scheme comprises a series of landscaped terraces (some with works of art), museum wings, lawns, and gardens. All the outdoor promenades are in fact marked by luxuriant planting and the changes of level and of spatial relationships that make exploration of the area a dramatic experience. The several buildings provide exhibition spaces for art, cultural history, and natural science, each with its own identity but tied together in a manageable whole that can be easily recognized. At nearby Berkeley, the interior of the University Art Museum presents a galaxy of tantalizingly ramped and tiered spaces, all bathed in illumination from a central skylight. The building's concept is based on five double-decked platforms of exhibition space, lapped like cards in a fan formation, all pivoting on the central, catalyzing entry court which also serves for displays of art.

OVERLEAF: *Sculpture by Alexander J. Calder, University Art Museum, University of California, Berkeley, Calif. (1968).* A superb steel composition by Calder introduces the angled, stepped-back concrete walls of the Berkeley museum.

Foothills College, Los Altos Hills, Calif. (1961). Ernest J. Kump with Masten & Hurd, architects

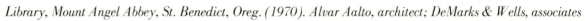

Library, Mount Angel Abbey, St. Benedict, Oreg. (1970). Alvar Aalto, architect; DeMarks & Wells, associates

Washoe County Library, Reno, Nev. (1966). Hewitt C. Wells, architect; Mitchell J. Servan, landscape architect

The thirty-nine buildings of Foothills College epitomize the California pavilion approach, and the college has understandably exerted enormous influence on instructional building. In general appearance Foothills looks like a well-knit, one-story, educational village of vaguely Japanese ancestry, with friendly residential scale. The wide overhangs of all buildings serve as outdoor corridors (there are no inner ones) creating a continuity (plus some exposure during the brief rainy season). The Mount Angel Abbey library, which is used by the Benedictine abbey's high school, college, and seminary, is one story in height at the entry level, then, taking advantage of its hillside site, develops three and a half floors, two of stacks plus a mezzanine, with a basement dropped below on the north side of the building. It is difficult to know whether to classify the Washoe County Library as a space for the perusal of books and periodicals or as an inviting botanical garden. The luxurious planting and several small fountains set the stage, with projecting disc-shaped platforms, for reading perched among the greenery.

Administration Building, East-West Center, University of Hawaii, Honolulu, Oahu Island, Hawaii (1963).
I. M. Pei & Partners with Young & Henderson, architects

A two-story lounge, flanked on both long sides by six substantial piers with arched heads, constitutes the kernel of the Administration Building of the East-West Center (the Center for Cultural and Technical Interchange Between East and West). On these piers rest twin continuous beams which run the full length of the building. At right angles atop these beams are placed a series of lateral beams that span the width of the structure and are cantilevered fifteen feet beyond the long sides. On top, the inset offices are capped by a deep, fasciaed roof. In the rear a delightful oriental garden, its stream stocked with large goldfish, lures the stroller. The Evergreen State College seems to be carved out of its bosky site. An intimacy with nature and a close relationship of students with professors accord the school's informal philosophy. An airy library with a high bell tower dominates a central mall, which is loosely enclosed by this and other buildings.

Daniel Evans Library, The Evergreen State College, Olympia, Wash. (1972).
Durham, Anderson, Freed Company, architects and planners

Garden, East-West Center

Student Union, San Francisco State University, Calif. (1975). Paffard Keatinge Clay, architect

The Student Union at San Francisco State University presents an imaginative profile akin to sculpture as well as to architecture. The vista is dominated by the two buildings with shiplike prows extending skyward with, on one, a stepped roof doubling as a dramatic open-air amphitheater and sunning spot. Its angled geometry extends an enthusiastic welcome to the student. On a two-thousand-acre rolling site John Carl Warnecke has designed a master plan for the University of California at Santa Cruz comprised of a series of individual colleges, each with its own dormitories, dining and recreation rooms, together with classrooms and faculty offices. Kresge College, illustrated below, resembles a gigantic stage set nestled amongst the redwoods. The white wood frame and stucco buildings enlivened by bold color accents are angled along a spinal path to create a small village atmosphere. The resulting spatial intimacy imparts a sense of belonging to the students.

Kresge College, University of California, Santa Cruz, Calif. (1974). MLTW/Moore, Turnbull Associates, architects

Kenneth Brooks and his firm have provided the Columbia Basin Community College of Pasco, Washington, with an exciting architectural complex for the arts. The startlingly plain exterior walls serve as giant screens on which, after dusk, movies or panoramas of scenic or art slides are projected by automatic machines built into the surrounding berms. The simple square exterior opens onto an unexpected inner labyrinth divided into four divisions for art, drama, music, and speech. Interior circulation is angled around corners with small courtyards on ground level and several bridges connecting the topmost floor.

Arts Complex, Columbia Basin Community College, Pasco, Wash. (1971). Kenneth W. Brooks & Partners, architects

OVERLEAF: *Weyerhaeuser Headquarters, Tacoma, Wash. (1971). Skidmore, Owings & Merrill, architects.* Set in a small open valley hemmed by trees at each end, an extraordinary corporate headquarters built up laterally in stepped layers fills in the space between. Its stretched-out mass is emphasized by extensions to parking areas. As the floors rise upward from the valley's contours, they increase in length and decrease in width, the sectional diminution filled in by planting boxes. Inside, all the office floors, except for small special rooms, are open and partitionless, with work spaces created by the use of movable standard components.

Situated on Sitka's harbor overlooking a panorama of sea, islands, and distant snow-capped mountains, the Centennial Building serves as a community and convention center. The handsome structure of local stone base and wood sides is dominated by its roof of well-sculptured planes. Occupying its front section is a small regional museum under the direction of the Sitka Historical Society. A colorful Tlingit Indian ceremonial canoe in front provides an appropriate introduction to the exhibits within, which include a thoroughly researched model of Sitka as of 1867. In Washington, overlooking the Spokane River is an opera house-convention center, the permanent building of Spokane's Expo 74. The auditorium roof angles upward to the stage area at the west and is separated from the one-level convention center at the east by a covered mall. Both units are wrapped in smooth concrete panels with dark glass for contrast. At the far end of the entry there are steps leading down to the river, where outdoor concerts are given in the summertime. The performers take their places on floating platforms and the audience occupies the steps.

Centennial Building, Sitka, Alaska (1967). Allen McDonald, architect

Riverpark Center, Spokane, Wash. (1974). Walker, McGough, Foltz-Lyerla, architects

In the last decade several cities in California have provided commendable public architecture to house their civic functions. The winning design for the limited competition for the Los Gatos Civic Center placed the buildings for administration, police, and library on an elevated square plaza, with the council chamber on the lower level. The construction materials of the well-scaled buildings—concrete with red brick walls—are repeated in the design of the attractive plaza surrounded by landscaped terraces. The design for the bold new civic center in Thousand Oaks atop its hill site was selected in a national competition. The two one-story buildings, strongly stated in concrete with heavy parapets which shield the band of windows and hide the roof-top parking area, are barely visible from the residential community below. San Bernardino has combined a city hall and convention center in one bold structure of dark brown glass. A spacious entry porch resting on pilotis welcomes the visitor to the elevated civic offices and the convention center. The building is stepped in profile and chamfered on the corners and edges to relieve the geometric insistence of its tightly wrapped glass skin.

Civic Center, Thousand Oaks, Calif. (1973). Robert Mason Houvener, architect

Civic Center, Los Gatos, Calif. (1965). Charles D. Stickney & William R. Hull, architects

*City Hall and Convention Center,
San Bernardino, Calif. (1972).
Gruen Associates, architects; Cesar Pelli, designer*

Seattle First National Bank, Seattle, Wash. (1969). Naramore, Bain,
Brady & Johanson, architects; Henry Moore, sculptor

The personality of the fifty-two-story Bank of America
Building in San Francisco derives primarily from the unusual angled bays that frame all four sides and form the
varying-height setbacks at the upper levels. Single-pane
windows are flush with the granite facing of the structure.
The serrated façades recall the bay windows so familiar to
San Francisco domestic architecture. Seattle's outstanding
skyscraper is the fifty-story square shaft of the city's First
National Bank. Its floors are supported by the four gigantic
aluminum-clad steel corner columns and the concrete inner
elevator core, no inner columns being used in the tower
floors. Henry Moore's "Vertebrae," placed in front of the
structure, is one of America's finest examples of urban
sculpture. The building is topped by a heliport.

OVERLEAF: *The Strip, Las Vegas, Nev.* In utter contrast to the
formal structural organization of these handsome bank
buildings stands the Strip at Las Vegas, an orgy of contemporary American folk art in flamboyant neon lights.

Bank of America, San Francisco, Calif. (1969). Wurster, Bernardi & Emmons with
Skidmore, Owings & Merrill, architects; Pietro Belluschi, consulting architect

COPPER CART

PRIME
RIB
STEAKS
COCKTAILS

CREDIT
CARDS

a musical laff riot
FUNNY
FARM
STARRING RIP TAYLOR

ALAD...

DESERT INN

FASHION SQUARE
SHOPPING
CENTER

TEXA

STARDUST
PARKIN

LIDO
SPECIAL 3RD SHOW
MOBY DIC

POST OFFICE

STEAKHOUSE   BREAKFA
DINNERS $4.95   24 HR. $1.19

INSIDE MOTEL

EL
MOR...
MOT...
RESTAU...
BEAUTY S
FRONT   AVIS
VALL
BAN
OF NEVA

L
La Concha
VACANCY
NEVADA CAR CORP
RENT·A·CAR
OFFICE IN LOBBY
LOW LOW RATES
RENT·A·CAR
OFFICE IN LOBBY
LOW LOW RATES

The Airport Business Center at Irvine, California, consists of twin sets of buildings—two rectangular one-story banks between two four-story office units. Solar bronze plate glass played against adroitly used weathering steel predominates in the construction. At San Rafael in California the Commerce Clearing House, a moderate-sized private office block, sensitively occupies its hillside site. A dining room has been angled out to provide a view of the Marin County hills. The Anchorage Natural Gas Building is one of the all-too-few meritorious structures in Alaska's first and largest city. A sculptured plaque, designed by Alex Duff Combs, an Alaskan artist, with semiabstract references to the state's wildlife and natural features, calls the attention of speeding motorists to this steel-frame building with its dark, anodized aluminum panels.

Airport Business Center, Irvine, Calif. (1969). Craig Ellwood Associates, architects

Commerce Clearing House Regional Headquarters, San Rafael, Calif. (1971).
Marquis & Stoller, architects

Anchorage Natural Gas Building, Anchorage, Alaska (1969).
Crittenden, Cassetta, Wirum & Cannon, architects

816

Salk Biological Research Institute, La Jolla, Calif. (1967). Louis I. Kahn, architect; Dr. August E. Komendant, structural engineer

The east-west–oriented court of the Salk Institute is lined with study towers, angled to face the ocean, that provide offices for thirty-six Fellows. These retreats are separated from two enormous blocks of laboratories by half-open, half-enclosed circulation "cloisters" where one encounters passages of sunshine and shadow, freedom and enclosure—an experience even more exciting than walking through the simple Italian cloisters which Dr. Salk (an eager client) initially had in mind.

OVERLEAF: *Court, Salk Biological Research Institute*. Hemmed by walls focusing on the immensity of the Pacific Ocean, the institute's court provides a brilliant formal setting on a gloriously informal site.

INDEX

Page numbers in italic indicate that the subject is illustrated.

A

A. Epstein & Sons: Federal Center, Chicago, Ill., *520*

A. N. Richards Medical Research Building and Biology Laboratory, Philadelphia, Pa., *258-59*

Aalto, Alvar: Mount Angel Abbey Library, St. Benedict, Oreg., *796, 797*

Academy of Sciences, Washington, D.C., 677

Acadian House, St. Martinville, La., *560, 561*

Ácoma, N.M., *550*

Actors' Theatre, Louisville, Ky., *350, 351*

Adam, James, 15, 177

Adam, Robert, 15

Adams, Abigail, 177

Adams, Henry, 429

Adams, John, 128, 131, 138

Adam style, 15, *63-65, 337*. *See also* Federal style.

Adam Thoroughgood House, Norfolk, Va., *291*

Adena (Thomas Worthington House), Chillicothe, Ohio, *436-37*

Adler, Dankmar, 428; Prudential (Guaranty) Building, Buffalo, N.Y., *224-25*; Wainwright Building, St. Louis, Mo., 669, *670-71*

Aiken, S.C., *412*

Air Force Academy, Colorado Springs, Colo., 626, 627, 686, *687-89*

Akron, Ohio, *510-11*

Albany Center, Albany, N.Y., *179*

Albright-Knox Art Gallery and Addition, Buffalo, N.Y., *252*

Alexander, James F.: Tippicanoe County Courthouse, Lafayette, Ind., *463*

Allegheny County Courthouse and Jail, Pittsburgh, Pa., *212-13*

Allen, Arthur, 291

Allen, Benjamin Franklin, 452

Allen, James, 146

Allen County Courthouse, Fort Wayne, Ind., *464-65*

Allentown, Pa., *146*

Alley Theater, Houston, Tex., *598-99*

Aloe Plaza Fountain, St. Louis, Mo., *674-75*

Altoona, Pa., *195*

Amana, Iowa, 425, 445, *446-47*

American Heritage Guide, Historic Houses of America, 7-8

Amesbury, Mass., 40, *42-44*

Ames Monument, Sherman, Wyo., *668, 669*

Ammann, Othmar H.: Golden Gate Bridge, San Francisco, Calif., *772*; Verrazano-Narrows Bridge, Staten Island, N.Y., 236, *238-39*

Ammann & Whitney: University of Illinois Assembly Hall, Urbana, Ill., *502*

Amon Carter Museum, Fort Worth, Tex., *616-17*

Amoskeag Manufacturing Complex, Manchester, N.H., *82-83*

Amoureaux House, Ste. Genevieve, Mo., *634, 635*

Anadarko, Okla., *540*

Anchorage, Alaska, 814, *815*

Andalusia, Andalusia, Pa., *195*

Anderson Hall, Kansas State University, Manhattan, Kans., *667*

Anderson Notter Associates: Old City Hall rehabilitation, Boston, Mass., *86, 87*

Andover, Maine, 98, *99*

Andrews, Frank M.: National Cash Register Company, Dayton, Ohio, *478-79*

Angell, Truman O., Mormon Tabernacle, Logan, Utah, *648-49*; Mormon Temple, Salt Lake City, Utah, 649, *650-51*

Annapolis, Md., 125, 129-30, *162*

Annunciation Greek Orthodox Church, Wauwatosa, Wis., *493*

Annunciation Priory, Bismarck, N.D., *682-83*

Anshen & Allen: Chapel of the Holy Cross, Sedona, Ariz., *606, 608-09*

Arcade, Cleveland, Ohio, *470-71*

Arcade, Providence, R.I., 100, *101*

Arcadia, Calif., *758*

Architectural Associates of Colorado: University of Colorado Engineering Science Center, Boulder, Colo., *691*

Arcosanti, near Dugas, Ariz., *603*

Arkwright, Sir Richard, 58

Arnold, Benedict, 166

Arnold, Eleazer: House, Lincoln, R.I., *28, 30-31*

Art deco style, 236

Art Museum of South Texas, Corpus Christi, Tex., *616-17*

Asawa, Ruth: Ghirardelli Square Fountain, San Francisco, Calif., *778, 779*

Ashland-Belle Hélène, near Geismar, La., *570, 571*

Ashley, Jonathan: House, Old Deerfield, Mass., *39*

Astor, John Jacob, 623, 705

Atheneum, Nantucket, Mass., *87*

Athens, Ala., *398, 399*

Athens, Ga., *356*

Atlanta, Ga., 282, 387, *394-95, 408-09*, 673

Auby, Eugene: Rothko Chapel, Houston, Tex., *612, 613*

Audubon House, Key West, Fla., *356*

Aurora, Ind., *450, 451*

Austin, Henry: Victoria Mansion (Morse-Libby House), Portland, Maine, *88-89*

Austin, Moses, 535, 559

Austin, Stephen, 535

Austin, Tex., 535

Ayala, Manuel de, 704

Aycock House, Fremont, N.C., *348, 349*

Ayres, James B.: P. L. Hay House, Macon, Ga., *365*

Aztec Ruins National Monument, Aztec, N.M., 540, *541*

B

Bacon, Henry: Lincoln Memorial, Washington, D.C., *232-33*

Bacon's Castle, Bacon's Castle, Va., *290, 291*

Bailey Library, Hendrix College, Conway, Ark., *604-05*

Baker, Elias, 195

Baker, T. J.: Iolani Palace, Honolulu, Hawaii, *734-35*

Baker Mansion, Altoona, Pa., *195*

Baldwin, E. J.: Guest Cottage, Arcadia, Calif., *758*

Baldwin and Pennington: Maryland Institute, Baltimore, Md., 204, *205*

Baldwin, Lord, 125

Baltimore, Md., 131, *165, 175, 180-81, 204, 205, 248-49*

Bandstand, Bellville, Ohio, *457*

Bank of America, San Francisco, Calif., *810*, 811

Bank of Pennsylvania, Philadelphia, Pa., 130

Banks, Nathaniel P., 567

Baptist Church, North Salem, N.Y., 216, *217*

Baranof, Alexander, 737

Barbone, Peter P.: Orange County Government Center, Goshen, N.Y., 250, *251*

Barker House, Edenton, N.C., 313, *314-15*

Barnes, Edward Larrabee: Crown Center Office Complex, Kansas City, Mo., *696*

Barnsdall House, Los Angeles, Calif. *See* Hollyhock House.

Barnstone, Howard: Rothko Chapel, Houston, Tex., *612, 613*

Barnum, Phineas T., 18

Bartlesville, Okla., *596*, 597

Bartram, John, 305

Basilica of the Assumption of the Blessed Virgin Mary, Baltimore, Md., 131, *180-81*

Baton Rouge, La., *564-65, 579-81, 604-05*

Battey & Childs: Union Tank Car Repair Facility, Baton Rouge, La., *604-05*

Bauduy, Pierre: Old Town Hall, Wilmington, Del., *174*, 175

Baum, Martin, 444

Beall, Burtch W.: Utah State University Fine Arts Center, Logan, Utah, *690*

Bear Run, Ohiopyle, Pa. *See* Fallingwater.

Beatrice, Nebr., *636, 637*

Beaufort, N.C., *318, 325*

Beaumont, Vivian: Theater, New York, N.Y., 270, *271*

Beaux-Arts style, *219, 228, 229, 480-81*, 709, *768-69*

Beaver, Utah, *640*

Bechtel Corporation: Owens-Corning Fiberglas Plant, Aiken, S.C., *412*

Beckhard, Herbert: St. Francis de Sales Church, Muskegon, Mich., *493*

Beinecke Rare Book Library, Yale University, New Haven, Conn., *118*

Beissel, Johann Conrad, 142

Bell, Calif., *774*

Bell, Josiah: House, Beauford, N.C., *325*

Bellamy House, Wilmington, N.C., 362, *363*

Belle Grove, near White Castle, La., *534*

Belle Meade, near Nashville, Tenn., *368-69*

Bellevue, La Grange, Ga., *362*

Bell Telephone Laboratories, Holmdel, N.J., *242-43*

Belluschi, Pietro, 711; Bank of America, San Francisco, Calif., *810*, 811; Commonwealth (Equitable) Building, Portland, Oreg., *774*; First Presbyterian Church, Cottage Grove, Oreg., *774*

Bellville, Ohio, *457*

Benicia, Calif., *754*

Benjamin, Asher, 17, 71

Benjamin Thompson & Associates: Design Research Shop, Cambridge, Mass., *100*

Bennett, A. A.: E. J. Baldwin Guest Cottage, Arcadia, Calif., *758*

Bennett & Dart: Civic Center, Chicago, Ill., *526-27*

Bentley, William, 12

Benton, Thomas Hart, 623

Bering, Vitus, 704

Berkeley, Calif. 769, *770-71, 793-95*

Berkeley, Sir William, 277, 291

Berkeley Plantation, Berkeley, Va., 19, *306*, 307

Bernard, Simon, 377

Bertrand Goldberg Associates: Marina City, Chicago, Ill., *524*

Bethesda Presbyterian Church, Camden, S.C., *338*

Bethlehem, Pa., *150-51*

Beth Sholom Synagogue, Elkins Park, Pa., *242-43*

Biddle, Nicholas, 195

Billings, Mont., *690*

Billopp House (Conference House), Tottenville, Staten Island, N.Y., *138*

Bingham, Hiram, 732

Bingham Canyon, Utah, 626

Birdair Structures, Inc.: Comsat Earth Station, Andover, Maine, 98, *99*

Birkerts, Gunnar. *See* Gunnar Birkerts & Associates.

Birmingham, Ala., 281

Bishop's House, Portland, Oreg., *742*

Bishop's Palace (Gresham House), Galveston, Tex., *590*, 591

Bismarck, N.D., *682-83*

Björk, Eric, 141

Blair Hall, Princeton University, Princeton, N.J., *230-31*
Blair Walk, Princeton University, Princeton, N.J., *230*
Bligh, William, 704
Bloomfield, Conn., *116-17*
Bloomfield, N.M., *543*
Blossom Music Center, near Akron, Ohio, *510*
Bodmer, Charles, 632
Bolduc House, Ste. Genevieve, Mo., *634*
Boley Clothing Company, Kansas City, Mo. *See* Katz Building.
Book of Architecture, A (Gibbs), 14, 60, 170, 326
Boone, Daniel, 279
Boston, Mass., 13, 16, 18, *38*, 39, *52*, 68, 69, *81*, *86*, 87, *92-95*, *102-05*
Boston Avenue Methodist Church, Tulsa, Okla., 592, *593*
Boston City Hall, Boston, Mass., *86*, 87, *102-03*
Boston Public Library, Boston, Mass., *92*, 93
Boulder, Colo., *691-95*
Boulder City, Nev., 627, 772, *773*
Bowers Mansion, near Carson City, Nev., *750*
Bowie, Jim, 532
Bowling Green Courthouse, Bowling Green, Ohio, *466*, 467
Boyington, William W.: Old Water Tower, Chicago, Ill., 452, *455*; Terrace Hill, Des Moines, Iowa, *452-53*
Bradbury Building, Los Angeles, Calif., *748*, 749
Bradt, Albert Andriesse, 126
Breuer, Marcel, 431; Annunciation Priory, Bismarck, N.D., *682-83*; St. Francis de Sales Church, Muskegon, Mich., *493*; St. John's University Abbey Church, Collegeville, Minn., *492*, 683; Whitney Museum, New York, N.Y., *254*
Bridgeport, Conn., 18
Bridger, Jim, 624
Brigham Young Winter Home, St. George, Utah, *644*
British Architect (Swan), 14
Broad Street Station, Richmond, Va., 384, *385*
Broadway, Skagway, Alaska, 739, *740-41*
Bronx Zoo, The Bronx, N.Y., *263*
Brooklyn, N.Y., *196-97*, *200-201*
Brooks, Kenneth W. *See* Kenneth W. Brooks & Partners.
Brown, Joseph: First Baptist Church, Providence, R.I., 60, *61*
Brown, Robert B.: George A. Smathers Plaza, 406, *407*
Brownington, Vt., *80*, 81
Brown Palace Hotel, Denver, Colo., 626, *673*
Brown's Ferry Nuclear Plant, near Athens, Ala., *398*, 399
Brown University, Providence, R.I., 128
Brumidi, Constantino, 220
Bryant Park, New York, N.Y., *219*
Brydges, Earl W.: Library, Niagara Falls, N.Y., *250*
Buckland, William, 130, 162, 308, 322
Bucklin, J. C.: Arcade, Providence, R.I., 100, *101*
Buffalo, N.Y., *224-25*, *252*
Buffalo Bill Cody House, North Platte, Nebr., *645*
Bulfinch, Charles, *16-17*; Boston State House, Boston, Mass., 16, *68*, 69; The Capitol, Washington, D.C., 17, 131, 220, *221*; First Church of Christ, Lancaster, Mass., *69*
Bull Run Steam Plant, near Knoxville, Tenn., *399*
Bunnell, Rufus H.: Bellamy House, Wilmington, N.C., 362, *363*
Burbank, James, 451
Burbank-Livingston-Griggs House, St. Paul, Minn., *451*
Burgee, John: Art Museum of South Texas,

Corpus Christi, Tex., *616-17*; Boston Public Library Addition, Boston, Mass., *93*; IDS Building and Crystal Court, Minneapolis, Minn., 515, *516-17*
Burgwin-Wright-Cornwallis House, Wilmington, N.C., *324*, 325
Burke, Edmund, 278
Burlington, N.J., *204-05*
Burnham, Daniel Hudson, 429: Flatiron (Fuller) Building, New York, N.Y., *227*; Union Station, Washington, D.C., *228*. *See also* Burnham & Root; Daniel H. Burnham & Company.
Burnham & Root: Monadnock Building, Chicago, Ill., *469*; The Rookery, Chicago, Ill., *469*
Burnside, John, 570
Burnside, La., *570*
Burroughs Wellcome Company, Research Triangle Park, N.C., 412, *413*, *414-15*
Burwell, Carter, 308
Burwell, Rebecca, 277
Business Men's Assurance Company Building, Kansas City, Mo., *696-97*
Butler, Miner: Sacramento State Capitol, Sacramento, Calif., 754, *755*
Butler Square, Minneapolis, Minn., *470*
Buttolph-Williams House, Wethersfield, Conn., *37*
Byrd, William II, 305

C

CBS Building, New York, N.Y., *268*, 269
C. F. Murphy Associates: Civic Center, Chicago, Ill., *526-27*; Federal Center, Chicago, Ill., *520*
C & I Bank, Memphis, Tenn., *412*
Cabeza de Vaca, Álvar Núñez, 531
Cabildo, New Orleans, La., 533, *559*, 562, *563*
Cable, George Washington, 562
Cabrillo, Juan Rodríguez, 703-04
Cades Cove Community, Cades Cove, Tenn., *348*, 349
Cahokia, Ill., *434*
Calder, Alexander: sculpture, University of California Art Museum, Berkeley, Calif., *794-95*; "Shiva," Crown Center, Kansas City, Mo., *696*
California bungalow style, 709, 764, *765*
California State Capitol, Sacramento, Calif., 754, *755*
California Water Project, 710
Calvary Presbyterian Church, Portland, Oreg., *743*
Cambridge, Mass.: 12, 18, 19, *91*, *100*, *110-13*
Camden, S.C., *338*
Cameron, E. A.: Union Station, St. Louis, Mo., *674-75*
Campbell, Colin, 129
Cannery, The, San Francisco, Calif., *779*
Canova, Dominique, 573
Canyon de Chelly National Monument, Chinle, Ariz., *542-43*
Cape Hatteras, N.C., *376*, 377
Cape May, N.J., *214-15*
Capen, Joseph, 34
Capitol, The, Washington, D.C., 17, 131, 220, *221*, 744
Carbondale, Ill., *504*, 505
Cardy, Samuel, 313
Carl Koch & Associates: Lewis Wharf Rehabilitation, Boston, Mass., *81*
Carl Schurz High School, Chicago, Ill., *479*
Carlyle, Thomas, 424
Carmel, Calif., *715*
Carpenter Center for the Visual Arts, Harvard University, Cambridge, Mass., *113*
Carpenters' Company of the City and County of Philadelphia, 128
Carr, E. T.: Anderson Hall, Kansas State University, Manhattan, Kans., *667*

Carrère & Hastings: Flagler College, St. Augustine, Fla., *383*; Jefferson Hotel, Richmond, Va., *382*, 383; New York Public Library, New York, N.Y., *219*
Carroll, Charles, 165
Carson, Pirie, Scott & Company Store, Chicago, Ill., 470, *472-74*
Carson, William: Mansion, Eureka, Calif., *758*, 759
Carson City, Nev., 744, 750
Carter, Amon: Museum, Fort Worth, Tex., *616-17*
Carter, Robert "King," 277, 300
Carter Dry Goods Building, Louisville, Ky., *380*, 381
Carter's Grove Plantation, Carter's Grove, Va., 277, 278, 308, *310-11*
Castillo de San Marcos, St. Augustine, Fla., 283, *284-85*
Catalano, Eduardo: City of Greensboro-Guilford County Center, Greensboro, N.C., *405*
Cataldo, Idaho, *638*, 639
Cathedral of St. Paul, St. Paul, Minn., *480*
Cathedral of St. Peter in Chains, Cincinnati, Ohio, *458*
Catlin, George, 632
Caudill, Rowlett, Scott: E. J. Thomas Performing Arts Hall, University of Akron, Akron, Ohio, 510, *511*; Fodrea Community School, Columbus, Ind., *496*, 497; Jesse H. Jones Hall for the Performing Arts, Houston, Tex., *610*
Cavaglieri, Georgio, 204
Cazenovia, N.Y., *216*
Cedarhurst, Holly Springs, Miss., *373*
Centennial Building, Sitka, Alaska, *806*
Center Family House, Shakertown (Pleasant Hill), Ky., *358-59*
Central Park, New York, N.Y., *222-23*
Chaco Canyon National Monument, Bloomfield, N.M., 531, *543*
Chadwick, Robert, 318
Chalfin, Paul: Vizcaya, Miami, Fla., *386*, 387
Chambers, Thomas, 126
Chapel of the Holy Cross, Sedona, Ariz., *606*, *608-09*
Charles Center, Baltimore, Md., *249*
Charles T. Main, Inc.: Garrison Dam, Riverdale, N.D., *698*
Charleston, S.C., 278, 283, 299, 308, *312-13*, *336-37*, 340, 347, 352
Charlottesville, Va., *332-33*, *335-36*
Chase, Samuel, 162
Chase-Lloyd House, Annapolis, Md., *162*
Chase Manhattan Building, New York, N.Y., *272*
Chase Mill, Fall River, Mass., *78*
Château de Mores, Medora, N.D., *645*
Chatham Towers, New York, N.Y., *264*, 265
Chattanooga, Tenn., *384*
Chenoweth, Lemuel: Covered Bridge, Philippi, W.Va., *348*, 349
Cheshire Mill, Harrisville, N.H., 78, *79*
Chester, Ill., *436-37*
Chew, Benjamin, 165
Cheyenne, Wyo., 625, *666*, 667
Chiang Kai-shek, Mme., 318
Chicago, Ill., 272, 425-30, 452, *455*, 466, 467, *468-69*, 470, *472-73*, 474, 479, *483-85*, *500-501*, *520-29*, 661
Chicago School, 427-31, 468-70, 472-75
"Chicago window," 474
Childs, N.Y., 184, *185*
Chillicothe, Ohio, *436-37*
Chimayo, N.M., *556*
Chinle, Ariz., *542-43*
Choo-Choo Hilton Inn, Chattanooga, Tenn., *384*
Chowan County Courthouse, Edenton, N.C., 316, *317*
Christ Church (Old North), Boston, Mass., 38, 39
Christ Church, Kilmarnock, Va., 300, *301*

Christ Church, Philadelphia, Pa., *160*, 161
Christ Church Lutheran, Minneapolis, Minn., *490*
Christian Science Center, Boston, Mass., *106*, 107
Chrysler Building, New York, N.Y., *236*
Church, Frederick Edwin, 132, 211
Church of the Assumption of the Virgin Mary, Kenai, Alaska, *738*
Church Creek, Md., *140-41*
Church of the Holy Family, Cahokia, Ill., *434*
Ciampi, Mario J.: University of California Art Museum, Berkeley, Calif., *793*
Cincinnati, Ohio, 425, *454-55*, *458-59*
Circle Campus, University of Illinois, Chicago, Ill., *500-501*
City of Greensboro-Guilford County Center, Greensboro, N.C., *405*
City National Bank, Lincoln, Nebr., *674*
City of Refuge National Historical Park, Honaunau, Hawaii, *726-27*, 728
Clark, William, 705
Clark & Enerson, Hamersky, Schlaebitz, Burroughs & Thomsen, City National Bank, Lincoln, Nebr., *674*
Clarke, C. J.: Carter Dry Goods Building, Louisville, Ky., *380*, 381
Clarke, George Hyde, 187
Classical style, 15-16, *86-87*, *92-93*, *456-57*, *480*, *754-55*. *See also* Greek Revival style.
Clay, Henry, 279, 366
Clay, Paffard Keatinge: San Francisco State University Student Union, San Francisco, Calif., *800*, 801
Clayton, Nicholas J.: Bishop's Palace (Gresham House), Galveston, Tex., *590*, *591*
Cleo Rogers Memorial County Library, Columbus, Ind., *496*
Cleveland, Ohio, *470-71*
Cliff dwellings, Mesa Verde National Park, near Cortez, Colo., 627, *628-29*
Climatron, St. Louis, Mo., *684-85*
Cliveden, Philadelphia, Pa., 165
Cobblestone House, Madison, N.Y., *184*
Cobblestone School, Childs, N.Y., 184, *185*
Cochrane, John C., 457; Lake County Courthouse, Crown Point, Ind., *463*
Cochrane & Piquenard: Des Moines State Capitol, Des Moines, Iowa, 456, 457
Cochrane, Stephenson & Donkervoet, Maryland Institute, Baltimore, Md., 204, *205*
Cody, "Buffalo Bill": House, North Platte, Nebr., *645*
Coeur d'Alene Mission of the Sacred Heart, Cataldo, Idaho, *638*, 639
Coffin, Jethro: House, Nantucket, Mass., *37*
College-Alumni Union, Rochester Institute of Technology, Rochester, N.Y., *260-61*
College Life Insurance Company of America, near Indianapolis, Ind., *508-09*
Collegeville, Minn., *492*, 502, 683
Collegiate Gothic style, *230-31*, 667
Colony House, Newport, R.I., 54
Colony Square, Atlanta, Ga., *394*
Colorado Springs, Colo., 626, 627, 686, *687*, *688-89*
Colt, Samuel, 18
Columbia, S.C., 338, *339*
Columbia Basin Community College, Pasco, Wash., *802-03*
Columbia Falls, Maine, *66-67*
Columbus, Ind., *494-97*
Columbus, Miss., *364*, 365
Columbus State Capitol, Columbus, Ohio, 448, 449
Commander's House, Fort Ross, Calif., *706*
Commerce Clearing House Regional Headquarters, San Rafael, Calif., 814, *815*
Commonwealth (Equitable) Building, Portland, Oreg., *774*
Comsat Earth Station, Andover, Maine, 98, *99*
Concordia Senior College, Fort Wayne, Ind., *492*
Conference House, Tottenville, Staten Island,

N.Y. *See* Billipp House.
Congregational Church, Middlebury, Vt., *71*
Congregational Meetinghouse, Midway, Ga., 318, *319*
Conway, Ark., *604-05*
Cook, Captain James, 704-05
Cooper, James Fenimore, 17, 72, 125, 126, 132
Cooperstown, N.Y., 132, *186-87*
Cope, Walter, 230
Cope & Stewardson: Blair Hall, Princeton University, Princeton, N.J., *230-31*
Copley Square, Boston, Mass., *93*
Corbett, Harrison & MacMurray: Rockefeller Center, New York, N.Y., *234-35*
Coronado, Calif., *760-61*
Coronado, Francisco Vásquez de, 531
Corona School, Bell, Calif., *774*
Corpus Christi, Tex., *616-17*
Cortez, Colo., 627, *628-29*, 630
Cosanti Foundation Workshop, Paradise Valley, Ariz., *602-03*
Cottage Grove, Oreg., *774*
Cotton Exchange, Savannah, Ga., 360, *361*
Cotton House, Green Bay, Wis., *444-45*
Country Builder's Assistant, The (Benjamin), 17
Covered bridge, Philippi, W.Va., *348*, 349
Covered bridge, Stark, N.H., 73, *74-75*
Coxe, Tench, 17
Craig Ellwood Associates: Airport Business Center, Irvine, Calif., *814*
Crawford, Thomas, 220
Creswell, N.C., *325*
Cret, Paul Philippe: Marion County Public Library, Indianapolis, Ind., *479*
Crèvecoeur, Michel Guillaume Jean de, 11
Creve Coeur, Mo., *682-83*
Crittenden, Cassetta, Wirum & Cannon: Anchorage Natural Gas Building, Anchorage, Alaska, 814, *815*
Crocker, Charles, 708
Crockett, Davy, 532
Croton-on-Hudson, N.Y., 138, *139*
Crown, S. R.: Hall, Chicago, Ill., *520*
Crown Center Office Complex, Kansas City, Mo., *696*
Crown Point, Ind., *463*
Crystal Court, IDS Building, Minneapolis, Minn., 515, *516-17*
Culbertson House, New Albany, Ind., *452*
Cummins Engine Company Technical Center, Columbus, Ind., *494*
Cupola House, Edenton, N.C., 316, *317*
Curtiss, Louis S.: Katz Building (Boley Clothing Company), Kansas City, Mo., *672*, 673
Cushing, Terrell & Associates: Fortin Educational Center, Rocky Mountain College, Billings, Mont., *690*
Custer State Park, Custer, S.D., *640*
Cutchogue, Long Island, N.Y., *136*, 137

D

Dailey, Gardner, 711
Dakin, James H.: Old State Capitol, Baton Rouge, La., *579*
Dallas, Tex., 598, 599, 612
Dalton, Van Dijk, Johnson: E. J. Thomas Performing Arts Hall, University of Akron, Akron, Ohio, 510, *511*
Dana, Richard Henry, 706
Daniel, Mann, Johnson & Mendenhall: Kukui Garden Housing, Honolulu, Hawaii, *787*
Daniel Evans Library, Evergreen State College, Olympia, Wash., 798, *799*
Daniel H. Burnham & Company: Flatiron (Fuller) Building, New York, N.Y., *227*; Reliance Building, Chicago, Ill., *468*, 469
Daniels, Howard: Old Courthouse, Dayton, Ohio, 444, *445*

Danville, N.H., 45, *46-47*
Dartmouth, Earl of, 279
Dartmouth Hall, Dartmouth University, Hanover, N.H., 128
Davenport, Isaiah: Davenport House, Savannah, Ga., 342, *343*
Davenport House, Savannah, Ga., 342, *343*
David B. Gamble House, Pasadena, Calif., *764*, 765
Davis, Alexander Jackson, 132, 190, 352; Columbus State Capitol, Columbus, Ohio, *448*, 449; Federal Hall National Memorial, New York, N.Y., *190-91*; Lyndhurst, Tarrytown, N.Y., *198*. *See also* Town & Davis.
Davis, Brody & Associates: Waterside Plaza, New York, N.Y., 264, *265*
Dayton, Ohio, 444, *445*, *478-79*
Deane House, Wethersfield, Conn., *56*
De architectura (Vitruvius), 14
Death Valley, Calif., *703*
Deere, John: Building, Moline, Ill., 505, *506-07*
Delaware Valley, *126-27*, 129
DeMarks & Wells: Mount Angel Abbey Library, St. Benedict, Oreg., *796*, 797
Demopolis, Ala., *362*
Denver, Colo., 625-27, *652-53*, 673, *678-79*, 696
Derby, Elias Hasket, 16
Derleth, Charles, Jr.: Golden Gate Bridge, San Francisco, Calif., *772*
Design Research Shop, Cambridge, Mass., *100*
Des Moines, Iowa, *452-53*, 456, 457
Desmond & Lord: Southeastern Massachusetts University, North Dartmouth, Mass., *114-15*
Detroit, Mich., 425, *502-03*
D'Evereux, Natchez, Miss., 366, *367*
Dey Mansion, Wayne, N.J., *154*, 155
Dickens, Charles, 130, 131
Dickinson, John: Mansion, Dover, Del., *155*
Dickinson, Samuel, 155
Dinkeloo, John. *See* Kevin Roche, John Dinkeloo & Associates.
Dodge City, Kans., 641, *642-43*
Dodge Gate, Princeton University, Princeton, N.J., *230*
Dover, Del., *155*
Downing, Andrew Jackson, 132, 198; Town Office Building, Cazenovia, N.Y., *216*
Downtown Presbyterian Church, Nashville, Tenn., *373*
Drake, Sir Francis, 704
Drayton, John, 308
Drayton, Michael, 276
Drayton Hall, Charleston, S.C., *308*
Dresden, Maine, 45
Dubuffet, Jean, 272
Dugas, Ariz., 603
Duke of Gloucester Street, Williamsburg, Va., *296*
Dulles Airport, Chantilly, Va., 400, *401*, *402-03*
Durham, Anderson, Freed Company: Daniel Evans Library, Evergreen State College, Olympia, Wash., 798, *799*

E

E. J. Baldwin Guest Cottage, Arcadia, Calif., *758*
E. J. Thomas Performing Arts Hall, University of Akron, Akron, Ohio, 510, *511*
Eads, James Buchanan: Eads Bridge, St. Louis, Mo., *654-55*, *700-701*
Eads Bridge, St. Louis, Mo., *654-55*, *700-701*
Earl W. Brydges Library, Niagara Falls, N.Y., *250*
Early American Architecture (Morrison), 8
Earth Lodge, Ocmulgee National Monument, near Macon, Ga., *286*, 287
East Haddam, Conn., 98

East-West Center Administration Building, University of Hawaii, Honolulu, Hawaii, *798*
Edbrooke, Frank E. *See* Frank E. Edbrooke & Company.
Edenton, N.C., 313, *314-15*, 316, *317*
Edmond, Okla., *604*
Edmonston-Alston House, Charleston, S.C., *347*
Edward Durell Stone & Associates: North Carolina State Legislative Building, Raleigh, N.C., *404*, 405
Eero Saarinen & Associates: Bell Telephone Laboratories, Holmdel, N.J., *242-43*; CBS Building, New York, N.Y., *268*, 269; Concordia Senior College Chapel, Fort Wayne, Ind., *492*; D. S. Ingalls Hockey Rink, Yale University, New Haven, Conn., *120-21*; Dulles Airport, Chantilly, Va., 400, *401-03*; Gateway Arch, Jefferson National Expansion Memorial, St. Louis, Mo., *700-701*; General Motors Technical Center, Warren, Mich., *505*; John Deere Administration Building, Moline, Ill., 505, *506-07*; Morse College, Yale University, New Haven, Conn., *121*; North Christian Church, Columbus, Ind., 494, *495*; Stiles College, Yale University, New Haven, Conn., *121*; TWA Terminal, John F. Kennedy International Airport, Queens, N.Y., *262*, 263; Vivian Beaumont Theater, Lincoln Center, New York, N.Y., 270, *271*
Egypt, Pa., *148-49*
Egyptian Building, Medical College of Virginia, Richmond, Va., *373*
Egyptian style, 18, 87, 373; 860-80 Lake Shore Drive, Chicago, Ill., 520, *521*
Eisenmann, John M.: Arcade, Cleveland, Ohio, *470-71*
Eleazer Arnold House, Lincoln, R.I., *28, 30-31*
Elkhorn, Mont., 656, *658-59*
Elkins Park, Pa., *242-43*
Ellenton, Fla., 362, *363*
Ellis, Harvey: Mabel Tainter Memorial Building, Menomonie, Wis., *467*
Ellis County Courthouse, Waxahachie, Tex., *591*
Ellwood, Craig. *See* Craig Ellwood Associates.
Elmslie, George G., 470, 477
Emery Roth & Sons: World Trade Center, New York, N.Y., 272, *273*
Emhart Manufacturing Company, Bloomfield, Conn., *116-17*
Emma, queen of Hawaii, 735
Empire State Building, New York, N.Y., 133, *236-37*
Engineering Science Center, University of Colorado, Boulder, Colo., *691*
Ephrata, Pa., 127, *142-43*
Epstein, A. *See* A. Epstein & Sons.
Equitable Building, Portland, Oreg. *See* Commonwealth Building.
Equitable Life Assurance Building, Atlanta, Ga., *394*
Esherick, Homsey, Dodge, and Davis: The Cannery, San Francisco, Calif., *779*
Eureka, Calif., 758, *759*
Evans, Daniel: Library, Olympia, Wash., 798, *799*
Evans, Rudolph: Jefferson Memorial, Washington, D.C., *232*
Evansville, Ind., *462*
Everson Museum of Art, Syracuse, N.Y., 254, *255*
Executive Office Building, Washington, D.C., *209*
Exeter, N.H., *115*

F

F. G. Peabody Terrace, Harvard University, Cambridge, Mass., *110-11*
Factor's Row, Savannah, Ga., *360*
Fairplay, Colo., *646*
Fallingwater, Ohiopyle, Pa., *240-41*
Fall River, Mass., 78
Falls Church, Va., 394, *396-97*
Farmers' Museum, Cooperstown, N.Y., *186-87*
Farmington, Conn., *36-37, 40*
Federal Hall National Memorial, New York, N.Y., *190-91*
Federal Hill, Ky., 280
Federal Reserve Bank, Minneapolis, Minn., 516, *518-19*
Federal style, 16-17, 54, *56-57, 62-73, 178-79*. *See also* Adam style.
Ferdinand Lindheimer House, New Braunfels, Tex., 536
54 Meeting Street, Charleston, S.C., 347
Fillmore, Lavius: Congregational Church, Middlebury, Vt., *71*; First Congregational Church, Old Bennington, Vt., *70-71*
Fine Arts Center, Utah State University, Logan, Utah, *690*
Fireproof Building, Charleston, S.C., *340*
First Baptist Church, Providence, R.I., 60, *61*
First Baptist Church and Chapel, Columbus, Ind., 494, *495*
First Church of Christ, Farmington, Conn., *40*
First Church of Christ, Lancaster, Mass., *69*
First Church of Christ, Scientist, Berkeley, Calif., 769, *770-71*
First Congregational Church, Old Bennington, Vt., *70-71*
First Congregational Church, Tallmadge, Ohio, 442, *443*
First Presbyterian Church, Cottage Grove, Oreg., *774*
First Presbyterian Church, Stamford, Conn., *108*
First Presbyterian Church, Troy, N.Y., *188-89*
First Unitarian Church, Rochester, N.Y., *259*
Flagler College, St. Augustine, Fla., *383*
Flatiron (Fuller) Building, New York, N.Y., *227*
Florida Southern College, Lakeland, Fla., *390*
Fodrea Community School, Columbus, Ind., 496, *497*
Folsom, William H.: Mormon Tabernacle, Salt Lake City, Utah, 649, *650-51*; Mormon Temple, Manti, Utah, *649*; ZCMI Department Store, Salt Lake City, Utah, 652
Foothills College, Los Altos Hills, Calif., *796*, 797
Ford, Jacob, Jr., 173
Ford Foundation Building, New York, N.Y., *260*
Ford Mansion, Morristown, N.J., *173*
Ford, Powell & Carson: Tower of the Americas, San Antonio, Tex., *594*
Forest Park Community College, St. Louis, Mo., *691*
Fort Abraham Lincoln State Park, near Mandan, N.D., *632-33*
Fort Astoria (Fort George), Oreg., *705*
Fort Belvoir, Va., *322-23*
Fort Davis National Historic Site, Fort Davis, Tex., 584, *585*
Fort George (Fort Astoria), Oreg., 705
Fort Harrod, Old Fort Harrod State Park, Harrodsburg, Ky., 279, *328, 329*
Fort Kaskaskia State Park, near Chester, Ill., *436-37*
Fort Laramie, Wyo., 624
Fort Larned, Larned, Kans., 640, *641*
Fort McClary, Kittery Point, Maine, 76, 77

Fort Michilimackinac, Mackinaw City, Mich., 431, *432-33*
Fort Pulaski, Savannah, Ga., *377*
Fort Ross, Calif., 704, 706
Fort Smith, Ark., *564*
Fort Snelling, Minn., 623
Fort Union, N.D., 623-24
Fort Washington, Pa., *155*
Fort Wayne, Ind., *464-65, 492*
Fort Worth, Tex., *582-83, 614-17*
Foster, Stephen Collins, 280
Founder's Hall, Girard College, Philadelphia, Pa., *195*
Fountain Elms, Munson-Williams-Proctor Institute, Utica, N.Y., 252, *253*
Fountain of Faith, National Memorial Park, Falls Church, Va., 394, *396-97*
Fowler, Orson Squire, 132
Frame House, Honolulu, Hawaii, 732, *733*
Frank E. Edbrooke & Company: Brown Palace Hotel, Denver, Colo., 626, *673*
Frank L. Hope & Associates: Stadium, San Diego, Calif., *785*
Frankfort, Ky., *351*
Franklin, Benjamin, 127-29, 138, 424, 621
Franzen, Ulrich. *See* Ulrich Franzen & Associates.
Frederick Church House, near Hudson, N.Y., 132
Fredericksburg, Tex., 536, *588*
Fremont, N.C., *348*, 349
French, Daniel Chester: Lincoln Memorial, Washington, D.C., *232-33*
Friedman Library, Tuscaloosa, Ala., *365*
Front Street Reconstruction, Dodge City, Kans., 641, *642-43*
Frost, Robert, 71
Fuller, Buckminster, 604, 685
Fuller Building, New York, N.Y. *See* Flatiron Building.
Furness, Frank: Pennsylvania Academy of Fine Arts, Philadelphia, Pa., *211*

G

Gaff, Thomas, 451
Gaggin & Gaggin: L. C. Smith Building, Seattle, Wash., *762*
Gaineswood, Demopolis, Ala., *362*
Galena, Ill., *425*
Gallatin, Albert, 131
Gallier, James, Jr., 534; Gallier House, New Orleans, La., 574, *575*
Gallier, James, Sr.: Ashland-Belle Hélène, near Geismar, La., 570, *571*
Gallier House, New Orleans, La., 574, *575*
Gallipolis, Ohio, 424
Gallus, Father: Old St. Mary's Church, Fredericksburg, Tex., *588*
Galveston, Tex., 536, *586, 590, 591*
Gamble, David B.: House, Pasadena, Calif., *764*, 765
Gamble Mansion, Ellenton, Fla., 362, *363*
Gardette, Joseph Coulon, 574
Garrison Dam, Riverdale, N.D., 698
Gassner-Nathan-Browne: C & I Bank, Memphis, Tenn., *412*
Gateway Arch, Jefferson National Expansion Memorial, St. Louis, Mo., *700-701*
Gaynor, J. P.: Haughwout Building, New York, N.Y., *202-03*
Geismar, La., 570, 571
Gemeinhaus, Bethlehem, Pa., *150-51*
General Motors Technical Center, Warren, Mich., *505*
Geneva, N.Y., *188*
Gensert, R. M. *See* R. M. Gensert Associates.
Geodesic domes, 604-05, *684-85*
George A. Smathers Plaza, Miami, Fla., 406, *407*
George Gund Hall, Graduate School of Design, Harvard University, Cambridge, Mass., *112*

Georgetown, Colo., 656-57
Georgetown, Washington, D.C., 169
Georgian style, 13-14, 39-41, 45-53, 60-62, 154-55, 162-67, 169, 173, 175, 296-97, 300-305, 310-11, 316-17, 322-23
Ghirardelli Square, San Francisco, Calif., 778, 779
Ghost town, Rhyolite, Nev., 750, 752-53
Gibbs, D. W.: Wyoming State Capitol, Cheyenne, Wyo., 666, 667
Gibbs, James, 14, 60, 170, 327
Gilbert, Cass: Minnesota State Capitol, St. Paul, Minn., 480-81; Woolworth Building, New York, N.Y., 19, 133, 226, 227
Gilbert Associates: Keystone Generating Station, near Shelocta, Pa., 255, 256-57
Gill, Irving J.: La Jolla Women's Club, La Jolla, Calif., 762-63
Gillette, William Hooker, 98
Gillette Castle, near East Haddam, Conn., 98
Glen, Alexander Lindsay, 126
Glessner House, Chicago, Ill., 466, 467
Goff, Bruce, 592; Hopewell Baptist Church, Edmond, Okla., 604
Goldberg, Bertrand. See Bertrand Goldberg Associates.
Golden Gate Bridge, San Francisco, Calif., 772
Golden North Hotel, Skagway, Alaska, 739, 741
Golden Plough Tavern, York, Pa., 142, 143
Gonzales Associates: Hopi Cultural Center, Oraibi, Ariz., 545
Goodell, Nathaniel D.: Governor's Mansion, Sacramento, Calif., 754
Goodhue, Bertram Grosvenor, 709; Academy of Sciences, Washington, D.C., 677; Nebraska State Capitol, Lincoln, Nebr., 676-77; St. Bartholomew's Church, New York, N.Y., 677
Goodwin, Governor: Mansion, Portsmouth, N.H., 56, 57
Goodwin, William A. R., 294
Goose Creek, S.C., 298-99
Gordon, J. Reilly: Ellis County Courthouse, Waxahachie, Tex., 591
Gordon Stockade, Custer State Park, Custer, S.D., 640
Gore, Christopher, 66
Gore Place, Waltham, Mass., 66
Goshen, N.Y., 250, 251
Gosling, Joseph: Nevada State Capitol, Carson City, Nev., 744
Gothic Revival style, 18-19, 90-91, 132, 196-99, 204, 206-07, 216-17, 226, 227, 288-89, 373, 381, 455, 646-47, 742-43
Governor Goodwin Mansion, Portsmouth, N.H., 56, 57
Governor John Langdon Mansion, Portsmouth, N.H., 62
Governor's Mansion, Sacramento, Calif., 754
Governor's Palace, Williamsburg, Va., 294, 296, 297
Graeme, Thomas, 143
Graeme Park House, Horsham, Pa., 143, 144-45
Graham, Anderson, Probst and White: Wrigley Building, Chicago, Ill., 520, 522
Grain elevators, Topeka, Kans., 679, 680-81
Grand Central Station, New York, N.Y., 228, 229
Grand Coulee Dam, Wash., 710
Grand Rapids, Mich., 490-91
Grauman's Chinese Theater, Los Angeles, Calif. See Mann's Chinese Theater.
Gray, Captain Robert, 705
Great Kiva, Aztec Ruins National Monument, Aztec, N.M., 540, 541
Greek Revival style, 17, 68-69, 87, 100-101, 130, 132, 188-95, 281, 312-13, 333-36, 338, 340-41, 344-45, 350-56, 362-69, 444-45, 448-49, 458, 479, 534, 536, 566-73, 578, 579, 638-39, 662. See also Classical style; Collegiate Gothic style.

Greeley, Horace, 625-27, 705-06
Green & Wicks: Albright-Knox Art Gallery, Buffalo, N.Y., 252
Green Bay, Wis., 434, 435, 444-45
Greene, Charles Sumner, 709, 765
Greene, Henry Mather, 709, 765
Greene & Greene: David B. Gamble House, Pasadena, Calif., 764, 765
Greenough, Horatio, 429
Greensboro, N.C., 405
Green Spring, Jamestown, Va., 277
Green-Wood Cemetery, Brooklyn, N.Y., 196-97
Gregory House, Torreya State Park, Fla., 357
Gresham House, Galveston, Tex. See Bishop's Palace.
Griffin, James S.: Rosalie, Natchez, Miss., 366
Griffith, Thomas M.: suspension bridge, Waco, Tex., 588-89
Griggs, Mary Livingston, 451
Grinnell, Iowa, 422
Gristmill, Spring Mill Village, Spring Mill State Park, Mitchell, Ind., 440-41
Gropius, Walter, 431
Grove Street Cemetery, New Haven, Conn., 87
Grow, Henry: Mormon Tabernacle, Salt Lake City, Utah, 649, 650-51
Gruen Associates: City Hall and Convention Center, San Bernardino, Calif., 808, 809
Guaranty Building, Buffalo, N.Y. See Prudential Building.
Guggenheim Museum, New York, N.Y., 241, 673, 777
Guilford, Conn., 28-29
Gund, George: Hall, Cambridge, Mass., 112
Gunnar Birkerts & Associates: Federal Reserve Bank, Minneapolis, Minn., 516, 518-19
Gunston Hall, Va., 130, 308-09
Guthrie, Tyrone: Theater, Minneapolis, Minn., 512

H

Haas-Lilienthal House, San Francisco, Calif., 702, 756, 757
Hackensack, N.J., 146, 147
Hager, Jonathan: House, Hagerstown, Md., 146, 147
Hagerstown, Md., 146, 147
Hale, Frederick A.: Old Main, University of Wyoming, Laramie, 667
Hall, Paul O. See Paul O. Hall & Associates.
Hallidie Building, San Francisco, Calif., 766
Halprin, Lawrence. See Lawrence Halprin & Associates.
Hamblin, Jacob: House, Santa Clara, Utah., 636
Hamlin, Talbot, 8
Hammel Green & Abrahamson: Orchestra Hall, Minneapolis, Minn., 512, 513
Hammond, Matthias, 130
Hammond-Harwood House, Annapolis, Md., 130, 162, 163
Hampton Mansion, near Baltimore, Md., 175
Hanalei, Kauai Island, Hawaii, 732, 733
Hancock, John: Center, Chicago, Ill., 522-23, 528, 529
Hancock, Mass., 76, 77
Hanover, N.H., 128
Hanson & Michelson: St. John's Preparatory School, Collegeville, Minn., 502
Hardie, James: D'Evereux, Natchez, Miss., 366, 367
Hardy Holzman Pfeiffer: Orchestra Hall, Minneapolis, Minn., 512, 513
Harpers Ferry, W.Va., 378, 379
Harris, Cyril M.: Orchestra Hall, Minneapolis, Minn., 512, 513
Harris, Harwell, 711
Harrison, Benjamin, 307

Harrison, Peter, 14, 52, 313; King's Chapel, Boston, Mass., 52; Redwood Library, Newport, R.I., 52, Touro Synagogue, 52, 53
Harrison, Wallace K.: First Presbyterian Church, Stamford, Conn., 108
Harrison & Abramovitz: Assembly Hall, University of Illinois, Urbana, Ill., 502
Harrison & Abramovitz and Abbe: U.S. Steel Building, Pittsburgh, Pa., 266, 267
Harrisville, N.H., 78, 79
Harrodsburg, Ky., 279, 328, 329
Harry Weese & Associates: Cummins Engine Company Technical Center, Columbus, Ind., 494; First Baptist Church and Chapel, Columbus, Ind., 494, 495; Forest Park Community College, St. Louis, Mo., 691
Hartford, Conn., 18, 90, 91, 108, 109
Harvard University, Cambridge, Mass., 12, 19, 91, 110-11, 112-13
Hasbrouck, Jean: House, New Paltz, N.Y., 138
Haughwout Building, New York, N.Y., 202-03
Hawaii Island, Hawaii, 726-27, 728-29, 730-31, 788-89
Hawaii State Capitol, Honolulu, Hawaii, 790
Hawks, John: Tryon Place, New Bern, N.C., 326-27
Hawthorne, Nathaniel, 12
Hay, P. L.: House, Macon, Ga., 365
Hazard of New Fortunes, A (Howells), 133
Hearst, William Randolph, 766
Henrich, John C.: Lake Point Tower, Chicago, Ill., 524, 525
Helena, Mont., 625, 660-61, 677
Hellmuth, Obata & Kassabaum: McDonnell Planetarium, St. Louis, Mo., 686; Priory of St. Mary and St. Louis, Creve Coeur, Mo., 682-83
Hendrix College, Conway, Ark., 604-05
Hennepin County Government Center, Minneapolis, Minn., 514-15
Henry Whitfield House, Guilford, Conn., 28-29
Hill County Courthouse, Hillsborough, Tex., 591
Hillforest, Aurora, Ind., 450, 451
Hillsborough, Tex., 591
Hingham, Mass., 32-33
Historic Restoration District, St. Augustine, Fla., 291, 292-93
Hitchcock, Henry-Russell, 8
Hoban, James, 220; White House, Washington, D.C., 131, 176-77
Hoffman, F. Burrel, Jr.: Vizcaya, Miami, Fla., 386, 387
Hollyhock (Barnsdall) House, Los Angeles, Calif., 765
Holly Springs, Miss., 373
Holmdel, N.J., 242-43
Holy Trinity (Old Swedes) Church, Wilmington, Del., 141
Home for All, A (Fowler), 132
Homestake Mining Company, 626
Homestead National Monument, near Beatrice, Nebr., 636, 637
Honaunau, Hawaii, 726-27, 728
Honolulu, Hawaii, 707, 732, 733, 734-35, 787, 790, 798, 799
Honolulu House, Marshall, Mich., 450, 451
Hood & Fouilhoux: Rockefeller Center, New York, N.Y., 234-35
Hood and Howells: Tribune Tower, Chicago, Ill., 520, 523
Hooker, Philip: Albany Center, Albany, N.Y., 179; Hyde Hall, near Cooperstown, N.Y., 186, 187
Hoover Dam, near Boulder City, Nev., 627, 772, 773
Hope, Frank L. See Frank L. Hope & Associates.
Hope, Henry, 155
Hope Lodge, Fort Washington, Pa., 155

Hopewell, Pa., *181-82*
Hopewell Baptist Church, Edmond, Okla., *604*
Hopi Cultural Center, Oraibi, Ariz., *545*
Hopkins, Mark, 708
Horse farms, Lexington, Ky., 387, *388-89*
Horsham, Pa., 143, *144-45*
Hotel del Coronado, Coronado, Calif., 708, *760-61*
Hôtel de Paris, Georgetown, Colo., *656*
Houmas House, Burnside, La., *570*
House of the Seven Gables, Salem, Mass., 12
Houston, Tex., 536, *570*, *598-99*, 610, *611*, 612, *613*
Houvener, Robert Mason: Civic Center, Thousand Oaks, Calif., *808*
Howard, Henry: Belle Grove, La., 534
Howe, Lord Richard, 138
Howell, Jehu, 175
Howells, William Dean, 133
Hoxie House, Sandwich, Mass., *23*
Hoyt, Burnham: Red Rocks Amphitheater, near Denver, Colo., 627, *678-79*
Hudson, N.Y., 132, *210-11*
Hudson's Bay Company, 706
Hudson Valley, 131-32, 138
Huizar, Pedro, 553
Hull, William R.: Civic Center, Los Gatos, Calif., 808, *809*
Humphreys, Kalita: Theater, Dallas, Tex., *598, 599*
Hunt, Robert Morris, 429, 744
Hunt, Richard Morris: Marble House, Newport, R.I., *96-97*; Tribune Building, New York, N.Y., 96
Hunter House, Newport, R.I., *54*
Huntington, Collis P., 708
Hyatt Regency Hotel, Atlanta, Ga., 394, *395*, 673
Hyde Hall, near Cooperstown, N.Y., *186*, 187

I

IDS Building, Minneapolis, Minn., 515, *516-17*
I. M. Pei & Partners: Christian Science Center, Boston, Mass., *106*, 107; Cleo Rogers Memorial County Library, Columbus, Ind., *496*; East-West Center Administration Building, University of Hawaii, Honolulu, *798*; Everson Museum of Art, Syracuse, N.Y., 254, *255*; National Center for Atmospheric Research, Boulder, Colo., *692-93*, *694-95*; University Plaza, New York, N.Y., *264*
Ice Houses, The, San Francisco, Calif., *779*
Illinois Institute of Technology, Chicago, Ill., *520*
Independence Hall, Philadelphia, Pa., 129, *156-57*
Independence National Historical Park, Philadelphia, Pa., *194*, 195
Indianapolis, Ind., *479*, *508-09*
Indian City U.S.A., near Anadarko, Okla., *540*
Industrial village architecture, 17, *24-25*, *58-59*, *78-79*, *82-85*, 133, *134-35*, 180, *182-83*
Institute of American Indian Art Outdoor Theater, Santa Fe, N.M., *598, 599*
International style, 431
Iolani Palace, Honolulu, Hawaii, *734-35*
Iowa State Capitol, Des Moines, Iowa, *456*, 457
Ipswich, Mass., *26-27*
Ironmaster's House, Saugus, Mass., *25*
Ironton, Mo., 620, *647*
Ironworks Reconstruction, Saugus, Mass., *24-25*
Irvine, Calif., *814*
Irving, Washington, 132
Isaac M. Wise Temple, Cincinnati, Ohio, *458-59*

J

Jackson, Andrew, 279
Jackson, Richard, 37
Jackson, Sheldon: Chapel, Fairplay, Colo., *646*
Jacob Hamblin House, Santa Clara, Utah, *636*
James, Thomas S.: Old City Hospital, Mobile, Ala., 352, *354-55*
Jamestown, R.I., *58*
Jamestown, Va., 276, *277*, 287
Jay, William: Owens-Thomas House, Savannah, Ga., *342*
Jean Hasbrouck House, New Paltz, N.Y., *138*
Jefferd's Tavern, York, Maine, *45*
Jefferson, Thomas, 130, 131, 277, 332, 621; Monticello, Charlottesville, Va., 277, *332*; University of Virginia Rotunda, Charlottesville, 332, *335-36*; Virginia State Capitol, Richmond, Va., 332, *333*
Jefferson Hotel, Richmond, Va., *382, 383*
Jefferson Market Library, New York, N.Y., *204*
Jefferson Memorial, Washington, D.C., *232*
Jefferson National Expansion Memorial, St. Louis, Mo., *700-701*
Jeremiah Lee Mansion, Marblehead, Mass., 56, *57*
Jesse H. Jones Hall for the Performing Arts, Houston, Tex., *610*
Jethro Coffin House, Nantucket, Mass., *37*
Johansen, John M.: Morris A. Mechanic Theater, Baltimore, Md., *248-49*; New Mummers Theater, Oklahoma City, Okla., 599, *600-601*. See also John M. Johansen & Associates.
John Andrews/Anderson/Baldwin: George Gund Hall, Graduate School of Design, Harvard University, Cambridge, Mass., *112*
John Carl Warnecke & Associates: Hennepin County Government Center, Minneapolis, Minn., *514-15*; Hawaii State Capitol, Honolulu, Hawaii, *790*
John Deere Administration Building, Moline, Ill., 505, *506-07*
John Dickinson Mansion, Dover, Del., *155*
John F. Kennedy Memorial, Dallas, Tex., *612*
John Hancock Center, Chicago, Ill., *522-23*, 528, *529*
John M. Johansen & Associates: Orlando Public Library, Orlando, Fla., *406*
Johnson, Philip: Amon Carter Museum, Fort Worth, Tex., *616-17*; Art Museum of South Texas, Corpus Christi, Tex., *616-17*; Bailey Library, Hendrix College, Conway, Ark., *604-05*; Boston Public Library Addition, Boston, Mass., *93*; IDS Building, Minneapolis, Minn., 515, *516-17*; John F. Kennedy Memorial, Dallas, Tex., *612*; Munson-Williams-Proctor Institute, Utica, N.Y., 252, *253*; Museum of Modern Art Sculpture Garden, New York, N.Y., *270*; Roofless Church, New Harmony, Ind., 496, *498-99*; Seagram Building, New York, N.Y., *247*. See also Philip Johnson Associates.
Johnson, S.C.: Offices, Racine, Wis., *486-89*
Johnson, Thomas, 639
Johnson, Walter S., 769
Johnson, Sir William, 173
Johnson City, Tenn., *329*
Johnson Hall, Johnstown, N.Y., *173*
Johnstown, N.Y., *173*
Jolliet, Louis, 622
Jonathan Ashley House, Old Deerfield, Mass., *39*
Jonathan Hager House, Hagerstown, Md., *146, 147*
Jones, Harry W.: Butler Square, Minneapolis, Minn., *470*
Jones, Jesse H.: Hall, Houston, Tex., *610*

Jonesboro, Tenn., 279
Jorasch, Richard: University of California Art Museum, Berkeley, *793*
Josiah Bell House, Beaufort, N.C., *325*
Joseph Manigault House, Charleston, S.C., *337*
Joseph Smith Mansion, Nauvoo, Ill., *442*
Jova-Daniels-Busby: Colony Square, Atlanta, Ga., *394*
Juneau, Alaska, *736, 737, 739*

K

Kahn, Louis I.: A. N. Richards Medical Research Building and Biology Laboratory, Philadelphia, Pa., *258-59*; First Unitarian Church, Rochester, N.Y., *259*; Kimbell Art Museum, Houston, Tex., *614-15*; Phillips Exeter Academy Library, Exeter, N.H., *115*; Salk Biological Research Institute, La Jolla, Calif., *816-17*, *818-19*
Kailua Village, Hawaii Island, Hawaii, 729, *730-31*
Kalakaua, king of Hawaii, 735
Kalita Humphreys Theater, Dallas, Tex., *598, 599*
Kallman, McKinnell & Knowles: Boston City Hall, Boston, Mass., *102-03*
Kamehameha I, king of Hawaii, 707
Kamehameha III, king of Hawaii, 708
Kamehameha IV, king of Hawaii, 735
Kansas City, Kans., *639*
Kansas City, Mo., 672, 673, *696-97*
Kansas State University, Manhattan, Kans., *667*
Katz Building (Boley Clothing Company), Kansas City, Mo., 672, 673
Kauai Island, Hawaii, 732, *733*
Kaufmann, Edgar J., 241
Kawaiahao Church, Honolulu, Hawaii, *732*
Kehoe & Dean: Ironworks Reconstruction, Saugus, Mass., *24-25*
Keith, Sir William, 143
Kellum-Noble House, Houston, Tex., *570*
Kelly & Gruzen: Chatham Towers, New York, N.Y., 264, *265*
Kenai, Alaska, *738*
Kennard, Thomas P.: House, Lincoln, Nebr., *644*
Kennedy, John F.: Memorial, Dallas, Tex., *612*
Kenneth W. Brooks & Partners: Columbia Basin Community College Arts Complex, Pasco, Wash., *802-03*
Kennecott Copper Corporation, 626
Ketchum, Morris. See Morris Ketchum, Jr., and Associates.
Kevin Roche, John Dinkeloo & Associates: College Life Insurance Company of America, near Indianapolis, Ind., *508-09*; Ford Foundation Building, New York, N.Y., *260*; Knights of Columbus Headquarters, New Haven, Conn., *122*; Oakland Museum, Oakland, Calif., *792-93*; Rochester Institute of Technology College-Alumni Union, Rochester, N.Y., *260-61*; Veterans Memorial Coliseum, New Haven, Conn., *122, 123*
Keystone Generating Station, near Shelocta, Pa., 255, *256-57*
Key West, Fla., *356*
Kiley, Dan: Oakland Museum, Oakland, Calif., *792-93*
Kilmarnock, Va., 300, *301*
Kimball, Fiske, 8
Kimball, John D.: Amoskeag Manufacturing Complex, Manchester, N.H., *82-83*
Kimbell Art Museum, Fort Worth, Tex., *614-15*
King's Chapel, Boston, Mass., *52*
King William Courthouse, King William, Va., *300*

Kino, Eusebio Francisco, 537, 556
Kittery Point, Maine, 56, 57, 76, 77
Kitt Peak Observatory, Kitt Peak, Ariz., 617-19
Kiva, Spruce Tree House, Mesa Verde National Park, near Cortez, Colo., 630
Klander, Charles Z., 691
Kline Biology Tower, Yale University, New Haven, Conn., 118, 119
Knights of Columbus Headquarters, New Haven, Conn., 122
Knoxville, Tenn., 399
Koch, Carl. See Carl Koch & Associates.
Kresge College, University of California, Santa Cruz, 801
Kukui Garden Housing, Honolulu, Hawaii, 787
Kump, Ernest J.: Foothills College, Los Altos Hills, Calif., 796, 797

L

L. C. Smith Building, Seattle, Wash., 762
Ladd & Bush Bank, Salem, Oreg., 746, 747
Ladd & Tilton Bank, Portland, Oreg., 746
Lady Pepperrell House, Kittery Point, Maine, 56, 57
La Farge, John, 95
Lafayette, Ind., 463
Lafever, Minard, 570; Old Whalers' First Presbyterian Church, Sag Harbor, Long Island, N.Y., 216
La Grange, Ga., 362
Laguna, N.M., 550, 555
La Jolla, Calif., 762-63, 816-19
Lake Anne Village, Reston, Va., 392-93
Lake County Courthouse, Crown Point, Ind., 463
Lake Point Tower, Chicago, Ill., 524, 525
Lake-Tysen House, Richmondtown Restoration, Staten Island, N.Y., 152-53
Lancaster, Mass., 69
Langdon, John, 62; Mansion, Portsmouth, N.H., 62
Laramie, Wyo., 667
Larimer Square, Denver, Colo., 652-53
Larkin, Thomas Oliver, 723
Larkin House, Monterey, Calif., 722-23
Larned, Kans., 640, 641
La Rochefoucauld-Liancourt, Duc François de, 278
La Salle, Sieur de, 280, 532, 622
Last Chance Gulch Restoration, Helena, Mont., 661
Las Trampas, N.M., 555
Lasuén, Fermín Francisco, 715, 718
Las Vegas, Nev., 811, 812-13
Latrobe, Benjamin Henry, 130-32, 577; Adena (Thomas Worthington House), Chillicothe, Ohio, 436-37; Bank of Pennsylvania, Philadelphia, Pa., 130; Basilica of the Assumption of the Blessed Virgin Mary, Baltimore, Md., 131, 180-81; Capitol, The, Washington, D.C., 17, 131, 220, 221
Latta House, Vineyard Village, Prairie Grove, Ark., 582
Lawrence Halprin & Associates: Auditorium Forecourt Fountain, Portland, Oreg., 779, 780-81; Ghirardelli Square, San Francisco, Calif., 778, 779
Lead, S.D., 626
Le Corbusier: Carpenter Center for the Visual Arts, Harvard University, Cambridge, Mass., 113
Ledyard, John, 704, 705
Lee, Francis Lightfoot, 300
Lee, Jeremiah: Mansion, Marblehead, Mass., 56, 57
Lee, Richard Henry, 300
Lee, Thomas, 300
Lee, Thomas H.: Sturdivant Hall, Selma, Ala., 362, 363

Le Moyne, Jean Baptiste, 533
L'Enfant, Pierre Charles, 13, 170, 220, 232
Le Prête House, New Orleans, La., 574
Lever House, New York, N.Y., 246-47
Lewis, Meriwether, 705
Lewis Wharf Rehabilitation, Boston, Mass., 81
Lexington, Ky., 387, 388-89
Libby Dam, Libby, Mont., 698-99
Lighthouse, Cape Hatteras, N.C., 376, 377
Liguest, Pierre Laclède, 623
Liliuokalani, queen of Hawaii, 735
Lincoln, Abraham, 426, 449
Lincoln, Nebr., 644, 674, 676-77
Lincoln, R.I., 28, 30-31
Lincoln Center, Vivian Beaumont Theater, New York, N.Y., 270, 271
Lincoln Memorial, Washington, D.C., 232-33
Lincoln's New Salem State Park, Petersburg, Ill., 436, 438-39
Lindheimer, Ferdinand: House, New Braunfels, Tex., 536
Link, Theodore C.: Union Station, St. Louis, Mo., 674-75
Link & Haire: Civic Center, Helena, Mont., 677
Lipchitz, Jacques, 496
Litchfield, Conn., 72-73
Little Rock, Ark., 578-79
Lloyd, Edward, III, 162
Locke, John, 278
Loebl, Schlossman: Civic Center, Chicago, Ill., 526-27
Logan, Utah, 648-49, 690
Log Cabin, Belle Meade, near Nashville, Tenn., 369
Loire, Gabriel, 108
Lompoc, Calif., 711, 712-13
Long, Robert C., Jr.: Baker Mansion, Altoona, Pa., 195
Longwood, Natchez, Miss., 282, 374-75
Los Altos Hills, Calif., 796, 797
Los Angeles, Calif., 703, 708, 748, 749, 765, 769, 776, 777
Los Cerritos Ranch House, Long Beach, Calif., 724, 725
Los Gatos Civic Center, Los Gatos, Calif., 808, 809
Louisville, Ky., 350, 351, 372, 373, 380, 381
Lundy, Victor A.: Unitarian Meetinghouse, Hartford, Conn., 108, 109
Lyndhurst, Tarrytown, N.Y., 198

M

MLTW/Moore, Turnbull Associates: Kresge College, University of California, Santa Cruz, 801
Mabel Tainter Memorial Building, Menomonie, Wis., 467
McArthur, John, Jr.: Philadelphia City Hall, Philadelphia, Pa., 209
McBean, Thomas: St. Paul's Chapel, New York, N.Y., 170, 171
McComb, John, Jr.: New York City Hall, New York, N.Y., 131, 178, 179
McDonald, Allen: Centennial Building, Sitka, Alaska, 806
McDonnell Planetarium, St. Louis, Mo., 686
McGregor Memorial Conference Center, Wayne State University, Detroit, Mich., 502-03
McIntire, Samuel, 16; Peirce-Nichols House, Salem, Mass., 62, 63; Pingree House, Salem, Mass., 63, 64-65
Mackay House, Virginia City, Nev., 750, 751
Mackie Building, Milwaukee, Wis., 460, 461
McKim, Mead & White, 133, 429; Boston Public Library, Boston, Mass., 92, 93; Pierpont Morgan Library, New York, N.Y., 218, 219; Racquet and Tennis Club, New York, N.Y., 246, 247

Mackinaw City, Mich., 431, 432-33
McLeansboro, Ill., 461
McMath, Robert R.: Telescope, Kitt Peak, Ariz., 617-19
Macon, Ga., 287, 365
Macpheadris-Warner House, Portsmouth, N.H., 49
MacPherson, John, 166
Madame John's Legacy, New Orleans, La., 533, 562
Madison, Ga., 387
Madison, James, 177
Madison, N.Y., 184
Main, Charles T. See Charles T. Main, Inc.
Manchester, N.H., 82-83
Mandan, N.D., 632-33
Mangin, Joseph François: New York City Hall, New York, N.Y., 131, 178, 179
Manhattan, Kans., 667
Manigault, Gabriel: Joseph Manigault House, Charleston, S.C., 337
Manigault, Joseph: House, Charleston, S.C., 337
Mann's (Grauman's) Chinese Theater, Los Angeles, Calif., 769
Manship, Paul, 235
Manti, Utah, 649
Manufacturers Hanover Trust Company, New York, N.Y., 269
Marblehead, Mass., 56, 57
Marble House, Newport, R.I., 96-97
Marietta, Ohio, 424
Marina City, Chicago, Ill., 524
Marin County Government Center, San Rafael, Calif., 782-83
Marine Midland Building, New York, N.Y., 269
Marion County Public Library, Indianapolis, Ind., 479
Market Hall, Charleston, S.C., 352
Mark Twain House, Hartford, Conn., 90, 91
Marquette, Jacques, 622
Marquis & Stoller: Commerce Clearing House Regional Headquarters, San Rafael, Calif., 814, 815
Marryat, Captain Frederick, 623
Marshall, Mich., 450, 451
Marshall Field Wholesale Store, Chicago, Ill., 427, 661
Maryland Blue Cross Building, Towson, Md., 243, 244-45
Maryland Institute, Baltimore, 204, 205
Mason, George, 130, 308
Mason, Thompson, 130
Masonic Hall, Victor, Colo., 656
Masqueray, Emanuel L.: Cathedral of St. Paul, St. Paul, Minn., 480
Massachusetts Institute of Technology, Cambridge, Mass., 91, 107
Massachusetts State House, Boston, Mass., 16, 68, 69
Massachusetts State Service Center, Boston, Mass., 103, 104-05
Masten & Hurd: Foothills College, Los Altos Hills, Calif., 796, 797
Matthias Hammond House, Annapolis, Md., 130
Mauna Kea Beach Hotel, Mauna Kea Beach, Hawaii, 788-89
Max, Elias: Tippecanoe County Courthouse, Lafayette, Ind., 463
Maybeck, Bernard R.: First Church of Christ, Scientist, Berkeley, Calif., 769, 770-71; Palace of Fine Arts, San Francisco, Calif., 709, 768, 769
Mechanic, Morris A.: Theater, Baltimore, Md., 248-49
Medical College of Virginia, Richmond, Va., 373
Medora, N.D., 645
Meigs, Montgomery C.: Old Pension Building, Washington, D.C., 208-09
Melville, Herman, 707

Memorial Hall, Harvard University, Cambridge, Mass., *91*
Memphis, Tenn., *412*
Menard, Pierre, 436; House, near Chester, Ill., *436-37*
Mendelsohn, Erich: Mount Zion Temple and Center, St. Paul, Minn., *490*
Menomonie, Wis., *467*
Merchants National Bank, Winona, Minn., *476, 477*
Mesa Verde National Park, near Cortez, Colo., 622, 627, *628-29, 630-31*
Metz, Christian, 425
Meyer & Holler: Mann's (Grauman's) Chinese Theater, Los Angeles, Calif., *769*
Miami, Fla., *386, 387, 406, 407*
Middlebury, Vt., *71*
Midway, Ga., 318, *319*
Mies van der Rohe, Ludwig, 431, 469, 524; 860-80 Lake Shore Drive, Chicago, Ill., 520, *521*; Federal Center, Chicago, Ill., *520*; S. R. Crown Hall, Illinois Institute of Technology, Chicago, Ill., *520*; Seagram Building, New York, N.Y., *247*
Miller, Hanson, Westerbeck, Bell: Butler Square, Minneapolis, Minn., *470*
Miller, J. Irwin, 494
Milles, Carl: Aloe Plaza Fountain, St. Louis, Mo., *674-75*; Fountain of Faith, National Memorial Park, Falls Church, Va., 394, *396-97*
Mills, Robert: Bethesda Presbyterian Church, Camden, S.C., *338*; Winnsboro Courthouse, Winnsboro, S.C., 340, *341*; Fireproof Building, Charleston, S.C., *340*; Robert Mills Historic House, Columbia, S.C., 338, *339*; Washington Monument, Washington, D.C., *220*
Milwaukee, Wis., *460, 461*
Minden, Nebr., *636*
Minneapolis, Minn., *470, 490, 512-19, 623*
Minnehaha County Courthouse, Sioux Falls, S.D., *664, 665*
Minnesota State Capitol, St. Paul, Minn., *480-81*
Minoru Yamasaki & Associates: World Trade Center, New York, N.Y., 272, *273*
Mission House, Stockbridge, Mass., *40-41*
Mississippi Valley, 426, 534
Mitchell, Ind., *440-41*
Mitchell, Robert S.: Old Courthouse, St. Louis, Mo., *662*
Mitchell Building, Milwaukee, Wis., *460, 461*
Mix, Edward Townsend: Mackie Building, Milwaukee, Wis., *460, 461*; Mitchell Building, Milwaukee, Wis., *460, 461*
Mobile, Ala., 352, *354-55, 357*, 369, *370-71*
Moffatt-Ladd House, Portsmouth, N.H., *48, 49*
Mohawk Valley, *131-32*
Moisseiff, Leon S.: Golden Gate Bridge, San Francisco, Calif., *772*
Moline, Ill., 505, *506-07*
Monadnock Building, Chicago, Ill., 469
Monroe, James, 17, 377
Monterey, Calif., 704, 706, *722-23*
Monticello, Charlottesville, Va., 277, *332*
Montpelier, Vt., *68, 69*
Moore, Henry, 270, 271; Large Arch, Cleo Rogers Memorial County Library, Columbus, Ind., *496*; "Vertebrae," Seattle First National Bank, Seattle, Wash., *811*
Moore, Isaac: Iolani Palace, Honolulu, Hawaii, *734-35*
Moore, Lydon, Turnbull & Whitaker: Sea Ranch Condominium, Sea Ranch, Calif., *786-87*
Moore, Turnbull Associates. *See* MLTW/ Moore Turnbull Associates.
Mooser, William: Santa Barbara County Courthouse, Santa Barbara, Calif., *769*
Morgan, Julia: San Simeon, San Simeon, Calif., *766, 767*

Morgan County Courthouse, Madison, Ga., *387*
Morgan Library, New York, N.Y., *218*, 219
Mormon Tabernacle, Logan, Utah, *648-49*
Mormon Tabernacle, Salt Lake City, Utah, 624-25, 649, *650-51*
Mormon Temple, Manti, Utah, *649*
Mormon Temple, Salt Lake City, Utah, 649, 650-51
Morris, V. C.: Building, San Francisco, Calif., *777*
Morris A. Mechanic Theater, Baltimore, Md., *248-49*
Morris Ketchum, Jr., and Associates: World of Birds Building, Bronx Zoo, The Bronx, N.Y., *263*
Morrison, Hugh, 8
Morristown, N.J., *173*
Morse College, Yale University, New Haven, Conn., *121*
Morse-Libby House, Portland, Maine. *See* Victoria Mansion.
Morton, John, 137
Morton Homestead, Prospect Park, Pa., *137*
Mortonson, Morton, 137
Mount Angel Abbey, St. Benedict, Oreg., *796, 797*
Mount Auburn Cemetery, Cambridge, Mass., 18
Mount Clare, Baltimore, Md., *165*
Mount Pleasant, Philadelphia, Pa., *166-67*
Mount Vernon, Fairfax County, Va., 329, *330-31*
Mount Zion Temple and Center, St. Paul, Minn., *490*
Muchow, W. C.: Engineering Science Center, University of Colorado, Boulder, Colo., *691*
Muchow Associates: Park Central, Denver, Colo., *696*
Mullet, Alfred B.: Executive Office Building, Washington, D.C., *209*; Old Post Office, St. Louis, Mo., *662-63*; Pioneer Post Office and Courthouse, Portland, Oreg., *744*
Mumford, Lewis, 18
Munday, Richard, 54
Munras, Estevan, 717
Munson-Williams-Proctor Institute, Utica, N.Y., *252, 253*
Murphy, C. F. *See* C. F. Murphy Associates.
Murphy & Mackey: Climatron, St. Louis, Mo., *684-85*
Murray-Jones-Murray: St. Patrick's Church, Oklahoma City, Okla., *606-07*
Museum of Modern Art, New York, N.Y., *270*
Muskegon. Mich., *493*
Myers, Elijah E.: Old City Hall, Richmond, Va., *381*
Mystic Seaport, Mystic, Conn., 83, *84-85*

N

Nantucket, Mass., *37, 87*
Naramore, Bain, Brady & Johanson: Seattle First National Bank, Seattle, Wash., *811*
Nashville, Tenn., *352, 368-69, 373*
Nassau Hall, Princeton University, Princeton, N.J., 157, *158-59*
Natchez, Miss., 281, 282, *366-67, 374-75*
Nathaniel Russell House, Charleston, S.C., *336-37*
National Cash Register Company, Dayton, Ohio, *478-79*
National Center for Atmospheric Research, near Boulder, Colo., *692-95*
Nauvoo, Illinois, 425, *442*
Nebraska State Capitol, Lincoln, *676-77*
Nentwig, Klaus Peter, 384
Nervi, Pier Luigi: Convention Hall, SCOPE, Norfolk, Va., *410-11*
Nesjar, Carl, 264

Nestor, John: Ladd & Bush Bank, Salem, Oreg., *746, 747*
Neutra, Dion: Orange County Courthouse, Santa Ana, Calif., *790, 791*
Neutra, Richard: Corona School, Bell, Calif., *774*; Orange County Courthouse, Santa Ana, Calif., *790, 791*
Nevada State Capitol, Carson City, Nev., *744*
New Albany, Ind., *452*
New Bern, N.C., 277, *326-27*
New Braunfels, Tex., *535-36*
New Castle, Del., *150, 157*
New Harmony, Ind., 425, 496, *498-99*
New Haven, Conn., 19, 87, *118-23*
New Iberia, La., *566-67*
Newman, Barnett: Rothko Chapel, Houston, Tex., 612, *613*
Newman, Robert, 39
New Market Block, Portland, Oreg., *746*
New Market Theater, Portland, Oreg., *706*
New Mummers Theater, Oklahoma City, Okla., 599, *600-01*
New Orleans, La., 533-34, 559, *562-63, 574-77*
New Paltz, N.Y., *138*
Newport, R.I., *52-55, 96-97*
New Roads, La., *561*
New St. Mary's Church, Burlington, N.J., *204-05*
New Salem State Park, Petersburg, Ill. *See* Lincoln's New Salem State Park.
Newsom, Samuel and Joseph C.: William Carson Mansion, Eureka, Calif., *758, 759*
New York, N.Y., 19, 96, 125-26, 131, 133, *170-71, 178*, 179, *190-91, 198-204, 218-19, 222-23*, 227, *228*, 229, *234-37, 241, 246-47, 254*, 260, *262-65, 267-73, 673*, 677, 777. *See also* Brooklyn, N.Y.; Queens, N.Y.; Staten Island, N.Y.
New York City Hall, New York, N.Y., 131, *178, 179*
New York Public Library, New York, N.Y., *219*
Niagara Falls, N.Y., *250*
Nogales, Ariz., 556, *557*
Noguchi, Isamu, 269
Norfolk, Va., *291, 410-11*
North Building, Shawnee Methodist Mission, Kansas City, Kans., *639*
North Carolina State Capitol, Raleigh, N.C., 352, *353*
North Carolina State Legislative Building, Raleigh, N.C., *404, 405*
North Christian Church, Columbus, Ind., *494, 495*
North Dartmouth, Mass., *114-15*
North Platte, Nebr., *645*
North Salem, N.Y., 216, *217*
North Tarrytown, N.Y., 133, *134-35*
Novelty Building, Helena, Mont., 6, *660-61*
Noyes, Eliot: Southside Junior High School, Columbus, Ind., *496, 497*
Nuestra Señora de la Purísima Concepción de Acuna, San Antonio, Tex., *554-55*
Nutt, Haller, 282, 374

O

Oahu Island, Hawaii, *732-35, 790, 798-99*
Oak Alley, Vacherie, La., *567-69*
Oakland, Calif., 784, 785, *792-93*
Oakland-Alameda County Coliseum, Oakland, Calif., *784, 785*
Oakland Museum, Oakland, Calif., *792-93*
Oakleigh, Mobile, Ala., *357*
Oak Park, Ill., *482, 483*
Oceanside, Calif., *718*
Ocmulgee National Monument, near Macon, Ga., *286, 287*
Octagonal Cobblestone House, Madison, N.Y., *184*

Octagon House, Washington, D.C., *177*
Ohio Land Company Office, Marietta, Ohio, 424
Ohiopyle, Pa., *240–41*
Ohio State Capitol, Columbus, Ohio, *448*, 449
Oklahoma City, Okla., 537, 599, *600–601*, *606–07*
Olana, Hudson, N.Y., *210–11*
Old Bennington, Vt., *70–71*
Old Burying Ground, Beaufort, N.C., *318*
Old City Hospital, Mobile, Ala., 352, *354–55*
Old College, Harvard, Mass., 12
Old Cove Fort, near Beaver, Utah, *640*
Old Custom House, Monterey, Calif., *722*, 723
Old Deerfield, Mass., *39*
Old Dutch House, New Castle, Pa., *150*
Old Fort Harrod State Park, Harrodsburg, Ky., *328*, 329
Old Fort Museum, Fort Smith, Ark., *564*
Old Fort Niagara, Youngstown, N.Y., *172–73*
Old House, Cutchogue, Long Island, N.Y., *136*, 137
Old Main, University of Wyoming, Laramie, *667*
Old Mill, Pigeon Forge, Tenn., *349*
Old North Church, Boston, Mass. *See* Christ Church.
Old Pension Building, Washington, D.C., *208–09*
Old Rock House, St. Louis, Mo., 623
Old St. Mary's Church, Fredericksburg, Tex., *588*
Old Salem Restoration, Winston-Salem, N.C., 279, *320–21*
Old Ship Meetinghouse, Hingham, Mass., *32–33*
Old Slater Mill, Pawtucket, R.I., *58–59*
Old Stone House, Brownington, Vt., *80*, 81
Old Swedes Church, Wilmington, Del., *141*
Old Tennent Church and Cemetery, Tennent, N.J., *161*
Old Trinity Protestant Episcopal Church, Church Creek, Md., *140–41*
Old Waioli Church, Hanalei, Kauai Island, Hawaii, 732, *733*
Old Water Tower, Chicago, Ill., 452, *455*
Old Whalers' First Presbyterian Church, Sag Harbor, Long Island, N.Y., *216*
Old Witch Totem Pole, Juneau, Alaska, *736*, 737
Olmstead, Frederick Law, 211, 536; Central Park, New York, N.Y., *222–23*
Olympia, Wash., *798*, 799
Omaha, Nebr., 625
Omni, Atlanta, Ga., *408–09*
1 Liberty Plaza, New York, N.Y., *267*
Oraibi, Ariz., *545*
Orange County Courthouse, Santa Ana, Calif., *790*, *791*
Orange County Government Center, Goshen, N.Y., 250, *251*
Orchestra Hall, Minneapolis, Minn., 512, *513*
Orlando Public Library, Orlando, Fla., *406*
Orton Plantation, near Wilmington, N.C., 342, *344–45*
Otis, Elisha, 203
Owatonna, Minn., *474*, *475*
Owen, Robert, 425
Owens-Corning Fiberglas Plant, Aiken, S.C., *412*
Owens-Thomas House, Savannah, Ga., *342*

P

P. L. Hay House, Macon, Ga., *365*
Pacheco & Graham: Institute of American Indian Art Outdoor Theater, Santa Fe, N.M., *598*, 599
Palace of Fine Arts, San Francisco, Calif., 709, *768*, *769*
Palace of the Governors, Santa Fe, N.M., 532, *544*

Paley, William S., 270
Palladio, Andrea, 14, 308
Palladio Londonensis (Salmon), 14
Palmer, Timothy, 40
Palmer-Epard Cabin, Homestead National Monument, near Beatrice, Nebr., 636, *637*
Palos Verdes, Calif., *774*, *775*
Panama-California Exposition, San Diego, Calif., 709
Panama-Pacific International Exposition, San Francisco, Calif., 709
Paradise Steam Plant, Paradise, Ky., *399*
Paradise Valley, Ariz., *602–03*
Park Central, Denver, Colo., *696*
Parker House, Log Cabin Village, Fort Worth, Tex., *582–83*
Parkman, Francis, 280, 532, 624
Parlange, near New Roads, La., *561*
Parson Capen House, Topsfield, Mass., *34–35*
Pasadena, Calif., 709, *764*, *765*, *774*
Pascal, Jean, 562
Pasco, Wash., *802–03*
Paseo del Rio, San Antonio, Tex., *594*, *595*
Paulding, William, 198
Paul O. Hall & Associates: Triple Water Tank, Southern Illinois University, Carbondale, Ill., *504*, 505
Paulsen, John C.: Novelty Building, Helena, Mont., 6, *660–61*
Pawtucket, R.I., *58–59*
Peabody, F. G.: Terrace, Cambridge, Mass., *110–11*
Pegram, George H.: Union Station, St. Louis, Mo., *674–75*
Pei, I. M.: Society Hill Apartments, Philadelphia, Pa., *168–69*. *See also* I. M. Pei & Partners.
Peirce-Nichols House, Salem, Mass., 62, *63*
Penn, William, 126, 128, 169
Pennsylvania Academy of Fine Arts, Philadelphia, *211*
Pennsylvania Hospital, Philadelphia, 129
Pennsylvania State House (Independence Hall), Philadelphia, 129
Pentagon Barracks, Baton Rouge, La., *564–65*
People's National Bank, McLeansboro, Ill., *461*
Peralta, Pedro de, 532
Perkins, Dwight H.: Carl Schurz High School, Chicago, Ill., *479*
Pepperrell, Sir William, 56
Perry, Shaw & Hepburn: Ironworks Reconstruction, Saugus, Mass., *24–25*
Petaluma Adobe State Historical Monument, Petaluma, Calif., *724–25*
Peters, William Wesley: Marin County Government Center, San Rafael, Calif., *782–83*; Van Wezel Performing Arts Hall, Sarasota, Fla., *409*
Petersburg, Ill., 436, *438–39*
Peterson & Brickbauer: Maryland Blue Cross Building, Towson, Md., 243, *244–45*
Pettigrew State Park, Creswell, N.C., *325*
Pfeiffer Chapel, Florida Southern College, Lakeland, Fla., *390*
Philadelphia, Pa., 128–31, *156–57*, *160*, 161, *164–69*, 190, *192–95*, 209, 211, *258–59*
Philadelphia City Hall, Philadelphia, Pa., *209*
Philadelphia House of Employment and Almshouse, Philadelphia, Pa., 129
Philip Johnson Associates: Kline Biology Tower, Yale University, New Haven, Conn., 118, *119*
Philippi, W. Va., *348*, 349
Philipsburg Manor and Gristmill, North Tarrytown, N.Y., 133, *134–35*
Philipse, Adolphus, 133
Philipse, Frederick, 133
Phillips Exeter Academy, Exeter, N.H., *115*
Picasso, Pablo, 264; "Woman," Civic Center, Chicago, Ill., *526–27*
Pierpont Morgan Library, New York, N.Y., *218*, 219

Pierre Menard House, Fort Kaskaskia State Park, near Chester, Ill., *436–37*
Pigeon Forge, Tenn., *349*
Pike, Zebulon, 534–35
Pingree House, Salem, Mass., 63, *64–65*
Pioneer Post Office and Courthouse, Portland, Oreg., *744*
Pioneer Square Historic District Redevelopment, Seattle, Wash., *749*
Piper & Burton: New Market Block and Theater, Portland, Oreg., *706*, *746*
Piquenard, Alfred H., 457
Pittsburgh, Pa., *212–13*, *266*, 267
Plaza Hotel, Atlanta, Ga., *394*
Pleasant Hill, Ky. *See* Shakertown, Ky.
Plimoth Plantation Reconstruction, Plymouth, Mass., 19, *20–22*
Plymouth, Mass., 19, *20–22*
Pohick Church, near Fort Belvoir, Va., *322–23*
Polk, Willis: Hallidie Building, San Francisco, Calif., *766*
Ponce de León, Juan, 275
Pope, John Russell: Broad Street Station, Richmond, Va., 384, *385*; Jefferson Memorial, Washington, D.C., *232*
Porlier, Joseph, 434
Port Authority Building, Savannah, Ga., 360, *361*
Porter, Lemuel: First Congregational Church, Tallmadge, Ohio, 442, *443*
Porteus, James, 128; Slate House, Philadelphia, Pa., 128
Portland, Maine, *88–89*
Portland, Oreg., 703, 706, 709, *742–44*, *746*, 779, *780–81*, *787*
Portland Center, Portland, Oreg., *787*
Portman, John C., Jr.: Hyatt Regency Hotel, Atlanta, Ga., 394, *395*
Portolá, Gaspar de, 704
Portsmouth, N.H., *37*, *48–51*, 56, *57*, 62
Poteaux-en-terre style, 434
Potter, Edward T.: Mark Twain House, Hartford, Conn., *90*, 91
Potts, Isaac, 146
Powder Magazine, Williamsburg, Va., *296*, 297
Powel, Samuel, 165
Powel House, Philadelphia, Pa., *164–65*
Power Block, Helena, Mont., *661*
Poweshiek County National Bank, Grinnell, Iowa, *422*
Pownalborough Courthouse, near Dresden, Maine, *45*
Prairie Grove, Ark., *582*
Pratt, Abner, 451
Preston, John Smith, 570
Preston, William Gibbons: Cotton Exchange, Savannah, Ga., 360, *361*
Price Tower, Bartlesville, Okla., *596*, 597
Princeton University, Princeton, N.J., 128, 157, *158–59*, *230–31*
Priory of St. Mary and St. Louis, Creve Coeur, Mo., *682–83*
Progressive Design Associates: St. Jude Church, Grand Rapids, Mich., *490–91*
Prospect Park, Pa., *137*
Proudfood, Bird & Monheim: City and County Building, Salt Lake City, Utah, *664*, 665
Providence, R.I., 60, *61*, 100, *101*, 128, *224–25*
Prybylowski & Gravino: Omni, Atlanta, Ga., *408–09*
Pueblo Bonito, Chaco Canyon National Monument, Bloomfield, N.M., *543*
Purcell, William G., 477
Purcell & Elmslie: Woodbury County Courthouse, Sioux City, Iowa, *477*
Purcell, Feick & Elmslie: Merchants National Bank, Winona, Minn., *476*, 477
Purísima Concepción Mission, Lompoc, Calif., 711, *712–13*
Puy, Louis de, 656

Q

Queen Anne style, *757, 760-61*
Queen Emma's Summer Palace, Honolulu, Hawaii, *735*
Queens, N.Y., *262, 263*
Quincy, Josiah, Jr., 278

R

R. M. Gensert Associates: Blossom Music Center, near Akron, Ohio, *510*
Racine, Wis., *486-89*
Racquet and Tennis Club, New York, N.Y., *246, 247*
Raeder, Frederick: Sanger-Peper Building, St. Louis, Mo., *652*
Rague, John F.: Old State Capitol, Springfield, Ill., *449*
Raleigh, N.C., 352, *353, 404, 405*
Ramberg & Lowrey: Orange County Courthouse, Santa Ana, Calif., *790, 791*
Ranchos de Taos, N.M., *548-49*
Randall, Robert, 190
Rapson, Ralph R.: Tyrone Guthrie Theater, Minneapolis, Minn., *512*
Ravalli, Anthony, 639
Red Rocks Amphitheater, near Denver, Colo., *627, 678-79*
Redwood Library, Newport, R.I., *52*
Reed & Stem: Grand Central Station, New York, N.Y., 228, *229*
Regency style, *342*
Rehoboth Church, Union, W. Va., *328, 329*
Reid & Reid: Hotel del Coronado, Coronado, Calif., *708, 760-61*
Reinhart & Hofmeister: Rockefeller Center, New York, N.Y., *234-35*
Reliance Building, Chicago, Ill., *468, 469*
Reno, Nev., *797*
Renwick, James: St. Patrick's Cathedral, New York, N.Y., *198-99*; Smithsonian Institution, Washington, D.C., 204, *206-07*
Research Triangle Park, N.C., 412, *413-15*
Reserve, La., *572-73*
Reston, Va., *392-93*
Revere, Paul, 16, 39, 69
Reynolds, Smith & Hills: Tampa International Airport, Tampa, Fla., *400*
Reynolds Metals Building, Richmond, Va., *405*
Rhoades, William, 77
Rhyolite, Nev., *750, 752-53*
Richard Jackson House, Portsmouth, N.H., *37*
Richards, A. N.: Building, Philadelphia, Pa., *258-59*
Richards, Joseph B., 69
Richards House, Ideal Cement Corporation, Mobile, Ala., *274, 369, 370-71*
Richardson, Henry Hobson, 18, 427, 467, 592, 625, 665, 777; Allegheny County Courthouse and Jail, Pittsburgh, Pa., *212-13*; Ames Monument, Sherman, Wyo., *668, 669*; Glessner House, Chicago, Ill., *466, 467*; Marshall Field Wholesale Store, Chicago, Ill., 427, 661; Trinity Church, Boston, Mass., 18, *94-95*
Richard Upjohn and Son: Greenwood Cemetery gates, Brooklyn, N.Y., *196-97*
Richmond, Vt., 77
Richmond, Va., 332, 333, *373, 381-82*, 383-84, *385, 405*
Richmondtown Restoration, Staten Island, N.Y., *152-53*
Ridgely, Charles, 175
Ritchie, W. A.: Spokane County Courthouse, Spokane, Wash., *744, 745*
Riverdale, N.D., *698*
Riverpark Center, Spokane, Wash., 806, *807*

Robert Mills Historic House, Columbia, S.C., 338, *339*
Robert R. McMath Solar Telescope, Kitt Peak Observatory, Kitt Peak, Ariz., *617-19*
Robie House, Chicago, Ill., *483-85*
Roche, Kevin. *See* Kevin Roche, John Dinkeloo & Associates.
Rochester, N.Y., *259-61*
Rochester Institute of Technology, Rochester, N.Y., *260-61*
Rockefeller, John D., Jr., 294
Rockefeller Center, New York, N.Y., *234-35*
Rockingham, Vt., *44*
Rocky Hill Meetinghouse, Amesbury, Mass., 40, *42-44*
Rocky Mountain College, Billings, Mont., *690*
Rocky Mount Historic Shrine, near Johnson City, Tenn., *329*
Rodia, Simon: Rodia (Watts) Towers, Los Angeles, Calif., *776, 777*
Rodia (Watts) Towers, Los Angeles, Calif., *776, 777*
Roebling, John Augustus: bridge, Cincinnati, Ohio, *454-55*; Brooklyn Bridge, Brooklyn, N.Y., *200-201*; 10th Street Suspension Bridge, Wheeling, W.Va., *378*
Roebling, Washington: Brooklyn Bridge, Brooklyn, N.Y., *200-201*
Rogers, Cleo: Library, Columbus, Ind., *496*
Roi, Joseph, 434
Roi-Porlier-Tank House, Green Bay, Wis., *434, 435*
Romanesque style, *94-95, 204-05, 466-67, 666*
Roofless Church, New Harmony, Ind., 496, *498-99*
Rookery, The, Chicago, Ill., *469*
Roper, James W., 357
Rosalie, Natchez, Miss., *366*
Rose, Thomas: Stanton Hall, Natchez, Miss., *366*
Rosedown Plantation, St. Francisville, La., *567*
Rose Hill, Geneva, N.Y., *188*
Rosewall Hall, Va., 277
Roth, Emery. *See* Emery Roth & Sons.
Rothko, Mark, 612
Rothko Chapel, Houston, Tex., 612, *613*
Round Church, Richmond, Vt., 77
Round Top, Tex., *584*
Rouse, William, 11
Rowan, John, 280
Row houses, Georgetown, Washington, D.C., 169
Rudolph, Paul: Burroughs Wellcome Company, Research Triangle Park, N.C., 412, *413-15*; Earl W. Brydges Library, Niagara Falls, N.Y., *250*; Massachusetts State Service Center, Boston, Mass., 103, *104-05*; Orange County Government Center, Goshen, N.Y., 250, *251*; Southeastern Massachusetts University, North Dartmouth, Mass., *114-15*; Tuskegee Institute Chapel, Tuskegee, Ala., *390, 391*
Ruggles, Thomas: House, Columbia Falls, Maine, *66-67*
Rumbold, William: Old Courthouse, St. Louis, Mo., *662*
Rush & Endicott: Boston Avenue Methodist Church, Tulsa, Okla., 592, *593*
Russell, Nathaniel, 337; House, Charleston, S.C., *336-37*
Russian blockhouse, Sitka, Alaska, *737*
Rutledge, Edward, 138

S

S. C. Johnson Offices and Research and Development Tower, Racine, Wis., *486-89*
S. R. Crown Hall, Illinois Institute of Technology, Chicago, Ill., *520*

Saarinen, Eero, 242, 505. *See also* Eero Saarinen & Associates.
Saarinen, Eliel, 242; Christ Church Lutheran, Minneapolis, Minn., *490*
Sabbathday Lake, Maine, *60*
Sacramento, Calif., 706, 710, *754-55*
Sag Harbor, Long Island, N.Y., *216*
Sailors' Snug Harbor, Staten Island, N.Y., *190*
St. Augustine, Fla., 275, 283, *284-85*, 291, *292-93*, 383
St. Bartholomew's Church, New York, N.Y., 677
St. Benedict, Oreg., *796, 797*
Ste. Genevieve, Mo., *634-35*
St. Francis de Sales Church, Muskegon, Mich., *493*
St. Francisville, La., *567*
Saint-Gaudens, Augustus, 668
St. George, Utah, *644*
St. James Church, Goose Creek, S.C., *298-99*
St. John's Preparatory School, Collegeville, Minn., *502*
St. John's University, Collegeville, Minn., *492, 502, 683*
St. Jude Church, Grand Rapids, Mich., *490-91*
St. Louis, Mo., 623, *652, 654-55, 662-63, 668, 669, 670-71, 674-75, 684-86, 691, 700-701*
St. Louis Cathedral, New Orleans, La., *533*
St. Louis Cemetery #1, New Orleans, La., *576, 577*
St. Luke's Church, Smithfield, Va., *288-89*
St. Martinville, La., 533, *560, 561*
St. Michael's Episcopal Church, Charleston, S.C., *312-13*
St. Nicholas Orthodox Church, Juneau, Alaska, *739*
St. Patrick's Cathedral, New York, N.Y., *198-99*
St. Patrick's Church, Oklahoma City, Okla., *606-07*
St. Paul, Minn., *442, 451, 480-81, 490, 623*
St. Paul's Chapel, New York, N.Y., 170, *171*
St. Paul's Church, Ironton, Mo., *620, 647*
St. Paul's Episcopal Church, Edenton, N.C., 316
St. Stephen's Church, St. Stephen, S.C., *322*
Salem, Mass., 12, 16, 62, *63-65*
Salem, Oreg., *746, 747*
Salk Biological Research Institute, La Jolla, Calif., *816-19*
Salmon, William, 14, 305
Salt Lake City, Utah, 624-25, 649, *650-52, 664, 665*
Samuel Paley Park, New York, N.Y., 270, *271*
Samuel Whitehorne House, Newport, R.I., *54*
San Antonio, Tex., 530, 532, 536, *552-55, 558, 559, 594-95*
San Bernardino, City Hall and Convention Center, San Bernardino, Calif., 808, *809*
San Carlos de Borromeo Mission, Carmel, Calif., *715*
San Diego, Calif., 704, 709, *714, 715, 785*
Sandwich, Mass., 23
San Estévan del Rey, Ácoma, N.M., *550*
San Francisco, Calif., *702, 704, 706-09, 756-57, 766, 768-69, 772, 777-800, 801, 810, 811*
San Francisco, Reserve, La., *572-73*
San Francisco de Asis, Ranchos de Taos, N.M., *548-49*
San Francisco State University, San Francisco, Calif., *800, 801*
San Gabriel Arcángel, San Gabriel, Calif., *716, 717*
Sanger-Peper Building, St. Louis, Mo., *652*
San Ildefonso Pueblo, N.M., *544-45*
San José de Gracia, Las Trampas, N.M., *555*
San José de Laguna, Laguna, N.M., *550, 555*
San José y San Miguel de Aguayo, San Antonio, Tex., *530, 552-53*

San José de Tumacácori, near Nogales, Ariz., 556, *557*

San Juan Capistrano Mission, San Juan Capistrano, Calif., 719, *720-21*

San Luis Rey de Francia, Oceanside, Calif., *718*

San Miguel Arcángel, Calif., *716-17*

San Rafael, Calif., *782-83*, 814, *815*

San Simeon, San Simeon, Calif., 766, *767*

Santa Ana, Calif., 790, *791*

Santa Barbara, Santa Barbara, Calif., 706, *719*

Santa Barbara County Courthouse, Santa Barbara, Calif., *769*

Santa Clara, Utah, 636

Santa Cruz, Calif., *801*

Santa Fe, N.M., 532, 535, *544*, 598, *599*

Santa Fe Railroad Station, Shawnee, Okla., *592*

Santuario de Chimayo, Chimayo, N.M., *556*

San Xavier del Bac, near Tucson, Ariz., 537, *538-39*, 550, *551*

Sarasota, Fla., *409*

Sasaki, Dawson, DeMay Associates: Copley Square redesign, Boston, Mass., *93*

Sasaki, Walker & Associates: John Deere Administration Building, Moline, Ill., 505, *506-07*

Saucier, Jean Baptiste, 434

Saugus, Mass., *24-25*

Savannah, Ga., 283, *342-43*, *360-61*, 377

Schafer, Flynn & Van Dijk: Blossom Music Center, near Akron, Ohio, *510*

Schipporeit, G. D.: Lake Point Tower, Chicago, Ill., 524, *525*

Schmidt, Peter R.: Haas-Lilienthal House, San Francisco, Calif., *702*, 756

Schmidt, Garden, and Erikson: Federal Center, Chicago, Ill., *520*

Schurz, Carl: High School, Chicago, Ill., *479*

SCOPE, Norfolk, Va., *410-11*

Scott, Dred, 623

Scottsdale, Ariz., 537, *596-97*

Scowden, Theodore R.: Water Company Pumping Station, Louisville, Ky., *372*, 373

Seagram Building, New York, N.Y., *247*

Sea Ranch, Calif., *786-87*

Sears Tower, Chicago, Ill., *272*, 528

Seattle, Wash., *709*, 710, *749*, *762*, *811*

Second Bank of the United States, Philadelphia, Pa., *194*, 195

Second Empire style, *96-97*, *209*

Security Bank and Trust Company, Owatonna, Minn., *474*, 475

Sedona, Ariz., *606*, *608-09*

Selma, Ala., 362, *363*

Sergeant, John, 40

Serra, Junipero, 704, *715*, 719

Sert, Jackson & Associates: Undergraduate Science Center, Harvard University, Cambridge, Mass., *112*

Sert, Jackson & Gourley: F. G. Peabody Terrace, Harvard University, Cambridge, Mass., *110-11*

Sert, José Maria, 235

Seward, William H., *709-10*

Shadows-on-the-Teche, New Iberia, La., *566-67*

Shaffer & Read: Power Block, Helena, Mont., *661*

Shaker barn, Hancock, Mass., *76*, 77

Shaker Heights, Ohio, 425

Shaker Meetinghouse, Sabbathday Lake, Maine, *60*

Shakertown (Pleasant Hill), Ky., *358-59*

Shasta Dam, Calif., 710

Shawnee, Okla., *592*

Shawnee Methodist Mission, Kansas City, Kans., *639*

Sheldon Jackson Memorial Chapel, Fairplay, Colo., *646*

Shelocta, Pa., *255*, *256-57*

Shepherd, Samuel: Amoskeag Manufacturing Complex, Manchester, N.H., *82-83*

Shepley, Rutan and Coolidge: Allegheny County Courthouse and Jail, Pittsburgh, Pa., *212-13*

Sheraton Palace Hotel, San Francisco, Calif., *707*

Sherman, Aaron: Thomas Ruggles House, Columbia Falls, Maine, *66-67*

Sherman, Wyo., *668*, 669

Shippen, Peggy, 166

Shirley Plantation, Shirley, Va., *306-07*

Shreve, Lamb & Harman: Empire State Building, New York, N.Y., 133, *236-37*

Shryock, Gideon: Actors' Theatre, Louisville, Ky., *350*, 351; Old State House, Frankfort, Ky., *351*; Old State House, Little Rock, Ark., *578-79*

Shutze, Philip T.: Swan House, Atlanta, Ga., *387*

Sibley, Henry Hastings, 442

Sibley House, St. Paul, Minn., *442*

Silloway, T. W., 69

Simon, Robert E., 393

Single Brothers' House, Old Salem Restoration, Winston-Salem, N.C., *279*, *320*, 321

Singleton, Henry: Old Courthouse, St. Louis, Mo., *662*

Sioux City, Iowa, 477

Sioux Falls, S.D., *664*, 665

Sitka, Alaska, 737, *806*

Skagway, Alaska, *739*, *740-41*

Skidmore, Owings & Merrill: Air Force Academy Chapel, Colorado Springs, Colo., *686*, *687-89*; Albright-Knox Art Gallery Addition, Buffalo, N.Y., *252*; Bank of America, San Francisco, Calif., *810*, 811; Beinecke Rare Book Library, Yale University, New Haven, Conn., *118*; Business Men's Assurance Company Building, Kansas City, Mo., *696-97*; Chase Manhattan Building, New York, N.Y., *272*; Circle Campus, University of Illinois, Chicago, Ill., *500-501*; Civic Center, Chicago, Ill., *526-27*; Emhart Manufacturing Company, Bloomfield, Conn., *116-17*; John Hancock Center, Chicago, Ill., *522-23*, 528, *529*; Ladd & Bush Bank, Salem, Oreg., *746*, 747; Lever House, New York, N.Y., *246-47*; Manufacturers Hanover Trust Company, New York, N.Y., *269*; Marine Midland Building, New York, N.Y., *269*; Mauna Kea Beach Hotel, Mauna Kea Beach, Hawaii, *788-89*; Oakland-Alameda County Coliseum, Oakland, Calif., *784*, 785; 1 Liberty Plaza, New York, N.Y., *267*; Portland Center, Portland, Oreg., *787*; Reynolds Metals Building, Richmond, Va., *405*; Robert R. McMath Solar Telescope, Kitt Peak Observatory, Kitt Peak, Ariz., *617-19*; Sears Tower, Chicago, Ill., *272*, *528*; Tenneco Building, Houston, Tex., 610, *611*; Weyerhaeuser Headquarters, Tacoma, Wash., 802, *804-05*

Slant Indian Village, Fort Abraham Lincoln State Park, near Mandan, N.D., *632-33*

Slate House, Philadelphia, Pa., 128

Slater, Samuel, 58

Sloan, Samuel: Longwood, Natchez, Miss., *282*, *374-75*

Smathers, George A.: Plaza, Miami, Fla., 406, *407*

Smith, George H.: Arcade, Cleveland, Ohio, *470-71*

Smith, George Washington, 709

Smith, Hamilton P.: Annunciation Priory, Bismarck, N.D., *682-83*; St. John's University Abbey Church, Collegeville, Minn., *192*, 683; Whitney Museum, New York, N.Y., *254*

Smith, John, 276

Smith, Joseph, 425, 442; Mansion, Nauvoo, Ill., *442*

Smith, L. C.: Building, Seattle, Wash., *762*

Smith, Robert, 128

Smith, Samuel F., 130

Smithfield, Va., *288-89*

Smithsonian Institution, Washington, D.C., 204, *206-07*

Soane, Sir John, 15

Society Hill Apartments, Philadelphia, Pa., *168-69*

Sod house, Pioneer Village, Minden, Nebr., *636*

Soleri, Paolo: Arcosanti, near Dugas, Ariz., *603*; Cosanti Foundation Workshop, Paradise Valley Ariz., *602-03*; Institute of American Indian Art, Outdoor Theater, Santa Fe, N.M., *598*, 599

Somerset Place, Pettigrew State Park, Creswell, N.C., *325*

Soong, Charlie Jones, 318

Southeastern Massachusetts University, North Dartmouth, Mass., *114-15*

Southern Illinois University, Carbondale, Ill., *504*, 505

Southside Junior High School, Columbus, Ind., *496*, 497

Spanish Governor's Palace, San Antonio, Tex., *558*, 559

Spanish Revival style, *275*, *383*, *709*, *762-63*

Spokane, Wash., *744*, *745*, 806, *807*

Spokane County Courthouse, Spokane, Wash., *744*, 745

Springfield, Ill., *449*

Spring Mill Village, Spring Mill State Park, Mitchell, Ind., *440-41*

Spruce Tree House, Mesa Verde National Park, near Cortez, Colo., 630, *631*

Stage Coach Inn, Harpers Ferry, W. Va., 378, *379*

Stamford, Conn., *108*

Stanford, Leland, 708

Stanley-Whitman House, Farmington, Conn., *36-37*

Stanton, Frederick, 281

Stanton Hall, Natchez, Miss., *366*

Stark, N.H., *73*, *74-75*

Staten Island, N.Y., *138*, *152-53*, *190*, 236, *238-39*

Steckel, Peter, 149

Steele, William L.: Woodbury County Courthouse, Sioux City, Iowa, 477

Stegner, Wallace, 703

Steuben, Friedrich von, 146

Stevens House, Wethersfield, Conn., *56*

Stewardson, John, 230

Stewart, Thomas H.: Egyptian Building, Medical College of Virginia, Richmond, Va., *373*

Stickney, Charles D.: Civic Center, Los Gatos, Calif., *808*, 809

Stiles College, Yale University, New Haven, Conn., *121*

Stockbridge, Mass., *40-41*

Stone, Edward Durell: Stuart Company, Pasadena, Calif., *774*. *See also* Edward Durell Stone & Associates.

Stone, Edward Durell, Jr., 406

Storey County Courthouse, Virginia City, Nev., *750*, *751*

Stratford Hall, Stratford, Va., 277, 300, *302-03*

Strauss, Joseph B.: Golden Gate Bridge, San Francisco, Calif., *772*

Strickland, William, 351, 369; Downtown Presbyterian Church, Nashville, Tenn., *373*; Nashville State Capitol, Nashville, Tenn., *352*; Second Bank of the United States, Philadelphia, Pa., *194*, 195

Strip, The, Las Vegas, Nev., 811, *812-13*

Strong, William K., 188

Stuart Company, Pasadena, Calif., *774*

Student Union, San Francisco State University, San Francisco, Calif., *800*, 801

Sturdivant Hall, Selma, Ala., 362, *363*

Stuyvesant, Peter, 125, 150

Sugar, Peter: City of Greensboro-Guilford

County Center, Greensboro, N.C., *405*
Sullivan, Louis H., 95, 241, 427-30, 477; Carson, Pirie, Scott & Company Store, Chicago, Ill., *470, 472-74*; Poweshiek County National Bank, Grinnell, Iowa, *422*; Prudential (Guaranty) Building, Buffalo, N.Y., *224-25*; Security Bank and Trust Company, Owatonna, Minn., *474, 475*; Transportation Building, World's Columbian Exposition, Chicago, Ill., 429, 777; Wainwright Building, St. Louis, Mo., 669, *670-71*; Wainwright Tomb, St. Louis, Mo., *668*
Surgeon's Quarters, The Dalles, Oreg., *742*
Sutter, John Augustus, 706, 754
Swan, Abraham, 14
Swan House, Atlanta, Ga., *387*
Synergetics, Inc.: Climatron, St. Louis, Mo., *684-85*; Union Tank Car Repair Facility, Baton Rouge, La., *604-05*
Syracuse, N.Y., 254, *255*

T

TVA: Brown's Ferry Nuclear Plant, near Athens, Ala., *398, 399*; Bull Run Steam Plant, near Knoxville, Tenn., *399*; Paradise Steam Plant, Paradise, Ky., *399. See also* Tennessee Valley Authority.
TWA Terminal, John F. Kennedy International Airport, Queens, N.Y., *262, 263*
Tacoma, Wash., 709, 802, *804-05*
Taft, Charles Phelps, 444
Taft, William Howard, 444
Taft House Museum, Cincinnati, Ohio, *444*
Tainter, Mabel: Building, Menomonie, Wis., *467*
Taliaferro, Richard, 278, 308
Taliesin Associated Architects: Marin County Government Center, San Rafael, Calif., *782-83*; Van Wezel Performing Arts Hall, Sarasota, Fla., *409*
Taliesin West, Scottsdale, Ariz., 537, *596-97*
Tallmadge, Ohio, 442, *443*
Tampa International Airport, Tampa, Fla., *400*
Tank, Nils Otto, 434
Taos Pueblo, Taos, N.M., 545, *546-47*
Tarrytown, N.Y., 132, 198
Tayloe, John, 177
Taylor, Bayard, 625
Taylor, Obed: ZCMI Department Store, Salt Lake City, Utah, *652*
Taylor-Grady House, Athens, Ga., *356*
Temple, Juan, 725
Temple Square, Salt Lake City, Utah, 649, *650-51*
TenEyck, Jacob, 216
Tenneco Building, Houston, Tex., 610, *611*
Tennent, N.J., *161*
Tennessee State Capitol, Nashville, Tenn., *352*
Tennessee Valley Authority, 282. *See also* TVA.
10th Street Suspension Bridge, Wheeling, W. Va., *378*
Terrace Hill, Des Moines, Iowa, *452-53*
The Dalles, Oreg., *742*
30 Meeting Street, Charleston, S.C., *347*
Thiry, Paul: Libby Dam, Libby, Mont., *698-99*
Thomas, E. J.: Performing Arts Hall, Akron, Ohio, 510, *511*
Thomas P. Kennard House, Lincoln, Nebr., *644*
Thomas Ruggles House, Columbia Falls, Maine, *66-67*
Thomas Worthington House, Chillicothe, Ohio. *See* Adena.
Thompson, Benjamin. *See* Benjamin Thompson & Associates.
Thompson, Martin E.: Sailors' Snug Harbor, Staten Island, N.Y., *190*
Thompson, Ventulett & Stainback: Omni, Atlanta, Ga., *408-09*

Thornton, William: Capitol, The, Washington, D.C., 17, 131, 220, *221*; Octagon House, The, Washington, D.C., *177*
Thoroughgood, Adam, 277, 291; House, Norfolk, Va., *291*
Thousand Oaks, Calif., *808*
Tillich, Paul, 490
Tippecanoe County Courthouse, Lafayette, Ind., *463*
Tolan, Brentwood S.: Allen County Courthouse, Fort Wayne, Ind., *464-65*
Tombstone, Ariz., 536, 586, *587*
Tombstone Courthouse Museum, Tombstone, Ariz., 586, *587*
Topeka, Kans., 679, *680-81*
Topsfield, Mass., *34-35*
Torreya State Park, Fla., *357*
Tottenville, Staten Island, N.Y., *138*
Touro Synagogue, Newport, R.I., 52, *53*
Tower of the Americas, San Antonio, Tex., *594*
Town, Ithiel, 352; Federal Hall National Memorial, New York, N.Y., *190-91*
Town & Davis, 570, 579; North Carolina State Capitol, Raleigh, N.C., 352, *353*; Old State Capitol, Springfield, Ill., *449*
Towson, Md., 243, *244-45*
Transportation Building, World's Columbian Exposition, Chicago, Ill., 429, 777
Trent, William, 155
Trent House, Trenton, N.J., *155*
Trenton, N.J., 155
Tribune Building, New York, N.Y., 96
Tribune Tower, Chicago, Ill., 520, *523*
Trinity Church, Boston, Mass., 18, *94-95*
Trinity Church, Newport, R.I., 54, *55*
Triple Water Tank, Southern Illinois University, Carbondale, Ill., *504*, 505
Trollope, Frances, 131, 534
Trout Hall, Allentown, Pa., *146*
Troxell, Peter, 149
Troxell-Steckel House, Egypt, Pa., *148-49*
Troy, N.Y., *188-89*
Tryon, William, 277
Tryon Palace, New Bern, N.C., *326-27*
Tucson, Ariz., 537, *538-39*, 550, *551*
Tulsa, Okla., 537, 592, *593*
Tuscaloosa, Ala., *365*
Tuscan Revival style, *88-89*, *372-73*, 644
Tuskegee Institute, Tuskegee, Ala., 390, *391*
Twain, Mark, 91
Twilight, Alexander, 81
2 Charles Center Apartments, Baltimore, Md., *249*
Tyrone Guthrie Theater, Minneapolis, Minn., *512*

U

U.S. Bureau of Reclamation: Hoover Dam, near Boulder City, Nev., 627, 772, *773*
U.S. Corps of Engineers: Garrison Dam, Riverdale, N.D., *698*; Libby Dam, Libby, Mont., *698-99*
U.S. Courthouse and Federal Building, Galveston, Tex., *586*
U.S. Steel Building, Pittsburgh, Pa., 266, *267*
Ulrich Franzen & Associates: Alley Theater, Houston, Tex., *598-99*
University of Akron, Akron, Ohio, 510, *511*
University of California, Berkeley, Calif., *793*, *794-95*
University of California, Santa Cruz, Calif., *801*
University of Colorado, Boulder, Colo., *691*
University of Hawaii, Honolulu, Hawaii, *798*, *799*
University of Illinois, Chicago, Ill., *500-501*
University of Illinois, Urbana, Ill., *502*
University of Virginia, Charlottesville, Va., 332, *335-36*
University of Wyoming, Laramie, Wyo., *667*

University Plaza, New York, N.Y., *264*
Upjohn, Richard: New St. Mary's Church, Burlington, N.J., 204, *205. See also* Richard Upjohn and Son.
Utah State University, Logan, Utah, *690*

V

V. C. Morris Building, San Francisco, Calif., *777*
Vacherie, La., *567-69*
Valdez, Juan, 553
Vallejo, Mariano Guadalupe, 725
Valley Forge State Park, Pa., 146, *147*
Van Alen, William: Chrysler Building, New York, N.Y., *236*
Van Cortlandt, Stephanus, 138
Van Cortlandt Manor, Croton-on-Hudson, N.Y., 138, *139*
Vancouver, George, 704, 705
Vancouver, Wash., 705
Vanderbilt, William K., 96
Vanderburgh County Courthouse, Evansville, Ind., *462*
Van Wezel Performing Arts Hall, Sarasota, Fla., *409*
Vaux, Calvert, 211; Central Park, New York, N.Y., *222-23*; Jefferson Market Library, New York, N.Y., *204*
Vermont State Capitol, Montpelier, Vt., 68, 69
Verrazano-Narrows Bridge, Staten Island, N.Y., 236, *238-39*, 772
Veterans Memorial Coliseum, New Haven, Conn., 122, *123*
Victor, Colo., 656
Victoria Mansion (Morse-Libby House), Portland, Maine, *88-89*
Victorian style, *88-89*, *214-15*, *374-75*, *381*, *451-53*, *457*, *460-61*, *573*, *590-91*, *645*, *656-57*, *660-61*, *664-65*, 702, 754, *756-57*, *759. See also* Gothic Revival style; Romanesque style; Tuscan Revival style.
Vieux Carré, New Orleans, La., 533, 562, 577
Village green, Litchfield, Conn., *72-73*
Village green, Washington, N.H., *72*
Virginia City, Nev., 750, *751*
Virginia State Capitol, Richmond, Va., 332, *333*
Vitruvius, 14
Vitruvius Britannicus (Campbell), 129
Vivian Beaumont Theater, Lincoln Center, New York, N.Y., 270, *271*
Vizcaya, Miami, Fla., *386*, 387
Volney, Constantin, 621
Voorlezer's House, Staten Island, N.Y., 153

W

Waco, Tex., *588-89*
Wagner, Ronald: University of California Art Museum, Berkeley, Calif., *793*
Wainwright Building, St. Louis, Mo., 669, *670-71*
Wainwright Tomb, St. Louis, Mo., *668*
Walker, McGough, Foltz-Lyerla: Riverpark Center, Spokane, Wash., 806, *807*
Wall, C. S.: Iolani Palace, Honolulu, Hawaii, *734-35*
Wallace, Kostritsky & Potts: Charles Center, Baltimore, Md., *249*
Walter, Henry: Ohio State Capitol, Columbus, Ohio, *448*, 449
Walter, Thomas U.: Andalusia, Andalusia, Pa., *195*; Capitol, The, Washington, D.C., 17, 131, 220, *221*; Founder's Hall, Girard College, Philadelphia, Pa., *195*
Waltham, Mass., 66
Ward, John Quincy Adams, 190

Ware, William R., 91
Ware & Van Brunt: Memorial Hall, Harvard University, Cambridge, Mass., *91*
Warnecke, John Carl: Kresge College, University of California, Santa Cruz, Calif., *801. See also* John Carl Warnecke & Associates.
Warren, Mich., *505*
Warren, Russell: Arcade, Providence, R.I., 100, *101*
Warren & Wetmore: Grand Central Station, New York, N.Y., 228, *229*
Washington, D.C., 13, 17, 131, 232, *169*, *176-77*, 204, *206-09*, *220-21*, 228, *232-33*, 677, 744
Washington, George, 52, 130, 146, 155, 165, 173, 279, 322, 327, 329, 424
Washington, N.H., *72*
Washington Irving house, Tarrytown, N.Y., 132
Washington Monument, Washington, D.C., *220, 232*
Washington's Headquarters, Valley Forge State Park, Pa., 146, *147*
Washoe County Library, Reno, Nev., *797*
Waterside Plaza, New York, N.Y., 264, *265*
Watmough, James, 155
Watts Towers, Los Angeles, Calif. *See* Rodia Towers.
Wauwatosa, Wis., *493*
Waverly Plantation, near Columbus, Miss., *364, 365*
Waxahachie, Tex., *591*
Wayfarer's Chapel, Palos Verdes, Calif., 774, *775*
Wayne, Anthony, 423
Wayne, N.J., *154, 155*
Wayne State University, Detroit, Mich., *502-03*
Webb House, Wethersfield, Conn., *56*
Webster, Daniel, 423
Webster, Noah, 14
Weeks, David, 567
Weese, Harry. *See* Harry Weese & Associates.
Wells, H. G., 133
Wells, Hewitt C.: Washoe County Library, Reno, Nev., *797*
Wentworth-Gardner House, Portsmouth, N.H., 49, *50-51*
Westover, Westover, Va., 277, 278, *304-05*
Wethersfield, Conn., 37, 56
Weyerhaeuser Headquarters, Tacoma, Wash., 802, *804-05*
Wheeling, W.Va., *378*
Wheelock, Otis E.: Burbank-Livingston-Griggs House, St. Paul, Miss., *451*
Whipple House, Ipswich, Mass., *26-27*
White, Edward B.: Market Hall, Charleston, S.C., *352*
White, Stanford, 429
White House, Canyon de Chelly National Monument, Chinle, Ariz., *542-43*
White House, Washington, D.C., 131, *176-77, 232*
Whitfield, Henry: House, Guilford, Conn., *28-29*
Whitney, Mount, Calif., 703

Whitney Museum, New York, N.Y., *254*
Whittlesey & Conklin: 2 Charles Center Apartments, Baltimore, Md., *249*
Whittlesey, Conklin & Rossant: Lake Anne Village, Reston, Va., *391-92*
William and Mary College, Williamsburg, Va., 294, *295*
William Carson Mansion, Eureka, Calif., 758, *759*
William of Orange, 13, 157
Williams, Warren H.: Calvary Presbyterian Church, Portland, Oreg., *743*
Williamsburg, Va., 276-77, *294-97*
Williams & Tazewell & Associates: Convention Hall, SCOPE, Norfolk, Va., *410-11*
Wilmington, Del., *141, 174*, 175
Wilmington, N.C., *324, 325*, 342, *344-45*, 362, 363
Wilson, James K.: Isaac M. Wise Temple, Cincinnati, Ohio, *458-59*
Winchell, John K.: Thomas P. Kennard House, Lincoln, Nebr., *644*
Windmill, Jamestown, R.I., *58*
Winedale Inn, near Round Top, Tex., *584*
Winnsboro Courthouse, Winnsboro, S.C., 340, *341*
Winona, Minn., *476*, 477
Winslow, Carlton M., 709
Winston-Salem, N.C., 279, *320-21*
Winthrop, John, Jr., 25, 26
Wise, Isaac M.: Temple, Cincinnati, Ohio, *458-59*
Withers, Frederick: Jefferson Market Library, New York, N.Y., *204*
Wolters, Henry: Vanderburgh County Courthouse, Evansville, Ind., *462*
Wood, J. A.: Baptist Church, North Salem, N.Y., 216, *217*
Woodbury County Courthouse, Sioux City, Iowa, *477*
Woolett, W. J.: Fountain Elms, Munson-Williams-Proctor Institute, Utica, N.Y., *253*
Woolley, Edmund, 129
Woolworth, Frank W., 227
Woolworth Building, New York, N.Y., 19, 133, *226*, 227
Works of Robert and James Adam, Esquires, The, 15
World of Birds Building, Bronx Zoo, The Bronx, N.Y., *263*
World's Columbian Exposition, Chicago, Ill., 428-30, 709
World Trade Center, New York, N.Y., 272, *273*
Worthington, Thomas, 436; House, Chillicothe, Ohio, *436-37*
Wren, Sir Christopher, 13, 39; Wren Building, William and Mary College, Williamsburg, Va., 294, *295*
Wright, Frank Lloyd, 95, 224, 241, 387, 427-31, 469, 537, 709, 711; Annunciation Greek Orthodox Church, Wauwatosa, Wis., *493*; Beth Sholom Synagogue, Elkins Park, Pa., *242-43*; Fallingwater, Ohiopyle, Pa., *240-41*; Guggenheim Museum, New York, N.Y., *241*, 673, 777;

Hollyhock (Barnsdall) House, Los Angeles, Calif., *765*; Kalita Humphreys Theater, Dallas, Tex., *598, 599*; Marin County Government Center, San Rafael, Calif., *782-83*; Pfeiffer Chapel, Florida Southern College, Lakeland, Fla., *390*; Price Tower, Bartlesville, Okla., *596, 597*; Robie House, Chicago, Ill., *483-85*; S. L. Johnson Offices and Research and Development Tower, Racine, Wis., *486-89*; Taliesin West, Scottsdale, Ariz., 537, *596-97*; Unity Temple, Oak Park, Ill., *482*, 483; V. C. Morris Building, San Francisco, Calif., *777*
Wright, Mrs. Frank Lloyd, 409
Wright, Lloyd: Wayfarer's Chapel, Palos Verdes, Calif., 774, *775*
Wrigley Building, Chicago, Ill., 520, *522*
Wurster, William Wilson, 711
Wurster, Bernardi & Emmons: Bank of America, San Francisco, Calif., *810*, 811; Ghirardelli Square, San Francisco, Calif., *778*, 779; Ice Houses, The, San Francisco, Calif., *779*
Wyman, George H.: Bradbury Building, Los Angeles, Calif., *748*, 749
Wyoming State Capitol, Cheyenne, Wyo., *666*, 667

Y

Yale University, New Haven, Conn., *118, 119, 121*
Yamasaki, Minoru: McGregor Memorial Conference Center, Wayne State University, Detroit, Mich., *502-03. See also* Minoru Yamasaki & Associates.
Yeon, John, 711
York, Maine, *45*
York, Pa., 142, *143*
York County Courthouse, York, Nebr., *665*
Yost & Packard: Bowling Green Courthouse, Bowling Green, Ohio, *466*, 467
Young, Ammi B.: U.S. Courthouse and Federal Building, Galveston, Tex., *586*; Vermont State Capitol, Montpelier, Vt., *68*, 69
Young, Brigham, 425, 624-26, 640, 644
Young & Henderson: East-West Center Administration Building, University of Hawaii, Honolulu, Hawaii, *798*
Youngstown, N.Y., *172-73*

Z

ZCMI Department Store, Salt Lake City, Utah, *652*
Zabriskie-Von Steuben House, Hackensack, N.J., 146, *147*
Zion & Breen Associates, Samuel Paley Park, New York, N.Y., 270, *271*
Zoar, Ohio, 425, *440-41*
Zoar Village Restoration, Zoar, Ohio, *440-41*